THROUGH STRANGERS' EYES

Purdue Studies in Romance Literatures

Editorial Board

Floyd Merrell, Series Editor
Jeanette Beer
Paul B. Dixon
Patricia Hart

Howard Mancing
Benjamin Lawton
Allen G. Wood

Associate Editors

French
Paul Benhamou
Willard Bohn
Gerard J. Brault
Mary Ann Caws
Gérard Defaux
Milorad R. Margitić
Glyn P. Norton
Allan H. Pasco
Gerald Prince
David Lee Rubin
Roseann Runte
Ursula Tidd

Italian
Fiora A. Bassanese
Peter Carravetta
Franco Masciandaro
Anthony Julian Tamburri

Luso-Brazilian
Fred M. Clark
Marta Peixoto
Ricardo da Silveira Lobo Sternberg

Spanish and Spanish American
Maryellen Bieder
Catherine Connor
Ivy A. Corfis
Frederick A. de Armas
Edward Friedman
Charles Ganelin
David T. Gies
Roberto González Echevarría
David K. Herzberger
Emily Hicks
Djelal Kadir
Amy Kaminsky
Lucille Kerr
Howard Mancing
Alberto Moreiras
Randolph D. Pope
Francisco Ruiz Ramón
Elżbieta Skłodowska
Mario Valdés
Howard Young

 volume 33

THROUGH STRANGERS' EYES

Fictional

Foreigners in

Old Regime

France

Sylvie Romanowski

Purdue University Press
West Lafayette, Indiana

Copyright ©2005 by Purdue University. All rights reserved.

♾ The paper used in this book meets the minimum requirements of American National Standard for Information Sciences—Permanence of Paper for Printed Library Materials, ANSI Z39.48-1992.

Printed in the United States of America
Design by Anita Noble

The Northwestern University Research Grants Committee has provided partial support for the publication of this book. We gratefully acknowledge this assistance.

Library of Congress Cataloging-in-Publication Data
Romanowski, Sylvie.
    Through strangers' eyes : fictional foreigners in old regime France / Sylvie Romanowski.
       p. cm. — (Purdue studies in Romance literatures ; v. 33)
    Includes bibliographical references and index.
    ISBN-13: 978-1-55753-406-4 (pbk.)
    ISBN-10: 1-55753-406-3 (pbk.)
    1. French literature—18th century—History and criticism. 2. French literature—19th century—History and criticism. 3. Outsiders in literature. 4. Aliens in literature. I. Title. II. Series.
    PQ265.R66 2005
    840.9'920691—dc22
                                          2005013496

To the Memory of
    Sarah Kofman (1934–1994)

Contents

- *x* **List of Illustrations**
- *xi* **Preface**
- *xiii* **Note on References**
- **1 Introduction**
  Ambiguous and Useful Strangers
- **15 Part 1**
  Montaigne's Cannibals
  - **17 Chapter One**
    Montaigne's Unknowable Cannibals
    - 17 Prologue: The Skeptical Crisis
    - 18 The New Strangers
    - 21 The Discoveries
    - 23 Montaigne's "Des Cannibales"
      - 23 1. Subjective and Objective Knowledge
      - 26 2. Unknowable Nature
      - 29 3. Objective and Subjective Knowledge
      - 31 4. A Reversal of Perspectives, or The Wise Cannibals
    - 34 Eighteenth-Century Inheritors of the Cannibals
- **39 Part 2**
  Montesquieu's Persians
  - **41 Chapter Two**
    The Men's Quest for Knowledge: The Impossibility of Transcendence
    - 41 Prologue: The Early Enlightenment
    - 44 The Strangers' Arrival
    - 45 The Voyage
    - 49 The Split Subjects of Knowledge
    - 52 Society without Origin nor Essence
    - 56 Double Subjects and Modernity

Contents

65 Chapter Three
Women's Knowledge: The Temptation of Equality
  65 Prologue: The Difficulties of Women's Learning
  70 The Persian Women as Objects
  74 The European Women's Ambivalent Freedom
  77 Liberation?

85 Chapter Four
Who Are the Eunuchs?
  87 The Text: Internal Clues
  89 Natural Roles in Question
  94 Nature/Artifice, or The Generalized Eunuch
  106 Two Forms of Power: Surveillance and the Sword
  114 Montesquieu, Naturalist or Artificialist?

118 Chapter Five
Montesquieu's "Introduction" and "Réflexions," and the Question of the "Secret Chain"
  120 The "Introduction," or The Author's False Modesty
  124 The Question of the "Secret Chain"

133 Part 3
Graffigny's Elusive Peruvian

135 Chapter Six
Graffigny's *Lettres d'une Péruvienne:* Giving (and) Reading
  135 The Preliminary Texts and Their Mandate
  140 The "Avertissement"'s Gifts
  147 The "Introduction historique aux *Lettres Péruviennes*": The Stranger's Gaze
  154 Zilia's Play: Place, Language, and Exchange: The Acts of Discovery and Self-discovery
    154 1. Act I: Exposition—The Voyage
    159 2. Act II: Self and Language
    168 3. Acts III and IV: Society's Contradictions

173 4. A New Kind of Exchange
176 5. Act V: The Dénouement—Zilia's Way, Imitable or Inimitable?

183 Part 4
Nature Affirmed and Nature Denied
185 Chapter Seven
Voltaire's *L'Ingénu* and Claire de Duras's *Ourika:* The Aristocracy's Betrayals
186 *L'Ingénu*, or Nature Confirmed
195 *Ourika,* or Nature Denied

210 Conclusion
Ambiguous Strangers and the Legacy of the Enlightenment
219 Notes
233 Bibliography
253 Index

List of Illustrations

96 Fig. 1
Jean Lecomte du Nouÿ, French, 1842–1923. *A Eunuch's Dream*, 1874.

Preface

Like a tree, this book has grown in concentric circles. The starting point was the idea that Montesquieu's only novel, the *Lettres persanes*, was a quest novel enacting a search for knowledge by its principal characters, Usbek and Rica, Persians who come to Europe to acquire wisdom. After further research, I became convinced that these characters could not be separated from the others they left behind in Persia. So the project grew to a study focused on the three genders present in the novel, men, women, and eunuchs. I searched for suitable companions to accompany my reading of Montesquieu and to situate his novel in a historical, literary, and philosophical context. I decided upon Montaigne's "savage" Cannibals, who can barely make themselves understood but who express some very scathing critiques of European society, and Graffigny's royal Peruvian Princess, whose elegantly discursive and persistent analyses serve as counterpoints to the Persian noblemen and the harem's women and eunuchs. Finally, Voltaire's Huron man and Claire de Duras's Senegalese Ourika joined this study of the "stranger-comes-to-visit-us" topos. These texts resonated no doubt with my own experience of being an outsider in the various places where I have lived, though I was never as complete an outsider as the cannibal and the other fictive strangers. It also became evident that this Old Regime topos, under the guise of topical and piquant outsider critique, enabled some philosophical questions to be asked about the foundations of culture, questions which persist into our own postmodern period.

The present book has been a long time in the making, often interrupted by other activities (some more welcome than others) that academic life throws in the path of the literary scholar and writer. Over the years, the support of colleagues and of many friends inside and outside academe has been crucial in assisting and sustaining my endeavor to write this book, and it is a pleasure to express my deep gratitude to the many people who have accompanied me in this work. I appreciate having been able to present my research to members of my own unfailingly supportive Department of French and Italian at Northwestern University, and I am grateful to the colleagues

Preface

who invited me to speak at Dartmouth College, De Paul University (Chicago), New York University, Ohio State University, the University of Kansas, the University of Miami, and the University of Texas. I wish to thank especially warmly some perspicacious interlocutors and readers whose various critiques, suggestions, and encouragement were essential at various stages of the project: Kerstin Behnke, Claire Carpenter, Eglal Henein, Dalia Judovitz, Robert Launay, Phyllis Lyons, Sara Melzer, William Paden, Lorraine Piroux, Suzanne Pucci, Susan Ross, Françoise Simon, Mary Trouille, Nancy VanBrundt, Maryline Weintraub, Connie Wood, Barbara Woshinsky. Finally, I am deeply grateful to two outstanding readers: Richard Allen for his precise and sensitive reading of almost the entire manuscript, and Ellen Wright for her instructive reading of the other sections at a crucial moment in its composition.

I wish to thank *Eighteenth-Century Fiction*, where the point of departure of this book and especially Chapter 3 appeared in an earlier French version as "La quête du savoir dans les *Lettres persanes*" (3 [1991]: 93–112). I am grateful to Northwestern University for a summer research grant which enabled me to read Montesquieu's sources at the Bibliothèque Nationale in Paris, and to the Alice Berline Kaplan Center for the Humanities for an Affiliate Fellowship awarded for a proposal describing this project. The Northwestern University Research Grants Committee has provided partial support for the publication of this book, for which I am also grateful.

Finally, I wish to remember here especially one person whose untimely disappearance I still regret deeply, and whose support never failed me: I dedicate this book to the memory of Sarah Kofman, feminist, philosopher, and friend.

Evanston, Illinois
SYLVIE ROMANOWSKI

Note on References

The references to Montaigne's text are from the edition by Albert Thibaudet and Maurice Rat, and references to the *Essay* number when necessary, are in roman numerals, followed by the page number. Quotations from Montesquieu's *Lettres persanes* and the fragments in the *Appendices* are from the edition by Paul Vernière. Graffigny's *Lettres d'une Péruvienne* is quoted from the edition by Joan DeJean and Nancy K. Miller. For both these novels, references in parentheses give the letter number, when necessary, followed by a colon and the page number of these editions: an arabic numeral by itself is a page number. Voltaire's *L'Ingénu* is quoted from the edition by Frédéric Deloffre and Jacques van den Heuvel. Claire de Duras's *Ourika* is quoted from the edition by Joan DeJean and Margaret Waller. Any translations and emphases (except for the ones in the epigraphs, which are the authors'), are my own, unless indicated otherwise.

Introduction
Ambiguous and Useful Strangers

> The stranger is thus being discussed here, not in the sense often touched upon in the past, as the wanderer who comes today and goes tomorrow, but rather as the person who comes today and stays tomorrow.
>
> Georg Simmel
> "The Stranger"

> Suddenly a stranger enters. The mother was just about to seize a bronze bust and hurl it at her daughter; the father was in the act of opening the window in order to call a policeman. At that moment the stranger appears in the doorway. This means that the stranger is confronted with the situation as with a startling picture.
>
> Walter Benjamin
> "What Is Epic Theater?"

Numerous imaginary strangers come calling from the ends of the earth to eighteenth-century Europe: from Turkey, China, Siam, Persia, Peru, Africa, and America, they come, observe, and criticize. The most famous of them were Usbek and Rica, Montesquieu's Persian noblemen who flee persecution in their homeland and resolve to instruct themselves in European manners and culture. Since these are not real foreigners writing, but European authors, this is really an exercise of the imagination both about the home culture and about the foreigner's culture that filters the home culture. Long before these fictive travelers came to European shores, some real newcomers

Introduction

showed up: the three men brought back to France in 1562, the unnamed Cannibals who appear at the end of Michel de Montaigne's essay "Des Cannibales." Their brief appearance and their short but scathing remarks could not be more different from the elegant discursive letters of the eighteenth-century travelers—yet these Cannibals are their ancestors.

Eighteenth-century writers were so fascinated by the strangers' appearance in Montaigne that they developed a flourishing topos, that of the outsider novel as cultural critique. In order to understand the stranger's role in the eighteenth century, I will focus first on the outsider as described by Georg Simmel and Walter Benjamin in the epigraphs of this Introduction. Then I will outline some tensions within the Enlightenment resulting from its own historical context, tensions that make the outsider a particularly attractive vehicle for cultural analysis. My interest is in exploring how the cultural outsiders were *used* in the eighteenth century, and how, despite their radical differences from their Cannibal ancestors, they continue to pose the same questions in the texts of Montesquieu, Françoise de Graffigny, Voltaire, and Claire de Duras.

First, the stranger as described by Georg Simmel and Walter Benjamin. Georg Simmel wrote a fascinating essay called "The Stranger" ("Der Fremde") published in his *Soziologie* (1908) as an excursus, well known to sociologists, appended to his chapter 9 on "Space and Spatial Organization of Society." First Simmel establishes who the stranger is:

> The stranger is thus being discussed here, not in the sense often touched upon in the past, as the wanderer who comes today and goes tomorrow, but rather as the person who comes today and stays tomorrow. He is [. . .] the *potential* wanderer: although he has not moved on, he has not quite overcome the freedom of coming and going. His position [. . .] is determined essentially by the fact that he has not belonged to it [the group] from the beginning, that he imports qualities into it, which do not and cannot stem from the group [. . .]. (402)

Simmel outlines several qualities of the stranger: first, that of being at once near and distant spatially, which introduces a certain tension: "A *special* proportion and reciprocal tension produce the particular, formal relation to the 'stranger.'" Thus the stranger is both "near and far *at the same time*" (407; Simmel's emphasis). What attracts Simmel to the figure of the stranger is the spatial and emotional ambiguity rather than the specific identity of the stranger. And it is this ambiguity that makes the stranger interesting from an epistemological point of view: capable of looking afresh at social mores, *and* capable of interpreting and understanding them in detail. Neither a blank slate nor a fully acclimated person, neither a passer-by nor a settler, the stranger is for Simmel a "peculiar unity [. . .] composed of certain measures of nearness and distance," having "a *special* proportion and reciprocal tension."

Walter Benjamin's stranger also occupies an ambiguous space, the doorway, but Benjamin, who is discussing the mechanisms of drama, stresses rather the effect of the stranger as he makes his appearance: he freezes the scene, turning it into a "startling picture." Benjamin emphasizes the difficulty of comprehending this picture by imagining a scene of domestic violence in which roles of mothering and fathering are reversed: the mother is about to attack her own daughter, and the father is helpless and must turn to the police to restore order. An extreme case, to be sure—but his point is well taken: to a true stranger, must not every scene he comes across and interrupts seem incomprehensible, standing outside any narrative or explanatory context? Both ambiguity of position and fragmentariness of perception are basic qualities of the stranger's perception of the new universe surrounding him.

The stranger is a subcategory of the more general notion of the foreigner, which Donald N. Levine analyzes in his important study *The Flight from Ambiguity*. He outlines a typology of strangers according to their interest and position in the host community: "the critical variable here is not the length of time spent in the host community, but the type of relationship which the stranger aspires to establish with the host group" (82). These factors distinguish between the guest or tourist who visits a country, a sojourner who resides in it, and a newcomer who aspires to membership in the host country (83). Between the tourist's short visit and the settler's desire to remain, is located that most ambiguous of persons, the sojourner, who interested Simmel and Benjamin.

Why were these qualities precisely the ones which made strangers interesting and useful to the writers of the eighteenth century? Why is the stranger, with his or her status as an interloper,

Introduction

and his or her peculiar perception, so prized by eighteenth-century authors and readers? In order to understand the role that such fictions played in the Enlightenment, we should, I think, situate them within their historical context vis-à-vis the century immediately preceding, because I believe that such a contextualization will allow us to understand the significance of outsider critics. While we postmodern readers cannot help but reinterpret the Enlightenment, as historians of literature we would be remiss if we did not recognize its specific historical context. Indeed, the postmodern view emphasizing the contextuality of knowledge and making all knowledge "local knowledge," in the words of Clifford Geertz, can also see previous periods as being "local" in their aspirations and achievements—though previous periods did not think of their achievements as being merely "local"—and the Enlightenment as a response to the seventeenth century's achievements.

Donald N. Levine and Stephen Toulmin characterize the seventeenth century as a "flight from ambiguity" (Levine's title), an ambiguity that characterized much of the sixteenth century—a state of crisis brought on by the religious wars of the sixteenth century and the skeptical crisis analyzed by Richard H. Popkin. Living in crisis is unsustainable for very long: "To live with the crisis meant accepting that in a fundamental sense our basic beliefs have no foundation and must be accepted on faith" (Popkin 217). The authorities and the thinkers of the seventeenth century thus sought to rebuild a society free from chaos and disorder; it was a period when order, and rational laws governing science, government, religion, and knowledge, were considered necessary. The seventeenth century can be characterized not only by a flight *from* disorder, but by a desire *for* order. This order, called by Toulmin the "modern scaffolding" and a "Counter-Renaissance" (chapter 2), is characterized by four principal changes from the Renaissance: written, formal logic replaced oral argumentation; universal principles replaced particular cases; general axioms replaced concrete, local diversity; and timeless principles replaced time-bound knowledge. Levine calls it the replacement of ambiguous discourse with univocal discourse (37). In the early seventeenth century, philosophy and the new sciences (astronomy, optics, physiology) led the way in resolving the skeptical challenge by Mersenne and above all by Descartes.

Introduction

In his *Histoire de la folie à l'âge classique* and especially in *Les mots et les choses*, Michel Foucault described the profound changes in the presuppositions of knowledge in the domains of representation, economics, and natural science. This new way of organizing knowledge, based on measure and order, sought to arrive at "une connaissance absolument certaine des identités et des différences" (*Mots* 69). What was happening on the level of ideas was not separable from changes in institutions, which sought centralization and clear lines of authority from the central figure of the king to all his subjects. As the historian Robert Muchembled states, in this period, "L'État absolu, appuyé par une Église régénérée, pousse des ramifications dans tout le corps social, auparavant très parcellisé" (226). He explains that this is achieved by giving power to the new overseers who seek to undermine and eradicate local authorities and unify the kingdom: "L'esprit des administrateurs proches du pouvoir royal est résolument hostile à la différence. Il s'agit d'appliquer partout la même loi" (281), resulting in a gradual disappearance of a multiplicity of local governments, beliefs, and customs that constituted a rich and very diverse culture.

The desire to have clear, distinct, and rational understanding pervaded many aspects of seventeenth-century thought and life. To give a few examples: philosophy and cosmology with the spreading of Cartesianism; esthetics with the separation of genres; linguistics with the purification of vocabulary and the reform of grammar; political organization with the centralization of government into the hands of Louis XIV and the centralization of the family around the figure of the father; the banishment of baroque illusions with the clear, linear perspectives of a Versailles; even the discipline of one's sexuality and one's bodily movements. And let us not forget the Counter-Reformation's imposition of a unified and generalized form of worship eliminating many local practices, and the banishment of Protestants from France for the sake of a unified religious realm. Little remained untouched by the desire for control, clarity, and order, so that ambiguity became relegated to odd corners occupied by estranged libertines, resistant remnants of popular culture, ridiculed preciosity, or the frisson of the "je ne sais quoi."

The seventeenth century's response (its form of "local knowledge") to the sixteenth century's diversity and disorder,

Introduction

and that century's establishment of unified, rational, and fundamental laws, both in thought and in institutions, what Toulmin calls the "cosmopolis" (67–69), can in turn be set in a much wider context. In the next section, I examine briefly a long-standing tension in Western thought between those periods dominated by a belief in the knowability and the regularity of nature and those skeptics who reject that idea.

There is an oscillation in Western philosophical thinking between the belief in a fundamental, underlying order—"l'existence d'un ordre universel, nécessaire et spontané" (Ehrard, *L'idée* 12)—and the rejection of that belief. This alternation has been described by Clément Rosset, who names the first approach the "naturalist mirage," and its opponents the "artificialists" who call belief in nature a "préjugé naturaliste" having at its core "un référentiel anthropocentrique [. . .] qui décide, dans tous les cas, de cette différence métaphysique entre la nature et l'artifice [. . .]" (10–11). The naturalist viewpoint is a "doctrine selon laquelle [. . .] certains êtres doivent la réalisation de leur existence à un principe étranger au hasard (matière) ainsi qu'aux effets de la volonté humaine (artifice)" (20). The idea of nature has the power to quiet some profound human anxieties. First, the anxiety that there is no ideal: "l'idée de nature permet à l'insatisfaction de *s'exprimer*" (25; Rosset's emphasis)—by setting a standard for what ought to be, a reference to an ideal. Second, the anxiety that all phenomena are not subject to any explanation, but are the product of chance: "l'idée de hasard, à laquelle elle [la nature] oppose, semble-t-il, le plus puissant des antidotes jamais élaborés par l'imagination des hommes" (25)—by providing a rational basis for explanation of phenomena. Rosset concludes by stating that "l'idée de nature apparaît donc comme une expression très générale de la pensée mythique" (29) which, as we know since Lévi-Strauss, is able to reconcile opposite concepts and provide the means of understanding both the conflict and its resolution. The idea of nature offers both an outlet for the expression of these major anxieties and the solution to them.

The affirmation that there is a constant tension in Western thought between reliance on "nature" and rejection of it by artificialist thought should be put in the past tense, according to Donna Haraway who is writing in the late twentieth century, "our time, our mythic time" (8). She states that this time has undergone "fundamental changes in the nature of class, race, and gender" so that there is no going back "ideologically or materially" (20–21): "The dichotomies between mind and body, animal and human, organism and machine, public and private, nature and culture, men and women, primitive and civilized are all in question ideologically" (22). There is a radically new "emerging system of world order" (20) that demands new ways of thinking and speaking, starting with her use of the neologism "cyborg." These fundamental changes give us the necessary perspective to understand and appreciate another period in Western philosophy when analogous struggles occurred but had a significantly different outcome.

As vigorous defenders of the artificialist point of view, Rosset and Haraway consider the idea of nature to be an illusion, a fiction that gives order and predictability to the material and human world. So does Montaigne, one of the prime artificialist thinkers in a time when the reconnection with the Ancients, the discoveries of the New World, the new sciences, and the Protestant Reformation destabilized and tore apart the medieval Christian-Catholic synthesis and led to an epistemological crisis. Into this picture, the Cannibals enter and pose a troubling question: can human nature be infinitely variable, more than what we can possibly imagine? As Francis Affergan maintains, most ethnographic thinking in the Renaissance, starting with Columbus himself, tended to transform radical alterity into difference that was more graspable: "très vite, cette altérité originaire va commencer à se dégrader par l'habitude et la durée. Le processus de transmutation de l'altérité en différence prendra certes du temps, mais il est déjà inscrit dans cette première perception comme un aveu insu" (77). Montaigne, however, is able to distinguish between mere difference and a radical alterity and stay firmly in the latter mode: "Montaigne représente dans ce contexte culturel [. . .] d'une part une sorte de retour aux sources de l'altérité, et d'autre part une critique virulente de ce qui s'annonce déjà sous le nom d'ethnologie" (81).

Despite the thought of such thinkers of artifice as Pascal, the seventeenth century, as I said, turned its back on that mode of thought, and gradually erected systems of thought that brought

Introduction

solutions to avoid ambiguity and institute order in most aspects of society, such as religion, language, government. These began to seem confining and burdensome at the end of the century—the Querelle des Anciens et des Modernes being an early symptom of this unease—and even more so after the death of the absolute monarch in 1715. New ideas and behaviors were facilitated by the rapid social and intellectual changes that took place in the early part of the eighteenth century, starting with the Regency period, during which Montesquieu wrote his novel.

In the Regency period, characterized by diversity and various libertinisms, both intellectual and physical, old rules and habits fell out of favor with an unusual rapidity noted by writers of the period. Historians of literature and culture have studied various aspects of the Regency. Jean Ehrard describes this period as an open and diverse period of transition: "Entre la 'Crise de la conscience européenne' et les grands systèmes qui s'édifieront après 1750, [. . .] la première moitié du XVIIIe siècle présente un caractère original qui a rarement retenu l'attention des historiens" (*L'idée* 20). Herbert Dieckmann states that "during the first part, the authors in France seem to be largely occupied with the liquidation of the past" ("Themes" 53), while in the second half of the century, building larger, more systematic ensembles of knowledge dominates the philosophes' efforts. Writing in 1741, Duclos describes this sudden change as his hero returns from abroad to the court after the death of Louis XIV:

> Je trouvai, en arrivant à la Cour, qu'elle avait absolument changé de face. [. . .] Le roi, en vieillissant, se tourna du côté de la dévotion, et dans l'instant toute la Cour devint dévote, ou parut l'être. Après sa mort, le tableau changea totalement, et sous la Régence on fut dispensé de l'hypocrisie. (222)

And Montesquieu describes the state of the country during the Regency as "le Pays du Désespoir" (338), a state of devastation caused by that nefarious stranger, Law, and as a succession of upheavals, "une succession de projets manqués et d'idées indépendantes; des saillies mises en air de système; un mélange informe de faiblesse et d'autorité" (339).

Launched in the unsettled days of the Regency, the movement for societal change continued and deepened as the eighteenth-century thinkers sought to reform the society they had inherited from the preceding century. They developed new values that promised more freedom, such as personal merit, individual advancement and intellectual achievement, slowly devaluing aristocratic lineage and grandeur, courtly life, and traditional religion. And they had ambitions of reforming political and religious institutions such as the Church, the monarchy, and the economic and political systems. One of the ongoing debates concerned the changing relations between men and women, as Alison Jaggar states: "Simultaneously with the new bourgeois man's revolt against the monarch's claim to absolute authority by divine right, therefore, the new bourgeois woman began to rebel against traditional male claims to authority over her" (27). However, and this is crucial, the unruliness and disorder of the Regency period meant that they did not want to abandon the "cosmopolis" that linked rational knowledge of nature (cosmos) with a rational organization of society (polis) as imagined by the seventeenth-century thinkers. As Toulmin says, "the Enlightenment philosophers did not reject the modern cosmopolis, [. . .] they accepted the system in its entirety but used it to fight *from within* the restrictive tendencies inherent in the nation-state" (142; Toulmin's emphasis).

The progressive Enlightenment thinkers wanted to reform society and change thought, but they did not want to go back to the sense of "mutability" that pervaded the sensibility of the sixteenth century; they wanted to balance reform, which is disquieting and potentially destructive, with a firm sense of groundedness in fundamental principles based in nature itself. Linda Nicholson remarks that the idea of progress, one of the driving "meta-narratives" of the eighteenth century, "contains at its core a key tension [. . .] between a commitment to historical change and universals of human existence" (1). This inner tension was felt by the eighteenth-century thinkers: witness D'Alembert, who is quoted at length by Ernst Cassirer at the beginning of his study:

> If one considers without bias the present state of our knowledge, one cannot deny that philosophy among us has shown progress [. . .] natural philosophy has been revolutionized; and nearly all other fields of knowledge have assumed new forms . . . *Nevertheless*, the discovery and application of a

Introduction

> new method of philosophizing, the kind of enthusiasm which accompanies discoveries [. . .] all these causes have brought about a lively fermentation of minds. [. . .] *this fermentation has swept with a sort of violence everything along with it which stood in its way.* (D'Alembert, in Cassirer 3–4)

Sweeping reforms in science, government, religion, thought, and culture had not only a positive effect, but a negative one, a sense of loss and a worry that with these reforms, little firm ground remained and too much was being changed. Such foundations must therefore be found or created: "The age of d'Alembert feels itself seized by a mighty movement and impelled forward, but it cannot and will not simply abandon itself to this movement" (Cassirer 3); it seeks "underneath the almost unlimited mutability of psychological phenomena a solid foundation and permanent and enduring fundamental elements" (Cassirer 20). Since Descartes and Locke, it was the task of knowledge and learning to find, underneath the multiple and the diverse, the "unity and the relative simplicity" (20–21) that lie at the source and ground of phenomena. Now the same task was expanded to understand social and psychological phenomena and to reform society as well. Order and clarity obtained in knowledge of the physical world was to be brought to understanding the fundamental principles and thereby bring a new order and rationality to society and human behavior.

The Enlightenment that emerges in this perspective is therefore a mixed one: on the one hand, the Enlightenment *philosophes* thought of themselves as emancipating and path-breaking, while on the other hand, they were reconnecting with a most Platonic type of inquiry, desiring firm foundations and natural principles to legitimate their reforms: "the intellect can and should begin with fundamental norms, which it creates from within itself, and then find its way to the formulation of the particular. For only so can it [. . .] achieve a system of law" (Cassirer 238). Even as they thought of themselves as daring and innovative, they also had a conservative side that needed systematic foundations—another example of a "local knowledge" that thought of itself as universally valid—and which perhaps, from our postmodern point of view, seems to have throttled their ambitious questioning.

Given this view of the Enlightenment, I suggest that imagining the reactions of some ambiguous strangers, visitors from faraway lands becoming familiar with the home culture, provides a safe mechanism to deal with the tensions between the desire for reform and the fear of mutability. For if these strangers, like Simmel's and Benjamin's, can reassure the home readers that their culture can be not only satirized and critiqued, but also understood and, even better, justified from the outsider's perspective, then a useful cultural work is accomplished. Skeptical and startled, these strangers accomplish just enough, but not too much of a critique, a critique that is fragmentary, cumulative, and yet not too systematic. In the end, by arriving at an understanding of some universal laws of human nature, these sojourners reassure the readers that these laws can indeed be discovered and understood, even by the most strange of outsiders.

Montaigne's critical and uncomprehending strangers had the effect of destabilizing completely any belief in fundamental nature. Or perhaps it would be more accurate to say that they confirmed an already existing view that the world was ambiguous, in flux, without any solid foundations. The Enlighteners, undertaking the task of reforming society's institutions and mores, wanted to dismantle without destroying, and they were haunted by the possibility that there was no firm foundation upon which to build human society. It is not surprising that the eighteenth-century travelers have a different function from the strangers who visited during the sixteenth century. The basic questions are the same, however, and they concern the idea of a foundation in nature.

How Montesquieu, Graffigny, Voltaire, and Claire de Duras use their strangers (Persians, Peruvian, Huron, Senegalese), disquieting by their ambiguity and reassuring at the same time, is the area of this study, which is divided into four distinct parts. As is the case for much of French literature, the point of departure is Montaigne, and the first chapter is on "Montaigne's Unknowable Cannibals"—how their brief and puzzled critiques at the end of the essay conclude what constitutes the central theme of the essay: an elaborate demonstration of the complete impossibility of knowing any foundational nature, linking together the topos of the outsider critic and the debate about nature.

Introduction

The largest section is on "Montesquieu's Persians," who obtain the lion's share of this study with four chapters. Montesquieu's polyphonic novel, which brought the fictional foreigner to prominence in European literature, has not one but three distinct genders and voices that should be understood in relation to each other, and which each fill one chapter: the male visitors who come to Europe on a search for wisdom, the wives who are left behind in the harem, and the eunuchs who guard the women for the absent husband. A final, fourth chapter concludes this section by offering an interpretation of Montesquieu's "Introduction" and his retrospective look in his "Quelques réflexions sur les *Lettres persanes*," which contains his famous and much debated statement that a "chaîne secrète" binds the letters together, a statement that can be recontextualized after the analysis of the philosophical thrust of the entire novel.

Graffigny's novel, consciously linked by its author to both Montaigne and Montesquieu, seems to have a simpler structure, with its one female voice writing to absent male interlocutors who never write back. However, her text is preceded by two preliminary essays, the "Avertissement" and the "Introduction historique aux *Lettres Péruviennes*," which give her monological novel more complexity and make her heroine into "Graffigny's Elusive Peruvian." This section devoted to her novel first analyzes the complex interplay between these two liminal essays, and how in turn they give significance to the novel. Then it explores the heroine's anxious search for a suitable modus vivendi in French society, a search that is structured like a classical five-act tragedy, but with a unique and untragic ending.

In the final section, "Nature Affirmed and Nature Denied," I continue the juxtaposition of a male and a female author, and the focus on gender issues which I believe to be central to the Enlightenment's debates about human nature and society. The chapter considers together Voltaire's *L'Ingénu* and Claire de Duras's *Ourika*, which illustrate contrasting outcomes for the stranger. Voltaire's Huron man successfully integrates himself completely into French society after having suffered from religious dogmatism; but the heroine, Mademoiselle de Saint-Yves, dies after having come to grief at the Versailles court.

Ourika, written at the beginning of the nineteenth century but set in the eighteenth century, portrays a young woman taken from her native Senegal who is brought to France before the Revolution. She becomes an outcast, finding no place in a society that prides itself on tolerance, refinement, and generosity, thus revealing the underlying prejudices that are momentarily undone in the Revolution, but then reconstitute themselves afterwards and lead the heroine to escape to a convent and ultimately into death.

This study concludes with a look at these "Ambiguous Strangers and the Legacy of the Enlightenment," considering first the esthetics of the genre and the brevity of its presence in literary history, and then analyzing how the passing of the genre reflects some wider transformations in society and philosophy. Finally, it offers some reflections on the importance of the debate about nature for the age of Enlightenment and its implications for our own society.

Part 1
Montaigne's Cannibals

Chapter One

Montaigne's Unknowable Cannibals

> The minds of others I know well;
> But who *I* am, I cannot tell:
> My eye is much too close to me,
> I am not what I saw and see.
> It would be quite a benefit
> If only I could sometimes sit
> Farther away; but my foes are
> Too distant; close friends, still too far;
> Between my friends and me, the middle
> Would do. My wish? *You* guess my riddle.
>
> <div align="right">Nietzsche
"Request," in <i>The Gay Science</i></div>

Prologue: The Skeptical Crisis

The Enlightenment's emphasis on the necessity of individual knowledge and the impact of that emphasis on society in general has its roots in the larger movements of philosophy and science occurring in the Renaissance. As successive crises overturned the previously accepted religious and philosophical dogmas of medieval culture, new ways of viewing the world took hold. The Protestant Reformation attacked the institutions and the dogmas of the Catholic Church; the Copernican revolution decentered the earth and challenged the anthropocentric view of the universe; and the new scientific, mechanistic thought battled the Aristotelian system. New discoveries in other continents decentered Europe from its privileged place on the planet, itself decentered in the cosmos.

Few areas of knowledge were left unshaken by these revisions. Accompanying this complete rebuilding of the world, this new confidence in reshaping human exploration and knowledge, there arose a skeptical crisis of great proportions. In their book on ancient skepticism, which was rediscovered and immediately influential from 1562 on, Julia Annas and Jonathan Barnes contend that this contradiction is only apparent: in an age in which knowledge is paramount, "scepticism will become an issue of the greatest importance once epistemology is regarded as the primary part of philosophy. Before embarking on their further inquiries, epistemologists ask how much they can expect to know. To this question the skeptic has an uncompromising answer: little or nothing" (5).

Rabelais, Bacon, and Montaigne were engaged in critiquing old habits of thinking, and in exploring and teaching new habits of thinking about the world. Rabelais abundantly satirized medieval learning and asked for more relevant knowledge suited to the new age. Rabelais's program of learning was copious, but it was balanced by physical activities, by conscience, with the famous saying "science sans conscience n'est que ruine de l'âme" (206), and by a free, hedonistic lifestyle of the "abbaye de Thélème," emblematized in the abbey's motto "Fay ce que vouldras" (159). Describing his ideal pedagogue in his essay "De l'institution des enfans," Montaigne wished for someone who has "plutost la teste bien faicte que bien pleine," and who has "plus les meurs et l'entendement que la science" (I, 26, 149), i.e., a person capable of sound reasoning rather than one who accumulates facts or speculates on useless abstract concepts. Francis Bacon attacked the Idols that stood in the way of objective, true scientific observation. But among the skeptics, both for his breadth of erudition and for his thoroughness and depth of reasoning, Montaigne stands alone—his "Apologie de Raymond Sebond" is unmatched in Western thought in its uncompromising philosophical rejection of any foundational basis and its dwelling in skepticism in complete serenity. This chapter examines the philosophical ramifications of Montaigne's encounter with the first visitors from the New World, the Cannibals of America, the shock of whose discovery remains fresh a century later.

The New Strangers

During the Middle Ages strange beings abounded in the popular imagination, in a tremendous variety of forms. Any traveler in Europe is familiar with the gargoyles, devils, and other fanciful beasts populating the cathedrals' doors and rooftops. Many other varied and wonderfully weird monsters also appear in words and especially in images. Some of the more common ones are: the *androgini,* or androgynes, who have genitals of both sexes; the *anthropophagi,* or man-eaters; the *astomi,* or mouthless ones, or apple smellers who live, smell, and die of bad odors; the *blemmyae,* or headless people; the *cyclopes* with one eye; the sciopods, who shade themselves with one huge foot; the *panotii,* with giant ears wrapped around themselves like shawls; as well as bearded ladies, men with dog's heads, dogs with men's heads, and pygmies and giants.[1] Add to this list devils, infidels, witches, and ogres, and you have a rich panoply of strange creatures that attract and repel, amuse and frighten.

Imagining most of these beings relied on easily discerned mechanisms: they were juxtapositions of odd characteristics, hybrids of animal and human, or exaggerations of normal traits. In the hierarchically ordered world of the medieval period, it was obvious that these creatures were ranked below human beings, even if they had some human characteristics. Extravagant but not truly frightening, these often other-worldly creatures tended to disappear from books and images toward the end of the Middle Ages: by the latter half of the fifteenth century, a more undifferentiated type of wild man dominated the imagination, a hairy woodsdweller usually carrying a large stick. It is amusing to learn that this wild man, associated with death and devils and clothed in bits of fur and feathers, has an eighteenth-century descendant in Harlequin's many colored, diamond-patched costume (Bernheimer).

None of these monsters ever showed up except in the imagination. The end of the fifteenth century brought an entirely different situation, one whose extraordinary difference and monumental importance is probably unparalleled in Western European history. I am speaking of the encounters from 1492 on with the entirely unknown and very real world of the Caribbean, of the Aztec and the Mayans, the "discoveries" of new lands and peoples by Columbus, Cortés, and numerous other explorers of both North and South America. Whereas medieval monsters had been fanciful, these peoples of the New World were real; whereas the medieval monsters seemed to occupy some other space and time, these were in the same space and time as the European explorers themselves. The paradox is that the medieval monsters were more fantastic but less threatening, whereas the encounters with the real peoples of the New World proved to be infinitely more unsettling. More than unsettling: destructive to the peoples of the New World, but this the Old World was not to comprehend till much later. From the end of the fifteenth century on, the question of the other was truly joined: these encounters demanded a response.

Almost a century later, Montaigne, still surprised at these discoveries, put words of social critique into the mouths of his New World Cannibals, who came to Europe and ate up European society as surely as they did the flesh of their enemies. Social critique has not been the same since. The topos of the naive and critical outsider was born, and the Persians are the descendants of the Cannibals, transformed and completely reshaped, yet unthinkable without their disquieting Cannibal precedents. Montaigne's essay "Des Cannibales" (I, 31), the ancestor to works by Montesquieu, Rousseau, and Diderot, among others, poses the questions of knowledge and of the self through confrontations with these new others.

The issues at stake in Montaigne's text are vastly different from those of Montesquieu's novel, over two centuries later. Reflecting on the unknown peoples represented by the extreme example of the Cannibal, Montaigne also confronts the problem of representing these peoples as other while also making them accessible to us. The issue of the essay becomes that of the representability of the other. Later, for Montesquieu, who is interested less in the other and more in his own culture, the issue is not the representability of the other, but, as I will discuss in Chapter 2 on Usbek and Rica, two modes of subjectivity available within his culture. Montaigne's essay is an exceptional text which, encompassing all the possibilities of discourse about the other, explores the relevant problematics in such a fascinating and extraordinary way that it resists being subsumed as mere "background" for my study of Montesquieu's novel, its intellectual, though distant, heir.

The Discoveries

The shock of encountering hitherto unknown lands and peoples in the New World was still fresh in the Old World's mind a century after Columbus's initial landfall in the West Indies, as is shown by Montaigne's statement: "ce monde nouveau que nous *venons de* descouvrir" (I, 31, 201).[2] The explorers of the fifteenth and sixteenth centuries went to the New World with a purpose, a mind-set, different from, for example, Marco Polo's two centuries before. Marco Polo also encountered new peoples on his way to China, yet his travels did not have the same immense impact that Christopher Columbus's and Hernando Cortés's travels did. The difference, of course, lay in the actions of the discoverers, their motivation, and their mind-set. Marco Polo went to observe and trade, even living abroad for long periods and immersing himself in various cultures. The later explorers' goals were to search for treasures and lands that could be transformed into funds to reclaim Jerusalem; in other words, the new worlds were not merely to be seen, experienced, and described, but renamed, possessed, and claimed by the explorers themselves in the name of the monarch and for the sake of Christianity—the Spanish and Portuguese divided the conquests along a line set initially by the Pope,[3] leading to what Stephen Greenblatt calls "Christian imperialism" (70). Greenblatt asks the central question, "Why did Columbus [. . .] think to take possession of anything [. . .]? It did not, after all, occur to Marco Polo in the late thirteenth century to claim for the Venetians any territorial rights in the East or to rename any of the countries; nor in the fourteenth century did Sir John Mandeville unfurl a banner on behalf of a European monarch" (53).

In the Renaissance, the concepts of the individual, of possession and control by a willful self, be they scientist, explorer, or monarch, were key defining concepts that eventually led to, and justified, colonization and even destruction of entire populations.[4] The desire to control and possess led to the elaboration of discovery as a process. The very words, "discovery" and "conquest," are revealing. Even though "conquest" seems more blatantly possessive, the word "discovery" is no less charged with intentionality, method, and purpose on the part of the

Chapter One

Europeans. "Discovery" is not a haphazard find, an event of stumbling upon a land or a people, but a rational, methodical process of seeking out land and peoples to possess: as Vitorino Magalhaes Godinho notes, "l'essentiel du 'découvrir' s'élabore pendant la première moitié du XVe et est déjà en place vers 1460 [. . .] L'essentiel: la saisie de l'espace [. . .] la saisie des peuples et civilisations [. . .] l'art de naviguer sans voir terre," and, very important, "ensuite savoir retourner à la même destination et rentrer de nouveau sain et sauf" (69, 73). However, in the planned "discovery" of a better route to China, Columbus came upon a land totally unknown to him. Justin Thorens describes the landfall of October 1492, when a sailor cried out "tierra, tierra," as a fact without precedent in both cultures: "le fait que deux mondes sans aucune référence commune se sont rejoints de façon brutale et inattendue" (36), "l'inattendu au sens propre" for Europeans, and, for the Amerindians "le choc psychologique absolu que représentait l'arrivée de ces êtres venus pour eux du néant, du ciel" (37). The process of discovery, however planned and methodical, was exceeded by an event so strange and unforeseen that no planning could ever prepare it. It is this conjunction of planned exploration and absolutely unexpected discovery that occurred in 1492 and can be called "find" or "encounter."[5]

In our modern age, I suspect that a similar combination of both the expected and the radically new might occur if, in our probes of deep space and other galaxies, we came upon other living beings that, however much we searched for them, would astonish us profoundly. Whether the impulse to conquer and colonize would also arise is another question that would depend not only on human attitudes but probably more on the nature of the environment discovered and its suitability for sustaining human life.

The desire to possess and conquer led to intense encounters with other truly different peoples, a confrontation that made Montaigne reflect on knowledge of the other in his essay. The encounter also changed the hitherto accepted view of the world, expanding the known world's configuration, a process that was to be assimilated intellectually rather slowly, starting with the first maps showing the New World in 1507. Indeed, the encounter, which stemmed from the impulse to conquer that

Greenblatt analyzes so fully, also reinforced another current of thought in the Renaissance. I am referring to the period's intense awareness of instability and mutability, the lack of belief in fixed essences, and the general view of the individual as "a creature of flux at sea in a world of flux."[6] The impact of the encounters with the New World was all the greater in that it impacted on both of these currents of thought, justifying the view of the world as changeable, as well as stimulating desires to conquer and possess the new lands and peoples.

Both these currents, one emphasizing individualism and control, and the other emphasizing contingency and instability (which are not exact opposites of each other, but obliquely divergent), imply different modes of knowledge, different representations of the world and the self. The individualistic, possessive self seeks certain, objective knowledge that one can possess and manipulate at will, whereas the unstable, changeable self cannot attain objective knowledge, for the knowledge that it claims remains dependent on the position of the subject: this is what Timothy J. Reiss calls "a perspectival and incomplete process of knowing" (25).[7] The concept of objective, impersonal, scientific knowledge (versus the unstable subjective views of individual perception) was to carry the day and dominate in the seventeenth century with the Cartesian construction of knowledge, but in the previous century, the situation was more fluid and allowed both types of concepts to coexist.[8] Both currents of thought and accompanying types of representations are present in uneasy coexistence in Montaigne's "Des Cannibales."

Montaigne's "Des Cannibales"

1. Subjective and Objective Knowledge

Montaigne's essay, though ostensibly about Cannibals, is really about us, with the Cannibals playing the role of "shifter," that is, they are readable only through reference to the context of the culture in which they are set. Specifically the essay is about the different processes and modes of knowledge about others: Cannibals are an example of strangers at their most extremely

Chapter One

and shockingly different. In other words, the essay's central problem is an epistemological question, and the Cannibals are an example, a tangent to the main movement of the essay. Its structure shows a succession of scenes exemplifying various attitudes and judgments in front of the reader titillated by the shock appeal of the title's "cannibals": in the sixteenth century "Indians" would have been the more usual word for the New World populations.[9] To use a theatrical analogy, Montaigne parades in front of our very eyes a variety of stances one can have about the other. Whether any of these presentations is ever given the nod as being "true" remains an open question even at the end of the essay.

The essay, which is in three sections plus the one-sentence coda, presents three sets of characters: the first section has philosophers and learned people as protagonists, the second gives a simple man's eyewitness account of the newly discovered peoples, and in the third section we hear the foreigners' own comments on French civilization. For the sake of convenience, I will refer to paragraphs, even though these are a modern editor's (Villey) addition to the text. That is the form in which Montaigne's *Essais* are known to contemporary readers: a Renaissance reader would have seen only a continuous text, with marginal glosses for a guide. Each section, which is accompanied by Montaigne's critical commentary, undermines or questions the previous one, and the coda, with a last, flippant comment, whose brevity belies its importance and its impact on the audience, functions as an exclamation point that resolves none of the ambivalences and reversals performed by the essay.

The opening paragraph performs a first, easy reversal of common prejudice by reason, when King Pyrrhus comments on the ordering of the armies of "barbarous" nations not being at all "barbarous." From this quote Montaigne deduces easily enough the moral, "il se faut garder de s'atacher aux opinions vulgaires, et les faut juger par la voye de la raison, non par la voix commune" (200). But in the next paragraphs, "reason" is undermined because it is inadequate to understand the earth, bigger and radically different as it shifts and changes shape under our very feet, as Montaigne took pains to stress with his later (b) additions about shifting continents, deviating rivers, and moving dunes. The earth is different from what Plato and

Aristotle ever imagined, and if Plato and Aristotle are wrong, what hope is there for lesser minds? "Nous embrassons tout, mais nous n'étreignons que du vent" (200). But do we *know* that we are grasping only wind? The essay reenacts several times this double gesture: we acquire knowledge, only to discover later that we were deluded and are left with hot air.

Montaigne affirms that the eyewitness account of an explorer is vastly preferable to the speculations of philosophers who might seem to represent "reason." Both Plato and Aristotle as well as the cosmographers are inventors, not reporters; they are "fines gens" whose drawback is interpreting too much: "les fines gens remarquent bien plus curieusement et plus de choses, mais ils les glosent" (202). Montaigne stresses the inferiority and unreliability of reason compared to the eyewitness account by stressing that the eyewitness is an "homme simple et grossier," "très-fidelle, ou si simple qu'il n'ait pas dequoy bastir et donner de la vray-semblance à des inventions fauces, et qui n'ait rien espousé" (202). For reason only gives "vraisemblance" and not truth like the simple man and his acquaintances, "matelots et marchans" (203), the opposites of the learned armchair travelers and cosmographers who invent tales about countries where they have never been. We might seem to be somewhat at an impasse, for on the one hand the reasonable man, Pyrrhus, judges better than the common man, and on the other hand the common man is less prejudiced and hence has better perceptions than the most illustrious philosophers.

At this point in the essay, we have not progressed much beyond a binary impasse: we have read that we should distinguish between *barbare* meaning foreign and *barbare* meaning "devoid of reason," that *barbare* as a denotation (foreign) should not be extrapolated to the connotation of "unreasoned." The confusion between the denotation and the connotation is made all the more piquant in that King Pyrrhus's "barbares" were not "Indians" from some primitive new world, but Romans, surely the epitome of civilization; that it is specifically the Roman army that was not "barbare" adds yet another layer of irony, in view of Montaigne's pacifist abhorrence of war and violence. Having undermined first the common man by an appeal to reason, then the learned men's views by an appeal to experience, Montaigne has shown the subjectivity of knowledge, which depends on one's learning and education. It

Chapter One

might be time for him to shift to another mode of knowledge, the more objective, impersonal kind given by an impartial, reliable observer. His next task might be to give the eye-witness's description of these foreigners. The reader is ready to read the simple man's faithful accounts of the New World foreigners.

2. Unknowable Nature

Montaigne delays in giving us these accounts, which will constitute the second part of the essay, and in this delay, or parenthesis, he comes to the crux of the essay, which is not in the announced topic of the title, but is given in the parenthesis we are about to read. He insists again on the distinction between two meanings of *barbare* and, much more important, he introduces the new and crucial concept "sauvage" adding it apparently casually in the topic sentence, "Or je trouve, pour revenir à mon propos, qu'il n'y a rien de barbare et de sauvage en cette nation" (203). Whereas *barbare* meant foreign, and not unreasoned, the same easy opposition between denotation and connotation of *sauvage* is impossible because *sauvage* has two meanings, as Montaigne explains: *sauvage* can mean, i.e., denote, "foreign" as a synonym of *barbare*, but it also means "natural": "*nous appellons* sauvages les fruicts que nature, de soy et de son progrez ordinaire, a produicts" (203). In this acceptation, *sauvage* means natural, and is opposed to *sauvage* meaning civilized, artificial, unnatural, i.e., "ceux que nous avons alterez par nostre artifice et detournez de l'ordre commun, que *nous devrions appeller* plutost sauvages" (203). The persistent reference to the act of naming indicates that Montaigne is presenting the reader not only with the problem of confusion between denotation and connotation, but between two problematic denotations. If *sauvage* means wild, destructive, and if the *barbares* are not *barbares*, then the people who are *sauvages* (natural) are not *sauvages* (wild) either. However, the denotation of *sauvage* as natural gives another much more substantial content to the word that the denotation of foreign, spatially removed, did not give to the word *barbare*.

The concept of *sauvage* as "natural," and the accompanying definition of nature as "pure" in the same paragraph constitute the crux of the essay. Montaigne stresses our difficulty of knowing the "sauvages" who are different and untouched by civilization, a product of "grande et puissante mere nature" whom we have so overlaid with "nos inventions, que nous l'avons du tout estouffée. Si est-ce que, par tout où sa *pureté* reluit, elle fait une merveilleuse honte à nos vaines et frivoles entreprinses" (203). The difficulty of knowing nature is part of a larger argument; it is an extremely important instance of our more general difficulty of knowing anything "pure": the "fines gens" never represent "les choses *pures*, ils les inclinent et *masquent* selon le visage qu'ils leur ont veu" (202). What these "choses pures" might be is spelled out two paragraphs later, while an intervening paragraph excoriates the cheating cosmographers who extrapolate from their limited travels and mislead the reader into believing their descriptions about parts of the world where they have never been: "Je voudroy que chacun escrivit ce qu'il sçait, et autant qu'il en sçait, non en cela seulement, mais en tous autres subjects: car tel peut avoir quelque particuliere science ou experience de la nature d'une riviere ou d'une fontaine, qui ne sçait au reste que ce que chacun sçait" (203). The insistent repetition of "sçait" indicates clearly enough what the topic of Montaigne's essay is: the problem of knowledge about nature, "sauvages," the "other" of civilization, our limited capacity to know something other than ourselves, to know something uncorrupted, "pure," untouched by language.

The following paragraph on nature abounds with the vocabulary of destruction and corruption to describe our modern attitudes and qualities: the fruits of nature have been "alterez par nostre artifice" and "detournez," our qualities are "abastardies," our taste is "corrompu," "rechargé," and the beauty of nature is "estouffée" (203). Two difficulties exist here side by side: one is the corruption of nature by civilized people, the other is the difficulty of even knowing what nature is, so corrupted is she and so incapable are we of approaching her. Put another way, those people who are in nature do not talk about it, and those who talk about nature are removed from that state and by definition incapable of knowing nature. Such is the aporia where Montaigne leads the reader.

Furthermore, Montaigne himself is nothing if not a member of the category of "fines gens," those who interpret too much and present a masked and altered view of reality. In short,

Chapter One

Montaigne is fighting fire with fire, using the mask he must wear as an intellectual to parade other viewpoints in front of the reader, to present the reader with a series of masks as he evokes the lost and unknowable purity of nature.

Since Montaigne is not proposing one view of nature or civilization as true, but presenting various epistemological positions, he is no more or less masked than his "fines gens." Montaigne too is presenting his opinion, "mon propos," but his "propos" is literally that: a proposal, a putting forward of possible perspectives. The only view he is espousing is that representation of the "natural" is impossible, a statement reinforced by two sets of images. The first set describes the little bird's nest and the spider's web as images of the unrepresentable nature: "tous nos efforts ne peuvent seulement arriver à *representer* le nid du moindre oyselet [...] non pas la tissure de la chetive araignée" (204). Secondly, the pure foreigner, the natural man, is out of the reach of our language and knowledge: "Ils [the philosophers] n'ont peu imaginer une nayfveté si pure et simple, [...] ny n'ont peu croire que nostre societé se peut maintenir avec si peu d'artifice et de soudeure humaine" (204). The natural man and society are described with the repeated negative "nul," a standard classical stylistic device of negation used to describe the Golden Age, later taken up by Rousseau.[10] Nature is not totally inaccessible, for he said earlier that "sa pureté reluit" (203), though it is unknowable. The philosophers cannot represent pure and simple nature, and are reduced to less verbal and intellectual means: "nous [la] voyons par experience" (204). It is inaccessible to language, representation, hence to knowledge, in an age where the correspondence between them constituted knowledge conceived as "not truth, but rather the semblance of truth, verisimilitude" (Harth, *Ideology* 27). If such representation is impossible, then knowledge is also outside our reach: "un tel entrelacement du langage et des choses, dans un espace qui leur serait commun, suppose un privilège absolu de l'écriture" (Foucault, *Mots* 53).

Why is Montaigne insisting that nature is so difficult to know, even if we have glimpses of her by nonverbal means? Because nature represents the most vexing and important case of epistemological difficulty of knowing the other: nature is an egregious example of something "pure," "other," and unknowable. Note that Montaigne introduces the impossibility of representing pure and simple things (202) *before* he discusses the impossibility of representing nature (203). The argument of the essay is about knowledge, about knowing the "sauvage," the other who is doubly inaccessible, as natural and as other, but not about the "sauvages" themselves, who are examples meant to draw the reader into his argument. In a complex move of involving and puzzling the reader at the same time, Montaigne embeds his main philosophical problem in the middle of the essay, making it both central and hidden to the reader. This placement of the argument is an illustration at the structural level of the philosophical point that nature is unknowable, and yet still shining through occasionally if one knows how to look, or how to read.

In the first section of the essay, Montaigne indicates that all knowledge is partial and dependent on what the subject sees, and on the denotations and connotations given to words: this is the Renaissance epistemology that Reiss has called "perspectival," dependent on the position of the subject with regards to the object of knowledge, a "moment of passage" between the medieval Christo-centric worldview and the "new certainty" of the seventeenth century's belief in absolute knowledge.[11]

3. Objective and Subjective Knowledge

After having presented the reader with the problem of naming, and with the knowledge that both reader and writer are caught in the web of language which hides nature as a mask, the essay's second section seems to do a complete about-face by presenting a detailed, objective description of the foreign peoples, their food and drink, their clothes, their buildings, their hunting, their marriage practices, their beds, the way they shave, their priests, and finally the way they make war and deal with their enemies. The relation between objective certainty and subjectivity of knowledge is reversed: whereas in the first part of the essay, relatively little factual knowledge was given about the New World peoples and emphasis was placed on the difficulty of knowing or saying anything about nature, here much objective factual knowledge is given and the observing subject intrudes only a few times. The eyewitness disappears

Chapter One

behind his account, which is presented as impersonal knowledge about unidentified "ils." Montaigne could be accused of reversing himself, because after having insisted on the inability to know anything without an overlay of interpretation, he gives us a factual description of the "them" in great detail. As a matter of fact, Montaigne has been accused of deception in another way, of relying on the very same cosmographers whom he had just accused of telling tales about places where they had never been (203).[12] But we have seen that this essay is not so much about Cannibals or natural peoples as about our difficulty in knowing about the truly other, i.e., peoples of and in nature.

By framing his apparently factual account with reminders of subjectivity, Montaigne indicates subtly that the type of account presented here is a mode of knowledge that also has to be interpreted. It is one more presentation in the parade of perspectives, not a true or definitive knowledge. The description is introduced by the reminder that Montaigne is listening to *his* eyewitnesses: "ce que m'ont dit mes tesmoings" (205), and the occasional introduction of the "je" throughout this section (205–07) indicates that even this anthropological description is not given as absolutely certain, but that all knowledge, even the objective, factual kind, is always obtained and received by an individual subject. And in the scheme of the essay, this second section is itself bracketed by the first and third sections, which show the difficulty of getting and interpreting knowledge about natural peoples.

Even within the second part's apparently objective account, Montaigne undermines the certainty of objective observation by emphasizing the subjectivity of judgment about something that might seem to be universal and beyond discussion: the taboo of cannibalism. Even such a seemingly unambiguous and horrific practice can be interpreted in varying ways: though cannibalism is repellent, the New World cannibalism represents vengeance carried out on dead bodies, whereas in European warfare cannibalism is torture done on living people, and thereby worse than the Cannibals' cannibalism. The presence of the personal pronoun *je* indicates that even on this topic, several viewpoints are possible: "Je ne suis pas marry que nous remerquons l'horreur barbaresque qu'il y a en une telle action [. . .] Je pense qu'il y a plus de barbarie à manger un homme vivant qu'à le manger mort" (207). Montaigne sums up this argument of the essay with the harsh pronouncement: "Nous les pouvons donq bien appeler barbares, eu esgard aux regles de la raison, mais non pas eu esgard à nous, qui les surpassons en toute sorte de barbarie" (208). Though this seems to be a repetition of the initial stance of the essay, which differentiated between *barbare* meaning foreign and *barbare* meaning uncivilized, we are at a different place intellectually, for we now know that there are no fixed certainties, no denotations or connotations that do not depend on one's point of view. The conclusion of the "objective" knowledge presented in the second part leads back to the realization that knowledge is unstable and contingent on one's capacity and situation.

Montaigne increases the presence of the subjective in the remainder of this second part of the essay, by reintroducing the *je* who hears a song and a poem written by the New World peoples. The song and the poem are both interpreted as having no "barbarie" (211, 212), and even their language is praised as being "doux," "qui a le son aggreable, retirant aux terminaisons Grecques," while their imagery is "tout à fait Anacreontique" (212). One cannot help but think that only a "fine gens" like Montaigne with his classical learning could come up with such a description. Both the subjective knowledge and the objective, impersonal knowledge coexist, but the latter is inseparable from the former. There is always a subject that sees, and one that receives: all knowledge is discursive, with a speaker and a listener, and even the most factual knowledge is mediated by two consciousnesses. Having shown that both types of claims made for knowledge really dissolve into subjective appreciation, Montaigne goes one step further, in an extraordinary move that pits the foreigners' perceptions against our own about ourselves. This plunge into otherness and into overt subjectivity will dominate the third part of the essay.

4. A Reversal of Perspectives, or The Wise Cannibals

After having shown the difficulty of knowing the other by giving us various modes of thinking about the other—philosophers, cosmographers, eyewitness accounts—all of which are more or less subjective, none of which are reliable, Montaigne

Chapter One

introduces another "je," one who is no longer one of "us," but one of "them." In the last two paragraphs (before the one-sentence coda), which are the culmination of the epistemological parade, the learned author's presence coexists with other subjects, the "ils" themselves who, I will suggest in this reading of the third section, are both the ancestors of the eighteenth-century Persians, as well as their opposite. The "ils" and the "eux" are never identified as being from any country, not even as "Indian." From the beginning of the essay, these anonymous peoples had been identified as being from "cet autre monde [. . .] l'endroit où Vilegaignon print terre, qu'il surnomma la France Antartique" (200), in a double gesture that masks them (*sur-nommer:* literally, to "nick-name"), simultaneously naming and hiding their identity. They are appropriated as objects by the explorer (they are from "la France Antartique") and remain elusive, abstract, and distant as unnameable "them" who lie beyond our capacity to name except in relation to the French writer.

The last section (the third- and second-to-last paragraphs) shows a tight intermingling of foreign and French voices and perspectives, and several breakdowns in communications. Although Montaigne puts himself in their place and imagines that the three of "them" will regret having come to Europe, there is no indication that this is indeed what they feel. With some honesty, Montaigne does indicate that this is pure speculation on his part: "je *presuppose* qu'elle [leur ruyne] soit desjà avancée" (212). They are shown around by the King with pomp and circumstance: "on leur fit voir nostre façon, nostre pompe, la forme d'une belle ville" (212), another parade for "their" benefit as well as the reader's. But the pageant fails to make the expected impression, since when the foreigners are asked what they have found most admirable, they are severely critical.

Their scathing and prophetic critiques will be taken up two centuries later by that other enemy of civilization, Jean-Jacques Rousseau: his summation of the *Discours sur l'origine de l'inégalité*—the ranting against the rule of a child-king over adults and the stark divergence between rich and poor—echoes the foreigners' critique in the essay.

When "they" are given a voice and asked to comment on French culture, only two of their three comments survive because Montaigne suffered a memory lapse at what must be a most inopportune moment. In a one-on-one exchange with one of these foreigners, Montaigne, having become presumably more attentive, is now plagued by a slow and incapable translator who spoils his pleasure: "un truchement qui me suyvoit si mal et qui estoit si empesché à recevoir mes imaginations par sa bestise" (213). Both foreigner and Frenchman remain strange to each other: the foreigners repeat how strange, absurd and unjust they find French civilization, and the Frenchman cannot penetrate their mind, asking only one fairly minor question about the advantage of high military rank—not the first question, perhaps, that comes to mind upon meeting a stranger from another continent. The bad translator and the memory lapses are more than mere glitches in communication: here I differ with Greenblatt who lessens their importance (148 and n42), and instead I emphasize this breakdown as central to the purpose of the essay, showing the other as unrepresentable except in a moment of breakdown.

The third section of the essay ends in a standoff, each person staying within the confines of his own culture. The irony is that the foreigner, introduced here as a person barely understood by the European observer, and emitting a strange opinion on Western society, will turn out, in the eighteenth-century version, to be a vehicle for an objective, impartial critique of European society. Here, at a time still close to the impact of the encounter between the Old and the New Worlds, the outsider remains outside, hardly audible and almost unintelligible, yielding few of his secrets.

Thus the extraordinary challenge of understanding the other, the foreigner from the New World's shores, ends in a stalemate. When Montaigne considered the problem of knowing the other, he went beyond the immediate problem in order to evoke the more general problem of knowing the pure other and pure nature that lie beyond our intellectual and linguistic capacities. The last flippant exclamation, "mais quoy, ils ne portent point de haut de chausses!" (213), might be said by the previously offstage "voix commune" to which King Pyrrhus replied at the very beginning of the essay. Harry Levin calls it a "parting shrug" (77), but one said by someone who notices the absence of "haut-de-chausses," an aristocratic garment, so that the "voix commune" of the beginning now becomes defined as aristocratic, or the aristocratic as "commun."

This coda again brings the reader back to the beginning—even before the beginning, since King Pyrrhus replies to the "popular" remark that is said before the essay begins—emphasizing a circular movement that underlines how little has been accomplished despite the essay's long disquisition. It is the one point of view that up till now has not been paraded before us, the silly person who judges everything by external appearances and who sends everyone else away with an ironic comment that all the "fines gens" are powerless to refute. In the next century, Pascal will say that the ignorant "gens du peuple" and the wise "fines gens" can meet: "Il faut avoir une pensée de derrière, et juger de tout par là, en parlant cependant comme le peuple."[13] The flippant rejoinder at the end of this essay suggests that neither point of view carries the day. There is no accomplishment of knowledge by the wise persons who are able to think like intelligent people and talk like the common people.

Eighteenth-Century Inheritors of the Cannibals

If we fast-forward to the eighteenth century, we see that the social critiques made by the strangers, partially rendered in the third part of Montaigne's text, have now expanded and become the basis for the texts of Montesquieu's *Lettres persanes*, of Graffigny's *Lettres d'une Péruvienne*, as well as for stories by Voltaire such as *Candide* and *L'Ingénu* and numerous other texts that have the "cultural outsider" as their premise. The point of Montaigne's entire essay was to demonstrate that despite our best attempts, the truly other was unknowable by us, though glimpses might be possible: what Montaigne wanted was to avoid relapsing into any absolute statement, to remain poised on the unstable thin line of ambiguity. Edgar Montiel simplifies a bit Montaigne's purpose by stating that Montaigne indeed "s'efforce de comprendre des hommes aux cultures et aux coutumes différentes, et jette ainsi les bases du relativisme culturel" (110): bases are hard to find in Montaigne, and the more one looks, they more they seem to vanish.

These others, as Montiel notes, become assimilated: they do so especially in light of the eighteenth century's desire for progress, improvement of humanity, and reform of institutions, as other peoples became an inspiration for philosophers, moralists, and artists: "L'Autre n'est plus un simple reflet dans le miroir; il fait désormais partie intégrante de la vision de l'Europe [. . .] ce sont les pièges de l'altérité" (119). Montaigne asked whether it is possible to understand other cultures on their own terms and was led to indicate the ultimate impossibility of doing so, because any certitude is impossible. On the contrary, the later loquacious eighteenth-century others—Persians, Turks, Chinese, Peruvians, etc.—are ambiguous "outsiders" who are also insiders. As Hans Blumenberg notes, the eighteenth century's interest in other worlds does not stem from an interest in "the full range of possibilities [of other worlds]." Rather: "The 'other worlds' provide a fictive exotic standpoint for criticism, just like the realms of 'noble savages' in the Enlightenment's travel romances" (163).

The confrontation with true others and with foreign cultures, as opposed to the creation of fictional and imaginary others, disappears as a concern during the eighteenth century with the possible exception of the *Supplément au Voyage de Bougainville*, when Diderot again comes to grips with the same question that intrigued Montaigne, what can we know about someone different, and how can we be sure that we are really understanding someone outside our own culture without imposing our understanding on them?

> A. Ô Aotourou! . . . que leur [his family] diras-tu de nous?
> B. Peu de choses, et qu'ils ne croiront pas.
> A. Pourquoi peu de choses?
> B. Parce qu'il en a peu conçues, et qu'il ne trouvera dans sa langue aucun terme correspondant à celles dont il a quelques idées.[14]

In this later text, the taboo of incestuous sexuality has replaced the other taboo of cannibalism as the sign of extreme otherness, perhaps an indication that, even in this daring text, the other is somewhat closer to us: sexuality, even the most free, is still less shocking than any cannibalistic practice. In our own time, postmodern and anguished over eurocentrism, multiculturalism, and empathy for the victims of conquests and colonialism, there is a "radical attempt to comprehend the foundations of modern Western society as it was taking shape," as one music critic noted when taking stock of the numerous operas being staged nowadays with cultural encounters at the center of their plot.[15] Perhaps the standoff at the end of the essay between the other peoples and one of the best minds of sixteenth-century Europe ought to give us pause. The epistemological problems Montaigne faced when confronting the other, the subjectivity of knowledge, the breakdown in linguistic communication, the incompatibility of points of view, all these problems make the other accessible only in short, awkward glimpses and "through a glass darkly," beyond our reach. Hence Montaigne's own choice was to present us with a succession of points of view that undermine each other. Montaigne's attempt to interact with the mind of the cultural outsider results in a breakdown in communication, which indicates precisely that something or someone radically different is facing us. Neither the "objective," "possessive" mode of knowledge, nor the "subjective," "perspectival" one is adequate to the task of knowing the other. The other, if known, is a product of our imagination, or if the other is truly an other, then the other remains outside our ken.

When Montesquieu imagined his Persians coming westward and looking at French people, he was not much concerned with knowing who Persians really were, for his focus was instead on the more pressing question: who are *we*? The ambiguous other of the eighteenth-century writers is a "shifter"[16] whose identity cannot be separated from the function of the critique it performs for the culture. The cultural outsider is now a convenient fiction, and often an amusing one, but given the difficulty of knowing the other, it is not surprising that this other is also us, representing the act of looking at ourselves. It is as if Montesquieu, Voltaire, Graffigny, and even Diderot took the foreigners' critique of the very last part of Montaigne's essay and expanded it to make it the basis of their whole text, but in so doing, they gave up any effort to represent the other as other, although such preoccupations sometimes surface briefly, for example, when Montesquieu posed but never answered the question, "Comment peut-on être Persan?" (30: 69); or when in the *Lettres d'une Péruvienne*, Graffigny attempts to render the strangeness of communicating by the knotted threads of the *quipus*, or, in what could be a phenomenological description, she renders the bodily and sensory perceptions of someone who has never been in a ship on the ocean. A trace of the other's presence remains, and the other never completely disappears from consciousness, for after the discoveries of the New World, the Old World could not ignore such awareness, even as it tried to repress and conquer these others. Indeed there remains in Western culture an unavoidable suspicion that there may be an entirely different way of comprehending reality, and it is perhaps this nagging suspicion, along with the eternal fascination both with ourselves and with foreigners that provide the foundation for the Enlightenment critique of society.

The "cultural outsider" topos constitutes a compromise between the absolutely other (and hence incomprehensible) and the completely similar (and therefore unable to critique society). The complete stranger, encountered in the sixteenth century, was appropriated and tamed for the purpose of social critique in the early eighteenth century. It lies in that middle distance, neither too close nor too far, neither too hostile nor too friendly, neither Cannibal nor European, that Nietzsche calls for in his poem cited at the beginning of this chapter. No one was to make better use of the topos, putting it on the literary map for the remainder of the eighteenth century, than Montesquieu.

Part 2
Montesquieu's Persians

Chapter Two

The Men's Quest for Knowledge
The Impossibility of Transcendence

> The human understanding is of its own nature prone to suppose the existence of more order and regularity in the world than it finds.
>
> Francis Bacon
> *Novum Organum*

Prologue: The Early Enlightenment

Although the *Lettres persanes* and its author are usually considered as belonging to the eighteenth century, they are actually both on the cusp of the Enlightenment. Montesquieu had a foot in both cultures. Born eleven years before the end of the seventeenth century, he was about 26 years old when Louis XIV's death definitively marked the passing of an era and 32 years old when his novel was published, already a mature age for that period—and the novel itself starts before the monarch's death.

The first three decades of the eighteenth century—the end of the Louis XIV era and the beginning of the Regency—constitute a particular moment of openness, of transition within what has been called the "Enlightenment project." Modern historians of literature and culture have attempted to define the early Enlightenment as a specific moment of passage from the seventeenth century to the Enlightenment itself. In studying the waning of the seventeenth century, Erica Harth describes the slow breaking apart of a unified system of esthetics based on the principle "ut pictura poesis" that spoke to the still powerful but waning aristocracy: "At the beginning of the seventeenth century, the arts possessed their own peculiar coherence. They were unified by common aesthetic laws and practices [. . .].

Chapter Two

With the deepening ideological crisis, the unity achieved in an earlier period slowly dissolved, and artistic representation entered a critical stage" (*Ideology* 23). In the eighteenth century, the aristocracy was slowly displaced by what she calls a "mandarin class" based in the bourgeoisie, and a new concept of objective truth emerged, divorced from the verisimilitude of rhetorical representation. From the vantage point of art history, Barbara Stafford and Rémy Saisselin have studied the long decline of Baroque culture, of a hierarchically organized culture that valued "an oral-visual mode of learning," "later condemned in the wake of the perceptual skepticism cast by Hume and others" (Stafford 1, 3). Baroque art, which started as "the art of the Church Triumphant, born of the victorious fervor of the Counter-Reformation" (Charpentrat 8), emphasized the outward spectacle as revealing of inner being. Slowly, this culture was replaced by a "Protestant culture of reading and writing" (Stafford 22), a print culture that was turned inward, that valued skepticism and logic, and that eventually developed democratic ideas and a market-driven economy based on individual merit and work. It was a period of change when prestige shifted from the declining, visually sumptuous Court culture to the new urban, middle-class elites, from a "traditional" or "customary" society to a "market" society studied by C. B. Macpherson in political history. In literary history, this was a time of destabilization of both social categories and moral categories of truth and virtue, described in detail by Michael McKeon.

Such shifts in cultural values did not escape the more keen-sighted writers of the times. Writing at the end of the seventeenth century, that sharp observer of mores, La Bruyère, opens his *Caractères* with the following aphorism: "Tout est dit, et l'on vient trop tard depuis plus de sept mille ans qu'il y a des hommes et qui pensent" ("Des ouvrages de l'esprit," 1). The sense of the passing of a societal system dominated by the "Grands"—the Court, and the monarchy—permeates the *Caractères*, whose disabused and ironic vision can be summed up in the following passage: "Rois, Monarques, Potentats, sacrées Majestés! [. . .] nous autres hommes nous avons besoin pour nos moissons d'un peu de pluie, de quelque chose de moins, d'un peu de rosée: faites de la rosée, envoyez sur la terre une goutte d'eau" ("Des esprits forts," 46). The criterion of usefulness for basic needs was completely at variance with the pompous and useless glory of high-sounding titles, and already points to the Enlightenment's concept of utility. The Querelle des Anciens et des Modernes that took place in France during the last years of the seventeenth century and at the beginning of the eighteenth was also a convenient signpost on the way to change. And the Regency marked a definite change in the esthetic and moral culture of the period. In short, it was a period when the first significant cracks appeared in the "cosmopolis" of the previous century.

It is in this period of change and fermentation that characterizes the early Enlightenment that Montesquieu's only novel was written and published. Written during the years 1717 to 1720, the *Lettres persanes* de-emphasizes the earlier period, which many historians of French culture consider to have ended decisively with the death of Louis XIV, even though fully half of the novel's 161 letters occur before 1715 (the monarch's death is mentioned in Letter 92). Certain seventeenth-century debates and attitudes are still evoked in the novel, such as the Baroque love for pomp and circumstance, the debates about religion, Jansenism, and the power of the Papacy, for example. But these topics by no means occupy center stage in the novel, which turns its back on the preceding times.

Forward-looking rather than nostalgic, the novel indeed has always been read as a text belonging to the Enlightenment. The text looks forward, in a remarkably prescient manner, to many of the new age's principal concerns: determining the foundations for a more just society, rejecting religious intolerance, re-examining relations between men and women. Its skepticism, its irony, its critiques of society, Christianity, and organized religion, its search for rational descriptions of cultural phenomena such as government and justice, all mark it as belonging to the Enlightenment. Yet, it reflects the instability of the Regency which marked a definite change in social attitudes, arts, and thought. It exhibits some features of a transitional period: questioning, uncertainty, ambiguity, as well as a wish to arrive at some firmly held values that can hold disquiet at a far distance from the mind. The text uniquely captures the openness of the period before the Enlightenment was a "project," a time when many ideas were in flux, and when the "buzz words" of the high Enlightenment were not yet established. Indeed, such a work as the *Lettres persanes* put into circulation many of the ideas that were to dominate philosophical and moral discourse later in the century.

The Strangers' Arrival

When two Persian noblemen, Rica and Usbek, leave their kingdom for Paris, they state in their first letter that their goal is to acquire knowledge about the Western world: thus from the very beginning of the work, the question of knowledge appears fundamental, and with it the question of the subject of this knowledge. In the very next letter, however, it is clear that the situation of Rica differs from that of Usbek, who has left behind a harem with many wives guarded by eunuchs. At the beginning of the text, there are four different subject positions: the man without a harem (Rica), the man with a harem (Usbek), the wives, and the eunuchs. There are hierarchical relationships that go beyond simple superior-inferior distinctions. Both Usbek and Rica are superior in that they are uncastrated, and free to leave their country in quest of knowledge, unlike the women who are confined to their seraglio, and the eunuchs who occupy a separate ground, for they are superior to the women under their surveillance and inferior to their master. As for the women, they are both superior to the eunuchs, but also inferior, since they must remain imprisoned and unable to undertake a quest of any kind, much less to a foreign land.

Thus all the subjects in the novel are shot through with ambiguity: Rica and Usbek are examples of the ambiguous stranger, the sojourner[1] who comes and stays in a foreign land, but who can reveal the workings of this foreign land to the readers back at home. However, the men will not find all the knowledge that they expected: thus Montesquieu questions the notion of universal and impersonal knowledge. The women will be the ones who find true knowledge despite their lack of freedom, which implies that knowledge is indeed attainable by anyone, no matter what the constraints are. Two movements coexist in the *Lettres persanes:* one movement demystifies universal knowledge and the universal subject, thus showing the dependence of knowledge on the subject's position, and the other movement recuperates it, affirming that any subject is free to acquire self-knowledge and wisdom regardless of any limiting position.

This chapter will focus on the men's quest and the two modes of subjectivity represented by Rica and Usbek, and it will show how this part of the novel leads to the demystification of the unitary concept of knowledge and of the transcendental subject. This position, which is close to the postmodern demystification of the unitary, centered self and the objectivity of knowledge, suggests the question that will conclude the chapter: can the *Lettres persanes* be considered in any way as contemporary? The recuperation and remystifying movement will be analyzed in a later chapter on the women. The men find many particular laws of society, but the women are the ones who reach universal laws transcending specific societies, reversing the usual association of men with abstract reason, and women with knowledge of details and feelings.

The Voyage

The *Lettres persanes* begin with that most classical gesture: a voyage, a quest, the beginning of so many tales and epics. By the eighteenth century, the voyage was also a feature of life for young aristocratic noblemen coming from England to educate themselves on the Continent, chiefly in France and Italy.[2] In the eighteenth century, such "grand tours" were not yet the stuff of the Bildungsroman of the nineteenth century nor the mass tourism of the twentieth, being limited to the aristocracy, and at the same time, they were no longer heroic quests for adventures, and no longer pilgrimages to religious centers or to urban centers of university learning.[3] In the case of our Persians, I prefer to use the word *quest* rather than *tour* in order to underline the still somewhat exceptional nature of their trip which they present loftily in their early letters as a quest for wisdom, for "sagesse."[4]

What could be simpler than the departure of these two Persian noblemen who renounce a life of leisure at court in order to "chercher laborieusement la sagesse" (1: 12)? They say that they are perhaps the first to leave their country with this

Chapter Two

objective in mind, suggesting a kind of archetypal situation: they are the first among their kind to seek wisdom. In so doing, they give birth to themselves as subjects capable of acquiring this knowledge.

However, the reason for their departure is not simple, and a close reading of Letter 8 reveals multiple ambiguities within the apparently simple gesture of embarking on a quest for learning. Thus the future strangers who will dwell in Europe are already ambiguous figures in their own homeland. The very first letter states their motivation for traveling as a desire for knowledge and for wisdom: "envie de savoir," "sagesse," and "connaissances" (12). However, behind the façade of the search for enlightenment, there might be something other than the pure desire for learning: this is hinted at by the request "Mande-moi ce que l'on dit de notre voyage," as Usbek asks his correspondent to relate the "on dit," rumors about his voyage that might be critical, for he adds the reassurance to his friend, "ne me flatte point," implying that the rumors might be less than entirely favorable (1: 12). But why bother to ask about what people say about him, when the search for knowledge should be enough to justify his bold enterprise? Why does he need the approval of others, even if these are few: "Je ne compte pas sur un grand nombre d'approbateurs"? The reason is that pure learning is not the motivation for the voyage, and perhaps not even the principal reason for it. In Letter 5, Rustan asks Usbek the reasons for his apparently unprecedented and totally incompréhensible departure: "On ne peut comprendre que tu puisses quitter tes femmes, tes parents, tes amis, ta patrie pour aller dans des climats inconnus aux Persans" (17).

In Letter 8, Usbek answers Rustan's letter and again takes up the question of the motivation for his and Rica's departure. And here, the pure search for learning which was proposed in Letter 1 is exploded, and with it the loftiness of Usbek's search for "savoir" and "sagesse." In Letter 8, there are no less than seven different moments or movements in Usbek's life from the time he was a youth to the time of his departure.

The first movement, begun in his youth, "ma plus tendre jeunesse" (8: 21), was one of being purely virtuous, but this first moment of unquestioned and undivided virtue is already sullied by its context: even in that first appearance at court, he had an awareness of the surrounding corruption, for he says, "mon cœur ne s'y corrompit point" (21). We can recognize here the topos of the corrupt court which, by the early eighteenth century, was well rehearsed. Critiques of court life were first formulated when the Renaissance courts became powerful institutions organized around an ever more centralized monarchy, and populated by noblemen no longer occupied by warfare and land management.[5] The disgust of the naive young Usbek upon his realization that court life is filled with vice led him to avoid the court, but this second moment was short-lived, and followed by a third, a return to the court, where, in a hubris characteristic of idealistic youth, he dared to state his criticism in no uncertain terms directly to the monarch himself who has overtones of spurious divinity: "je portai la vérité jusques au pied du *trône* [. . .] j'étonnai en même temps les adorateurs et *l'idole*" (21).

The third movement removed him from a state of virtue in his avoidance of vice, and took him into the realm of discourse: "j'y parlai un langage jusqu'alors inconnu" (21). This new, additional language about virtue, which is added to being virtuous, illustrates both aspects of the supplement analyzed by Jacques Derrida: in the first aspect, the supplement is the rival of plenitude, "un surplus, une plénitude enrichissant une autre plénitude" and in its second aspect it is a poor substitute, "un adjoint, une instance subalterne [. . .]. En tant que substitut, [. . .] sa place est assignée dans la structure par la marque d'un vide" (*Grammatologie* 208). For Usbek, speech about virtue is equal to his being virtuous, but at court, the courtier's language is a powerless substitute that can never fill the lack of virtue there. Usbek's situation differs from what Derrida has shown about Rousseau: for Rousseau, writing was a dangerous supplement to speech, whereas for Usbek, speech is a dangerous supplement to being and to silence.

The iconoclast cannot last long in a social system based on lies and idolatry: in a fourth movement, Usbek stumbled as he realized, first, that he had made some powerful enemies—"la jalousie des ministres" (21) in a foreshadowing of a theme, the corrupt ministers, that will recur toward the end of the novel—and second, that even his own inner sense of virtue and resolve was fading fast. The new role of defender of virtue made Usbek

Chapter Two

hesitate: the one who had just described himself as incorruptible, now admits that "dans une cour corrompue, je ne me soutenais plus que par une faible vertu" (21) when he was attacked.

Now that he had entered the discursive chain that was to lead him away from virtue, Usbek found himself obliged to act against his will: in a fifth movement, he decided to retire from the court. In this moment, we recognize another topos regarding the critique of corrupt courts—retreat into a life of simplicity and virtue in the country: "je me retirai dans une maison de campagne." In order to return to the innocence of his youth? On the contrary, in this fifth moment, he dwelt in inauthenticity: "je *feignis* un grand attachement pour les sciences." In yet another (sixth) reversal, the feint became real and the pretense to search for learning became a genuine love of learning: "à force de le *feindre*, il [l'attachement pour les sciences] me vint *réellement*" (22). Does the word "réellement" have any meaning at this point? His identity as a quester for knowledge is founded upon pretense and weakness.

Despite his passage from feigned to "real" love for the sciences in the silence of his country house, Usbek was still threatened: from the inside and from the outside. Even though he was no longer lying, and had become a genuine lover of sciences, he could see that his retreat did not protect him from the evil enemies: "je restais toujours exposé à la malice de mes ennemis." Another move was necessary: "Je résolus de m'exiler de ma patrie, et ma retraite même de la Cour m'en fournit un *prétexte* plausible" (22), which constitutes the seventh and last move into exile.

Having already pretended to search for knowledge in the solitude of the countryside, he can now manufacture a second, elaborate feint for the benefit of the credulous ruler, in two successive arguments. The first argument, "Je lui marquai l'envie que j'avais de m'instruire dans les sciences de l'Occident," gives priority to the West, which might offend an Oriental monarch, so with a consummate politician's skill, Usbek adds a second reason that would be seductive to his ruler: "Je lui insinuai qu'il pourrait tirer de l'utilité de mes voyages." "Insinuai" indicates the oblique approach, and "utilité" appeals to the ruler's practical and selfish interests. This entire speech is, however, a façade hiding a personal motivation for traveling abroad: "je dérobai une victime à mes ennemis" (22). Under the pretense of learning and benefiting the king lurks the very real fear for his life and the desire to save his own skin. Discourse in defense of virtue, which had endangered his very being and life, now saves him from death: like Scheherazade, Usbek saves himself through skillful tales and is able to escape to another world, to the West, and to the center of the West, France and Paris.

After these multiple feints and lies, Letter 8's concluding sentence seems rather comic: "Voilà, Rustan, le *véritable* motif de mon voyage" (22). Truth is shot through with lies, desire for learning disguises self-preservation, and the word *véritable* is crossed out by irony. In a final paragraph that testifies to his permanent fall from being into the economy of the discursive supplement, he expresses curiosity about what people might say about him: "On parle de moi à présent." Why does he even ask the question, if not because he himself has entered the world of discourse, of the supplement. He knows that people speak about him, and that unsettles him, but the possible future silence of being forgotten worries him even more, so much so that he leaves his thought unsaid as if too horrible to contemplate: "Peut-être ne serai-je que trop oublié, et que mes amis . . . Non, Rustan, je ne veux point me livrer à cette triste pensée: je leur serai toujours cher" (22). He counts on their words, the only testimony of friendship, which may not be forthcoming. Usbek is definitely within the realm of discourse, where words create friendship, and language is the source of value, death, and life. The search for truth and knowledge has fallen from that purity of being into the networks of language, of pretext and subtext. The separation from initial wholeness of being will dominate the following considerations on the constitution of Usbek and Rica as subjects of knowledge.

The Split Subjects of Knowledge

Usbek and Rica have begun to constitute themselves as knowing subjects, a long and laborious process of separation from the previous existence in the mother country.[6] Not for nothing are these travelers Persians, exiles from the Orient, that symbol of bliss and ignorance that has fascinated the West. As Edward

Chapter Two

Said says, the West's "kind of free-floating mythology of the Orient" (53) was defined by views that the "Orient is irrational, depraved (fallen), childlike, 'different'" (40). In the case of our text, the Orient is a locus of both ignorance and corruption, to be replaced by life in the West where "the European is rational, virtuous, mature, 'normal'" (40). Prefiguring Kant's pronouncement in his 1784 essay, "An Answer to the Question: What Is Enlightenment?," that becoming enlightened is "emergence from [. . .] self-imposed immaturity" (41), Montesquieu's text places the Orient in the position of representing what must be left behind in a process of individual maturing: just as an embryo's development in the womb reproduces the evolution of the species, so does the two adults' coming to maturity reproduce the passage from child to adult. The first letter foregrounds the image of birth in both the literal and the figurative sense, for after their literal birth—"nous sommes nés dans un royaume florissant" (12) in a paradisiacal land—the Persian travelers must undergo a symbolic death and rebirth into the intellectual adulthood of the European Enlightenment.

This second birth might be laborious and problematic, as the second sentence of the novel slyly suggests, by evoking death and repeated birth in close coexistence: "Lorsque nous eûmes fait nos dévotions sur le tombeau de la Vierge qui a mis au monde douze prophètes" (1: 11). Contradictions abound here: the prophet's mother must be a pure Virgin but she gives birth—a good example of a split subject, if there ever was one. She gives birth to not one but twelve prophets, as if she by herself produced not only one divine person, but all twelve apostles. No less than twelve miraculous births are necessary to proclaim divine truth to an obtuse humanity, so that the Virgin mother has indeed earned the adoration of the faithful at her tomb. Even though Montesquieu's use of the word *Virgin* is taken from genuine Muslim texts relating to the pilgrimage to Kom, as Vernière notes (11n2), the European reader may indeed see in this passage "une impertinence" (Vernière's word) that foreshadows the religious satire to come.

Not only is the possibility of a unitary subject left behind with the exile, the multiple and contradictory virgin births, and the travels to a new land: the "nous" is also split mainly into Rica and Usbek, who are the principal letter writers, but occasionally "nous" refers to several other writers as well. Rhédi, another traveler, is one of the most important other Persians: he conveniently stays in Venice, providing a Persian interlocutor and correspondent situated in Europe but not in Paris. Like Usbek, he too stresses the necessity of acquiring learning and maturity by leaving his native land: "je sors des nuages qui couvraient mes yeux dans le pays de ma naissance" (31: 70). He is like Usbek in that he prefers to discuss serious subjects like the possibility of an ultimate weapon (Letter 105), the loss of nature's fecundity (Letter 112), or universal history (Letter 131). He is a serious and philosophical thinker who is the recipient of many letters written by Usbek, both satirical and philosophical, but unlike Usbek, he seems unencumbered by a harem.

Critics have often noticed that Rica's letters have a different tone from those written by Usbek. Usbek is seen as being more serious than Rica, and indeed Usbek does draw a sharp difference between himself and Rica early in the novel, in Letter 25: "La vivacité de son esprit fait qu'il saisit tout avec promptitude. Pour moi, qui pense plus lentement, je ne suis en état de te rien dire" (58). Usbek prefers to treat such philosophical subjects as ritual purity and impurity (Letter 17), the difference between religious practices (Letter 33), the Last Judgment (Letter 35), the various types of government (Letters 80, 102–104), depopulation (Letters 112–122), the origin of society (Letter 94), and the nefariousness of evil ministers (Letter 146). However, he does also treat lighter subjects such as the differences between Oriental and French women (Letter 26), the Parisian cafés (Letter 36), and the mad scientist (Letter 145). Rica writes many amusing, satirical letters on various curious aspects of Parisian life, such as theater, opera, relations between spouses, and all the odd people he meets, in characterizations that recall La Bruyère's *Caractères*. However, it is Rica who writes the important Letter 38 on the subordination of women to men. It is not Usbek, but Rhédi who writes Letter 105 on the danger that a weapon may be devised that will destroy entire nations—a letter that seems more prophetic in our age of atomic and other weapons of mass destruction than Usbek's optimistic reply in Letter 106, that the law of nations would unanimously consent to destroy such a "fatale invention" (220).

Chapter Two

In short, though each of the writers has a general tendency to write about a certain type of topic, each is not confined to it. No character is pure, each having mixed traits and concerns, in keeping with the view, stated earlier, that Montesquieu questions the existence of unalloyed, pure concepts and characters.

The Persians' desire for life and knowledge initiate both the process of their own maturing as subjects of a new knowledge and also the process of the text itself, of all the letters. Letter upon letter builds up a portrait of French society in the early part of the eighteenth century, as experience upon experience gradually enables the Persians to evolve from ignorance to learning. It is in these many astute and perspicacious letters that the Persians fulfill their roles as useful strangers: they state what is interesting and important about society, ranging from amusing social commentary to fundamental statements about such profound topics as the nature of justice or the ideal government for happiness. If Usbek and Rica can discover these fundamental laws and principles, cannot any Frenchman or Frenchwoman also acquire them?

And yet, there is another aspect of society that makes it impossible to know it well or to know it at all, and an inherent difficulty in ascertaining any fundamental bedrock principles. Before the travelers make landfall in Europe and describe the particular peoples and societies they encounter, Montesquieu places a set of letters that have been the object of much analysis, a cautionary tale about the Troglodytes (Letters 10–14), which examines an imaginary society in order to foreground the topic of the origins and nature of society.

Society without Origin nor Essence

The central question is posed in Letter 10: "si les hommes étaient heureux par les plaisirs et les satisfactions des sens, ou par la pratique de la vertu" (27). One can readily guess what the answer *should* be. But Montesquieu plays a trick on his readers who are in search of a fundamental answer, a universal truth valid for all humanity, by presenting the answer in his cautionary tale of the "cave dwellers," if one reads the tale not as a depiction of utopia, but as a utopia that is "sous rature," crossed out by its frame of initial violence and final downfall from grace into dystopia.

The Troglodytes story has often been read as depicting a utopia, for example by Jean Ehrard: "Le bonheur des Troglodytes, c'est celui d'un âge d'or qui ne connaît pas le péché" (*L'idée* 348), but this applies only to the middle section, Letters 12 and 13. A close reading of the story shows a more complex interplay between utopia and dystopia. Letter 11 shows the ancient Troglodytes who were horribly violent and completely anarchic: "si méchants et si féroces qu'il n'y avait parmi eux aucun principe d'équité ni de justice. Ils avaient un roi d'une origine étrangère, qui, voulant corriger la méchanceté de leur naturel, les traitait sévèrement" (28–29). Not only have the good Troglodytes issued from ancestors who were violent, but they had a foreign king powerless to reform them. And that is only the first stage of their ancient history and dystopia: there is a second stage when the people, newly liberated from their monarch, elect magistrates, and again liberate themselves from these by murder, in order to live in a generalized state of war as described by Hobbes. Only two families survive, and these are finally the foundation for the good Troglodytes and the well-known utopia of Letters 12 and 13.

It is obvious, then, that goodness and virtue are not inherent in human nature: virtuous society has a dim ancestry in a cruel past. There is no inherent nature, only a slim continuity between the past and the present—only two families survive—and more discontinuity: the two surviving families found a radically different kind of society.[7] Furthermore, the new virtue is not everlasting, and the danger comes not from elsewhere, but from inside, from its very success. The resulting overpopulation makes lack of government inefficient: "Comme le Peuple grossissait tous les jours, les Troglodytes crurent qu'il était à propos de se choisir un roi" (14: 36). The slide into domination by a monarch and into a life of criminality is predicted by the elderly man chosen to be king, who warns them against having any other rule than that of Virtue. In short, no pure virtue can exist without its dangerous opposite, just as out of evil some good can result. There is no pure concept without its dangerous supplement, its opposite that splits it from within. As Jean-Luc Nancy has shown, there is always a split into any ideal, any pure concept: "la loi de l'écart" (28) that undermines every essence, every idea: "L'érection et l'inauguration *mêmes* du Sujet ont provoqué l'effondrement de sa substance" (Nancy

33; Nancy's emphasis). The answer to the question that started the tale, are men made happier by pleasure and the senses or by virtue, refutes the very notion of a pure pleasure or a pure virtue.

The portrait of French society emerging from the letters written principally by Rica as well as some written by Usbek also offers a critique of stability, of essences, in that the society they observe has no certain and predictable characteristics and constantly changes under their very eyes and ears. The tone is given in the first sentence of Letter 24, written by Rica, when they arrive in Paris: "nous avons toujours été dans un mouvement continuel" (54). Rica describes what he sees: the surface of things and people, and what he sees is precisely a society that lives on the surface, that tries to impress, a society in which what is represented on the surface may not or does not correspond to anything else. The monarch himself gives the example "Le roi de France [...] a plus de richesses [...] parce qu'il les tire de la vanité de ses sujets, plus inépuisable que les mines" (24: 55), in a doubling of representation: his wealth does not rest on any gold reserve, but on the boundless pretense of his subjects. The monarch can, if he wants, make them think that one coin is worth two, that paper is money (56). The Pope, that other monarch of the Old Regime, is the king's equal in legerdemain: "Ce magicien s'appelle *le Pape*. Tantôt il lui [le roi] fait croire que trois ne sont qu'un, que le pain qu'on mange n'est pas du pain, ou que le vin qu'on boit n'est pas du vin, et mille autres choses de cette espèce" (56; Montesquieu's emphasis). Nothing is what it seems to be on the surface: the court is ruled not by its ruler, but by women, who Rica declares to be "d'une création inférieure" (how very different an opinion from his own Letter 38 where he will raise the feminist question of inequality of women due to their education). And there are invisible enemies of the kingdom who live not outside of the kingdom but in its very heart: "ils sont à sa cour, dans sa capitale, dans ses troupes, dans ses tribunaux [...]. On disait qu'ils existent en général, et qu'ils ne sont plus rien en particulier: c'est un corps, mais point de membres" (57–58), almost a vision like Deleuze's vision of a "corps sans organes." Usbek validates this vision in the next Letter 25 by marveling at Rica's liveliness of mind which leads to great perspicacity: "il saisit tout avec promptitude" (58)—this liveliness of mind makes Rica much more suited to grasping this fluid and indefinable society than Usbek, the slow thinker.

Rica sees everything and everyone as being dominated by the urge to be seen. Many of his letters begin by an allusion to sight: "Je vis hier une chose assez singulière" (28: 63); "Lorsque j'arrivai, je fus regardé" (30: 68); "On peut avoir vu toutes les villes du Monde et être surpris en arrivant à Venise" (31: 69); other examples occur in Letters 32 and 70; Letters 45 and 91; Letters 49 and 104. Even virtue, the announced topic of Letter 50, "si naturelle" in some people (105), is something that is given to see, as much as entirely fictive qualities: "Je vois de tous côtés des gens qui parlent sans cesse d'eux-mêmes: leurs conversations sont un miroir qui présente toujours leur impertinente figure" (106). From Letter 50 on, hearing is added to sight, and Rica, having been all eyes, now becomes all ears as well: "J'étais ce matin dans ma chambre, qui, comme tu sais, n'est séparée des autres que par une cloison fort mince et percée en plusieurs endroits; de sorte qu'on entend tout ce qui se dit dans la chambre voisine" (113–14). Usbek also listens to a religious who elaborately and elegantly justifies bending the rules through casuistry, in a letter with a tone reminiscent of Pascal's *Provinciales,* which ends with Usbek's refusing to hear any more (57: 119–22). Listening and seeing, Rica understands that this society does not hide anything, because it has no depth, and is laid out for everyone to see and hear. There is no underlying substance, only an infinitely scintillating and changing play of surfaces. Letter 84, which describes this play of appearances, indicates how these take the place of substance:

> Quel spectacle de voir rassemblées dans un même lieu toutes ces victimes de la Patrie, qui ne respirent que pour la défendre, et qui, se sentant le même cœur, et non pas la même force, ne se plaignent que de l'impuissance où elles sont de se sacrifier encore pour elle!
> Quoi de plus admirable que de voir ces guerriers débiles [. . .] chercher leur dernière satisfaction dans *cette image de la guerre*, et partager leur cœur et leur esprit entre les devoirs de la religion et ceux de l'art militaire! (177)

Fiction becomes reality, appearance becomes the only reality, if these words still have any meaning. Modern society is the reverse image of the ancient cave dwellers: it is not a cave, but "une ville bâtie en l'air, qui a six ou sept maisons les unes sur les autres [. . .] extrêmement peuplée [. . .] dans la rue, il s'y fait un bel embarras" (24: 54). Any substance has disappeared, and just as there was underlying no stable identity or fixed origin to the Troglodytes, so in modern France, all is image and surface that constantly shifts under our observation.

The initial question about the essence and origin of society was critiqued in the Troglodytes fable, and the portrait of French society as all surfaces and no depth reinforces this nonessentialist view. Yet Montesquieu, though willing to let Rica speak in this demystifying mode, was also unwilling to forego any stable basis for society. Haunted, perhaps, by the dangers posed by anarchy and instability, he places in Usbek's voice the basis of society in human nature, specifically in family bonds: "rechercher [. . .] l'origine des sociétés [. . .] me paraît ridicule [. . .] ils [les hommes] naissent tous liés les uns aux autres [. . .] voilà la société et la cause de la société" (94: 193–94). A similar move occurs in the discussion of justice: refusing to see justice as essentially divine, he situates justice as inherent in relationships among things: "La Justice est un rapport de convenance, qui se trouve *réellement* entre deux choses; ce rapport est toujours *le même*" (83: 174). Justice, however, is hard to perceive, as it gets overwhelmed by human emotions: "elle a peine à se faire entendre dans le tumulte des passions" (175). Significantly, the conclusion of Letter 83 is less than a ringing endorsement of humanity's capacity to listen to justice: "la Justice est éternelle et ne dépend point des conventions humaines; et, *quand elle en dépendrait, ce serait une vérité terrible, qu'il faudrait se dérober à soi-même*" (175). That last sentence betrays, ever so briefly, that Montesquieu might have been haunted by a fear of anarchy, and by a suspicion that any belief in essential sociability is a self-delusion—but the alternative of a contractual, artificially constructed society dependent only on human conventions (Hobbes's view) is too horrible to contemplate and must be quickly repressed.

Double Subjects and Modernity

Rica and Usbek exemplify two modes of being in society. Rica enters into this fragmented, unsubstantial society: by abandoning his identity as a Persian, he becomes someone (else). When he removes his exotic dress, he puts on a mask of being someone he is not, a Frenchman, but then being a Persian was also a mask (Letter 30). He removes his Persian dress, which, by attracting too much attention, makes him unable to discern his objective worth: "Cela me fit résoudre à quitter l'habit persan [. . .] pour voir s'il resterait encore dans ma physionomie quelque chose d'admirable" (69).[8] The search for his real worth will lead not to the answer about his worth, but to a discarding of the notion of true worth altogether: "Cet essai me fit connaître ce que je valais réellement: libre de tous les ornements étrangers, je me vis apprécié au plus juste. [. . .] J'entrai tout à coup dans un *néant affreux*" (69); the emphasized phrase will return in a later letter by Usbek. Rica draws the only possible conclusion: he has no underlying identity, other than the mask imposed by social costumes and customs. That, I believe, is the meaning of the famous last question, "Comment peut-on être Persan?" One cannot *be*, neither Persian nor Parisian.

This position lies beyond cultural relativism, which though more flexible than belief in fundamental, unchanging values, still makes reference to a center, to some fixed point: relative is still relative to something. And this point of reference can become quickly a fixed center, which makes us, for example, create an image of a supreme being in our own image, reversing the usual statement that the divinity made human beings in its image. Rica makes this point in Letter 59: "Il me semble, Usbek, que nous ne jugeons jamais des choses que par un retour secret que nous faisons sur nous-mêmes" (124). He concludes, in keeping with his position: "quand je vois des hommes qui rampent sur un atome, c'est-à-dire la Terre, qui n'est qu'un point de l'Univers, se proposer directement pour modèles de la Providence, je ne sais comment accorder tant d'extravagance avec tant de petitesse." In Letter 63, the last, logical stage of his evolution is accomplished: he dissolves into the surrounding society: "Je me répands dans le monde, et je cherche à le connaître. Mon esprit perd insensiblement tout ce qui lui reste d'asiatique, et se plie sans effort aux mœurs européennes" (131). The Persian subject loses all identity and becomes other. Rica has grasped that in this society, there is no underlying identity beneath the masks, that everything is mask and depth at once: "La dissimulation, cet art parmi nous si pratiqué et si nécessaire, est ici inconnue: tout parle, tout se voit, tout s'entend; le cœur se montre comme le visage" (131). Rica is well on the way to being not a stranger-sojourner, but a much more assimilated newcomer who loses his status as ambiguous observer, and loses himself in the host society.

Usbek had already seen this aspect of Rica and anticipated his friend's assimilation into society, thanks to his "santé parfaite," his "gaieté naturelle" (27: 62), so that "la vivacité de son esprit fait qu'il saisit tout avec promptitude" (25: 58). By contrast, Usbek complains that he is slow to think, cannot even say anything (Letter 25), and in Letter 27 he feels sad and empty: "Mais, pour moi, [...] mon corps et mon esprit sont abattus; je me livre à des réflexions qui deviennent tous les jours plus tristes; ma santé, qui s'affaiblit, me tourne vers ma patrie et me rend ce pays-ci plus étranger" (62). He wants a double recentering: toward himself (note the words "mais pour moi," and the frequent use of the "je me" reflexive construction) and toward his homeland. But he suffers many losses: he will not know who he truly is, he will not understand society and its people, and he will be unable to return to his homeland.

French society has revealed some of its secrets to him, but not all, and it seems all the more dangerous and corrupt that it seems impenetrable: the searing indictment of the dishonest ministers of Letter 146 leaves Usbek entirely without any hope or empathy for this society: "Que dira la postérité lorsqu'il lui faudra rougir de la honte de ses pères?" (323). As Usbek looks backward to an era when honesty existed, when originally there was truth and value, he bemoans the fall into present-day nothingness: "Je ne doute pas que les nobles [...] ne laissent la génération présente dans l'affreux néant où elle s'est mise" (323). The process of complete alienation is accomplished in Letter 155, when the "affreux néant" of society becomes Usbek's own. Following the long jeremiad of Letter 146, against the "climat barbare" in which he lives, Usbek pours forth many lamentations regarding his own situation: "Une tristesse sombre me saisit; je tombe dans un accablement affreux; il me semble que je m'anéantis, et je ne me retrouve moi-même que lorsqu'une sombre jalousie vient s'allumer et enfanter dans mon âme la crainte, les soupçons, la haine et les regrets" (329). With an almost Baudelairian venting of spleen, he complains of his many losses, ironically repeating the now empty pronouns *je*, *me*, and *moi*: "Malheureux que je suis! je souhaite de revoir ma patrie, peut-être pour devenir plus malheureux encore! Eh! qu'y ferai-je?" Having lost his sense of self, worried, with good reason, that he has lost his position as husband and possessor of a harem, Usbek has even lost the support of Rica, who seems to have forgotten "sa patrie, ou plutôt il semble qu'il m'ait oublié moi-même" (329). Writing to one of his eunuchs, Usbek concludes with a statement of rejection on a cosmic scale: "Rebut indigne de la Nature humaine, esclaves vils dont le cœur a été fermé pour jamais à tous les sentiments de l'amour, vous ne gémiriez plus sur votre condition si vous connaissiez le malheur de la mienne" (330). At this point, Usbek can live nowhere, not able to continue being the sojourner in France, nor able to return to his homeland.

Rica and Usbek show two types of alienation: one allows integration into society (Rica), the other excludes the subject from society, from himself (Usbek).[9] Rica alienates himself from his Persian identity in order to know French society; Usbek remains the same and remains permanently alienated from everything and everyone. Rica becomes other in order to be the same as everyone, and Usbek remains the same and is other to everyone and to himself. It might be tempting to prefer Rica's attitude, since it allows society to exist and human beings to coexist. By insisting at such length and with such forceful language on Usbek's suffering, Montesquieu seems to suggest that Rica's solution of adaptability might be a better one than Usbek's resistance, for it is a strategy of survival that allows the subject to live, though decentered, fragmented, and mobile. Usbek's immobility and despair is literally unlivable. However, as we will see in Chapter 3 on the women's knowledge, neither Rica's nor Usbek's position will represent the answer to this dilemma.

The coexistence of two such different modes of subjectivity raises the question: how can the author even envisage two such radical positions, one that is modern and one that is postmodern or contemporary? By "modern" I refer to the mode of subjectivity, initiated in the seventeenth century, that believes in the stable self in command of its will and in the objectivity of knowledge: as Reiss states, this is an "individual *I* in search of knowledge" (190) who seeks "personal possession" of this knowledge and also seeks to impose his knowledge on the world.

Chapter Two

The contemporary, "postmodern" questioning of this notion of the self, which has been variously identified with such writers as Nietzsche, Freud, Foucault, and Derrida, questions the ability of the self to impose a will on itself and on the outside world, to find certain, objective knowledge. These writers envision the self as split, discontinuous, and subject to external and internal forces not within its control.[10] This brings to the foreground the question of whether there could be a contemporary mode of subjectivity within the modern period. Reiss discusses this question at the end of his *Discourse of Modernism*, saying that "the indication within discourse of an unfamiliar discursive class may be thought of as a 'potentiality,' not as anything like 'an entity in its own right'" (382); it would be "*non-sensical* because what it would signify [. . .] could never 'fit' the other signifieds of the discourse, or *how* it would signify could not do so. It thus becomes *excessive*" (382–83; Reiss's emphasis). Refusing any possibility of the supplement, Reiss does not believe that literature might be "an eternal questioning of dominant discursive structures" (383) because that gesture makes questioning permanent, and only reinforces the dominant model: such critics who have this view of literature (Reiss quotes Paul de Man, Geoffrey Hartmann, J. Hillis Miller, Derrida, among others) "are in fact caught up in the same discursive space as the traditional critics whose practice they seek to 'deconstruct'" (383n45). I would like to argue for a more complex position that would admit the possibility of questioning, even for the necessity of it; agreeing with Reiss, I do not wish to posit questioning as a permanent feature of literature, but I refuse to deny any such questioning for literature or, for that matter, philosophy.

Can this novel, then, be viewed as going beyond the modern? Did a kind of questioning of the modern "cosmopolis" similar to the postmodern questioning of metaphysics take place in the eighteenth century? If one views the demystifying thrust of the novel as contemporary, then is that not saying that such a kind of questioning always existed? There are two competing views here.

Some see postmodernity as starting in a given period, namely, the late nineteenth or the twentieth century, and refuse to admit that an avant-garde could exist in any other time than in the twentieth century (for example, Renato Poggioli). Foucault's classification of epistemic changes would fall into this category. Like François Lyotard, one can consider that postmodernity is a radically separated period that rejects the legitimizing discourses of the Enlightenment (*La condition postmoderne*). Others (e.g., Frederick Karl), on the contrary, see in history a permanent questioning of metaphysics, and hence a coexistence of two strata in all texts. This view is argued by Jacques Derrida, Paul de Man, and Roger Laporte. The first opinion preserves the specificity of each period but has difficulty accounting for historical changes. The other view holds that there is a permanent questioning of metaphysics and hence a coexistence of two strata in all texts: but this view has difficulty defining what is specific for each period, and ends up also having difficulty talking about change, since these features are permanent in texts throughout history.

Since I have argued that there are two philosophical thrusts in Montesquieu's novel, I might want to agree with the second view, that of Derrida, Laporte, and de Man, and stay there. Indeed, I think it is fair to say that such demystification carried out by Montesquieu and more obviously by others such as Diderot and Sade, is what made possible the more general demystification of metaphysics carried out much later by Nietzsche and Heidegger. Derrida cites some authors (Mallarmé, Artaud, for example) who have been able to "opérer des frayages ou des effractions" (*Positions* 93) and "marquer et organiser une structure de résistance à la conceptualité philosophique qui aurait prétendu les dominer" (*Positions* 94). The critical aspect of the *Lettres persanes* is what makes this text so appealing and so fascinating to a contemporary audience. However, it is also clear that Montesquieu wanted to find some foundational truths that he represents as being important enough to die for. One could sum up the position of the *Lettres persanes* as a text that stages, through the mechanism of the letters' juxtaposition, the tension between the (deconstructive) resistance to the system and what resists this resistance, the foundations of truth and nature—which, as Rosset claims, constitute the basis of most philosophies of Western thought.

I would like to get away from this binary aporia that leads to enclosure in history or eternal sameness throughout time, the choice between the impossibility of something like postmodernity before our period, and the eternal presence of the postmodern kind of questioning throughout history. One way to do this is to try to keep both the specificity of historical periods and open them up to inner contradictions. In a chiasmic movement, one would first historicize the critique of metaphysics, and show what *that* particular critique did within *that* textual and historical period; secondly, what is thus rehistoricized is then what exists in our own time, or more accurately it is what makes our own specific critique possible.

This chiasmic procedure is, however, not completely satisfactory, for it too stays within the paradigm of truth and error, of contradiction and oneness. As Heidegger has said, a simple reversal of metaphysics stays entirely inside metaphysics ("Dépassement de la métaphysique" [91]). Other metaphors, other ways of thinking about thought, can be sought in order to evade the binary opposition within which my own figure of the chiasm remains caught. I prefer to say that inasmuch as Montesquieu's text brings me to do this, it is a text that lies within our modern horizon. The concept of *horizon* is suggested by Kostas Axelos in his essay "Science opérante et pensée questionnante" in *Problèmes de l'enjeu* (62–96), and explored more fully by Gianni Vattimo in *La fin de la modernité*: "une expérience de la vérité comme horizon et fond sur lesquels, discrètement, nous nous déplaçons, et non comme objet que l'on s'approprie et que l'on transmet" (19). The horizon is a stable, yet shifting line, sometimes visible, sometimes not, occulted and yet present. The multifaceted, unstable nature of this enterprise, Axelos warns us, is what defines contemporary thought: "Ce qui domine l'homme de la modernité [...] comporte un grand nombre de paramètres (ou de variables). Il est difficile d'envisager le jeu de tous les paramètres, jouant simultanément. Ce qui ne signifie pas que l'on puisse se tirer à bon marché de l'embarras, en bavardant sur le jeu multifactoriel de la réalité" (96).

One of the multifaceted aspects of Montesquieu's text that may indeed have escaped us is its particular form of contradiction, its own aporia which may not be ours. Can we try to get out of ours and think another? For what Montesquieu may have faced is not what Derrida has analyzed powerfully: the impossibility of thinking something nonmetaphysical in a logocentric language, leading to his use of words under erasure and various metaphors of folds, supplements, poisons, and invagination. Montesquieu, who had one foot in the seventeenth century and one in the eighteenth and who was truly present at the passing of an era, may have sensed something like the menace of disorder, not in language, but in society, where codes of behavior seemed to be crumbling dangerously in the free-wheeling world of the Regency. In such an environment, he would be faced with the difficulty of making order in an unraveling world threatened with the deprivation of foundational truth. I would suggest that, from his point of view, one of his problems was not how to *de*construct, but how to *re*construct.[11] It is in this light that Montesquieu's famous statement, that there is a "secret chain" linking the various parts of his novel, will be considered in a later section of this study. The Enlightenment eventually reconstructed social order based on rejection of traditional religious and mythical narratives, on the belief in progress and individual merit, and eventually elaborated democratic, egalitarian laws to replace the old, hierarchical aristocratic order that seemed increasingly outmoded.[12] This enterprise, radically different from the one in the late nineteenth and twentieth centuries that questioned this Enlightenment construction, is brought to our consciousness in our very interrogation of the *Lettres persanes* as a contemporary text. The result, somewhat paradoxically, is that our attempt to reclaim it for our contemporary age leads us to refute (at least partially) its relevance for us.

In trying to get away from simple yes or no answers, I will again cite Vattimo, who suggests that in our time, "la valeur du nouveau, radicalement dévoilée, a perdu elle-même toute valeur fondatrice et toute possibilité de valoir à nouveau" (112). As Vattimo concludes his book with the proposition that we may be only "faiblement nouveau" (185), I propose that Montesquieu may have been feebly postmodern.

This is an incomplete answer, for the men's quest for knowledge is not the only one in the novel: it is set in a context consisting of the women's progress from submission to rebellion, and the eunuchs' steadfast, yet contradictory position of domination and submission. Indeed the men, women, and eunuchs

Chapter Two

provide contexts for each other, but the most powerful relation obtains between the men and the women in relation to the pursuit of wisdom. It is time to consider the place of the women in the quest for knowledge, for here lies the answer to the men's uncompleted quest.

Chapter Three

Women's Knowledge
The Temptation of Equality

> [. . .] we, daughters of educated men, are between the devil and the deep sea. Behind us lies the patriarchal system [. . .]. Before us lies the public world [. . .]. The one shuts us up like slaves in a harem; the other forces us to circle, like caterpillars head to tail, round and round the mulberry tree, the sacred tree, of property. It is a choice of evils. Each is bad.
>
> Virginia Woolf
Three Guineas

Prologue: The Difficulties of Women's Learning

Where do women fit into this general scheme? Kant has a telling sentence in the essay "What Is Enlightenment?": "The guardians who have so benevolently taken over the supervision of men have carefully seen to it that the far greatest part of them (including the entire fair sex) regard taking the step to maturity as very dangerous, not to mention difficult" (35).[1] "Women's knowledge" can be understood in two ways: women as subjects of knowledge, and women as objects of (other people's) knowledge. The ambiguity of my title suggests that there is an interaction between what women themselves were allowed to learn, and what the culture's discourses either prescribed, described, or forbade them to know. Furthermore, there is the symbolic value attached to women, and what they represented for the culture: these representations also interact with both the women's activities and the cultural discourse about their learning. Women's learning, their being, and their symbolic value are distinct and yet so intertwined as to be inseparable.

Chapter Three

Like many novels in French and indeed Western literature, the *Lettres persanes* has a plot line that is initiated and oriented by men: men's desires impel the novel forward, and their point of view structures it.[2] Though the Persian women actually write only 11 out of the 161 letters of the novel, they are present as topics of discussion in about 36 other letters, and their presence is crucial in a disproportionate manner to the number of letters they write. The novelty of this work is that the women's subplot turns out to be crucial to the main plot, since the women's plot brings the story to a conclusion. Women do not initiate the search for knowledge nor move it forward, but they provide the ending for the men's adventures—Montesquieu deliberately rearranged the last 15 letters, which are written principally by women and eunuchs (I will deal with the eunuchs in the next chapter)[3] from their chronological order in the fiction, in order to group them together at the end.[4]

In their quest for knowledge and in their satirical observations about the West's mores, laws, literature, arts, and philosophy, Usbek and Rica also develop self-knowledge, each doing so in rather different ways. Usbek tries to retain his identity, unwilling to forego his innate, autonomous self as a Persian nobleman, while Rica is willing to accept a fragmented, decentered, and flexible self in order to integrate himself into the surrounding social milieu. The paradox is that Usbek is the one who ends up fragmented and desperately unhappy, without any place to call properly his own on earth, and Rica is the one who finds an agreeable modus vivendi in France. We can now integrate the women into this plot. Having thus reached a philosophical impasse with these two opposite modes of identity, the text finds a dramatic conclusion by means of the women's subplot. The women's story provides an ending that the men's stories could not. For in the meantime back in the seraglio, Usbek's wives, despite the harsh control of the eunuchs, gradually become more independent and eventually rebel against their masters' rule. Upon Usbek's orders, they are put to death, or they commit suicide, but not before declaring their independence and their hatred of despotism.

One of the novel's principal thrusts, as I have shown,[5] is to demystify certain notions that pertain to innateness of ideas, transcendence of self, virtue, and truth, centered around Usbek, in order to set forth the advantages of much more contemporary views which refute idealist positions relating to truth, virtue, and human nature, represented by Rica. However, this is only one aspect of the novel; another competing aspect is the opposite attempt to validate the notions of innate ideas, virtue, transcendent self, in a battle that Montesquieu was waging against such artificialist thinkers as Hobbes, who viewed the basis of society as contractual, and emphasized its artificial, arbitrary construction. Although critics debate whether to place Montesquieu into the artificialist, contractual camp, or the essentialist, idealist one, I do not think that he can be very easily classified.[6] Both *De l'Esprit des lois*[7] and the *Lettres persanes* can be read in both ways, and I would like to show how this ambivalence is located in the novel particularly with relation to the women. I will argue that the significance of the women in this text is linked with considerations about women in the eighteenth century, both as subjects and as objects of discourses which restrict them in their intellectual and social aspects, and that the promise of equality and liberation through knowledge, though attractive as a solution, proves to be illusory.

Women, considered as agents of knowledge, were kept very separate from men. Their education took place in separate schools, with very different curricula and expectations. Their lives were separate too, with different social roles expected of them, and generally few avenues to self-esteem open to them.[8] For most women there were only two options: either marriage or the convent, "aut maritus aut clausus." This did not prevent inventive attempts by women to find other modes of existence by mitigating these two options. For example, the *précieuses* attempted to opt partially out of marriage by advocating platonic marriage. Religious women tried to lessen the rigors of conventual life by imagining religious communities of lay women not bound by solemn vows.[9]

Women were also continually the objects of discourses and debates about their nature. The war between the sexes, the opposition in the seventeenth century between the "femme forte"[10] concept and its mysogynist refutations (for example, in the work with the suggestive title *Alphabet de l'imperfection et malice des femmes*, 1617), the various treatises on women's

Chapter Three

education, and the debates about quietism and flight into piety (for example, by Jeanne Guyon), all these controversies kept women visible as an object of debate in the culture. In general, there seemed to be little middle ground when it came to discussing women's nature and roles, and, for the women themselves, these debates did not open up new possibilities beyond the ones already available to them, the social roles of nun or wife and mother.

In the eighteenth century, women who were active in circles where learning had been possible to them in the seventeenth century saw their situation change for the worse.[11] Seventeenth-century Cartesianism had set forth the duality of mind and body, which meant that the mind was distinct from the body: this uncoupling of body and mind was favorable for women, who had always been viewed as overly determined by their bodies, allowing them to claim access to universal knowledge as unsexed minds. It is no accident that the most feminist, rigorously equal definition of the sexes was proposed in the seventeenth century by a follower of Descartes, Poullain de la Barre. In the eighteenth century, several simultaneous strands reduced the influence of Cartesian dualism. With Locke, and with materialism, the emphasis on the senses as the source of ideas led to the reintroduction of the body as a locus of learning[12] and the diminishing of the idea of the unsexed mind. The Regency culture saw the rise of libertinism in men-women relations and a new emphasis on the bodily and the erotic. As Erica Harth has discussed in *Cartesian Women*, science moved away from pure abstract thought and hypotheses and toward experimentation and manipulation of nature in laboratories, and concurrently learning was moving away from women-dominated salons to male-dominated *académies* and eventually to laboratories. All these trends reduced the sharp dualistic separation of thought from matter, and made it more problematic for women to claim that their minds were not influenced by their bodies. These changing aspects of learning in the eighteenth century that tended to exclude women from the places of learning paralleled a move that excluded women from the public sphere of discourse, from the political arena, as Landes has shown. The social aspect of scientific learning, which dictates who may participate in scientific learning, introduces a breach in the universality claimed by and for science. This exclusion, Evelyn Fox Keller states, "is a symptom of a wider and deeper rift between feminine and masculine, subjective and objective, indeed between love and power" (7).

There is a further link between reason and gender, which is more indirect, but profound and pervasive, more insidious because it is less visible. That the ideal of rationality is gendered, and not sex-neutral, has been discussed by several critics, such as Keller, Lloyd, and Lorraine Code, who analyze not only the practical implications of the separateness of women's lives for science, but also the deep link between the system that places objective reason over subjective feeling, culture over nature, mind over matter, and the same system of values that places man over woman. As Genevieve Lloyd summarizes:

> What does exactly the "maleness" of Reason amount to? [. . .] Our ideas and ideals of maleness and femaleness have been formed within structures of dominance—of superiority and inferiority, "norms" and "difference," "positive" and "negative," the "essential" and the "complementary." And the male-female distinction itself has operated not as a straightforwardly descriptive principle of classification, but as an expression of values. (103)

Keller also states: "Just as science is not the purely cognitive endeavor we once thought it, neither is it as impersonal as we thought: science is a deeply personal as well as a social activity" (7).[13] Lorraine Code aptly summarizes these findings: "Reason [. . .] persists as an ideal that incorporates attributes valued as masculine and is defined in terms of them" (118).

My argument thus far can be summarized in three main points. First, in the eighteenth century women were increasingly excluded from learning and major roles in political and social life by an asymmetrical system of social values.[14] Second, claiming equality on the basis of the ideal of neutrality and objectivity may seem appealing and serve a useful purpose for women, in reaction to a highly differentiated and asymmetrical value system. Third, ultimately the appeal to equality and objectivity draws on the very system that by being gendered makes the women secondary and excludes them, and therefore the solution to the women's quandary may not be an

Chapter Three

appeal to equality and symmetry, but a much more profound reform in thought.[15]

The Persian Women as Objects

Similar to the women of their times, the women in the *Lettres persanes* are first depicted as highly differentiated from men, unequal, visibly marked as sexual beings, imprisoned by their husband who is able to travel to France and acquire knowledge. Second, the women, especially Roxane, rebel and claim to find equality and liberation with the ideals of truth, virtue, and independence that they discover toward the end of the novel. This they achieve in spite of their enclosure in the seraglio, without the benefit of learning or travel, by introspection, suggesting that these ideas and ideals are innate and accessible to anyone who thinks. Third, these ideals prove to be unrealizable for these women and useless in their search for recognition and for equality, as is indicated by their fate at the end of the novel: they die at the hand of their master, who commands the eunuchs to kill them.

There are four moments when women are present in the novel. First, the Persian women describe themselves at the beginning of the novel when they have just been left by Usbek, and they remember scenes of love-making in better days past (Letters 3 and 7); a little further in the novel, there is another group of letters written by these same women on diverse aspects of their fate, Letters 47, 53, 62, and 70, to which may be added Letter 51. Second, European women are described by the astonished Persians upon their arrival in Italy and France in several letters. A third category of textual occurrences dealing with women is not a specific moment in the narrative, but the three embedded stories (Letter 67, Aphéridon and Astarté; Letter 125, the Hindu widow who does not want to burn herself on her husband's pyre; Letter 141, Ibrahim and Anaïs, itself framed within the story of the wise Zulema). Fourth, there are the last 15 letters where the Persian women's lives again occupy center stage at the end of the novel.

It is no accident that the first woman we hear in the novel talks about her body (Letter 3), and that the first body which is described is that of a woman (Letter 2) in a letter written by

Usbek to give instructions to his First Black Eunuch on how to treat his wives during his absence.[16] The Persian *men*'s bodies are hardly ever evoked, let alone described, thus reinforcing the observation that women are often seen as being primarily bodily beings, and that bodies are seen only when belonging to women.

The women are not only seen as bodies, but are seen by men. The gaze of the narrator, of the one who desires, is primarily male, as has been discussed by several critics of narrative and also and most perceptively by several writers in the fields of the visual arts, painting, and especially film (Berger, Mulvey, Kaplan, de Lauretis). At the point of entry of the woman/body in the novel—i.e., Letters 3 and 7 by Zachi and Fatmé—Zachi recalls "cette fameuse querelle entre tes femmes" (3: 14–15), a beauty contest imagined by their husband Usbek to determine which woman would have his attention. She is looking at herself when he is looking at her: "je me voyais en ce lieu où, pour la première fois de ma vie, je te reçus dans mes bras" and "je me vis [. . .] devenir la maîtresse de ton cœur" (3: 15). John Berger has analyzed the difference between the way men and women act and are seen in the world, and the consequent splitting of women's self-understanding:

> According to usage and conventions which are at last being questioned but have by no means been overcome, the social presence of a woman is different in kind from that of a man. A man's presence is dependent upon the promise of power which he embodies. [. . .] By contrast, a woman's presence expresses her own attitude to herself [. . .]. To be born a woman has been to be born, within an allotted and confined space, into the keeping of men.

As he goes on to explain, this has led to

> a woman's self being split into two. A woman must continually watch herself. [. . .] And so she comes to consider the *surveyor* and the *surveyed* within her as the two constituent yet always distinct elements of her identity as a woman. (45–46; Berger's emphasis)

In Letter 3, Zachi is not only splitting herself into subject and object, as indicated by the reflexive verbs, but is adopting the

Chapter Three

man's point of view: she is looking at herself primarily as she is seen by him.

The authors of Letters 3 and 7, Zachi and Fatmé, do not question the basic assumption that they are indeed the husband's possession. Furthermore, they state their past satisfaction in terms that resemble, and are even derived from, the dominant, male-oriented, value system that seeks to establish superiority and dominance. The beauty contest between the women, instigated by the man, sparked a contest of wills among the women, a desire for glory and victory, a desire to dominate:

> *Je* comptais pour rien la pudeur: *je* ne pensais qu'à *ma gloire*. [. . .] *Je* te l'avoue, Usbek: une passion encore plus vive que l'ambition me fit souhaiter de te plaire. *Je* me vis insensiblement devenir la maîtresse de ton cœur [. . .]. *Je* sus te retenir: *le triomphe fut tout pour moi*, et le désespoir pour *mes rivales*. [. . .] Plût au ciel que mes *rivales* eussent eu le courage de rester témoins de toutes les marques d'amour que je reçus de toi! (3: 15)

So much for solidarity among the oppressed! and so much for female consciousness at this stage of the novel. This will begin to change soon, as we shall see.

In Letter 7, however, Fatmé, another wife, the woman-object-body, dares to talk back to the man-subject-mind. In spite of the reduction to being bodies, the women are expected to function as whole human beings, complete with mind. This is a classic case of double-bind: be what I, the Persian man, ask you to be—mere bodies for my pleasure—but also be whole human beings with minds and feelings.[17] This double bind is stated in clear terms by Fatmé in her somewhat angrier Letter 7: "Vous êtes bien cruels, vous autres hommes! Vous êtes charmés que nous ayons des passions que nous ne puissions satisfaire; vous nous traitez comme si nous étions insensibles, et vous seriez bien fâchés que nous le fussions [. . .]" (20–21).

As she starts to find her own voice, Fatmé feels strongly the sense of injustice suffered at the hands of her husband, but she is still dominated by the despotic, authoritarian system from which she sees no escape: her feelings of dissatisfaction are only a hint of a more independent consciousness yet to come. This initial sign of displacement will continue, and become amplified in the novel until a final emancipation of the women and their all-too-brief seizing of control over their sexual and intellectual lives.

Another group of Letters (47, 53, 62, 70) written by the Persian women, as well as Letter 51, with a letter written by another woman embedded in it, also deal with the women's subordination and the disadvantages of their situation. These letters are not unified around a single theme, but rather expand on various different aspects of the women's situation of separateness and powerlessness. The lack of material freedom to move about is described in Letter 47, precisely when Zachi describes the disasters befalling the women when they travel to the countryside—they nearly drown in a box that carries them across a river and their outing causes an imprudent man to be executed when he comes too close to the convoy. "Que les voyages sont embarrassants pour les femmes!" (47: 98) she exclaims—emphasizing the difference between the ease with which men travel abroad and the difficulty with the women's mere excursion into the countryside—adding that men can lose their lives, but women can lose both their lives and their virtue, another example of the double standard. Zachi has just taken a further step on the road to understanding the oppressive system that defines that virtue, but has not yet come to full understanding of the system's functioning.

Just as there had been a contest between the women for love and pleasure, there is a contest of another kind, to discover who is the most miserable. In Letter 51, the Muscovite woman complains that she is not beaten by her husband, unlike her sister whose husband does beat her and thus shows his love for her: a situation even more abject than that of the Persian women who are merely abandoned by their husband, making the latter look relatively fortunate. Letter 53 by Zélis discusses the strange kind of pleasures that eunuchs may experience with women, and the subservience of her slave Zélide, who agrees to marry Cosrou, a white eunuch. The inferiority of women is surpassed here by the inferiority of the eunuchs. But there remains some

Chapter Three

uncertainty about who has the greater misery: the women, whose bodies are left whole but who are subordinated to the men, or the men, whose bodies have been mutilated but who rule over the women.

The last two letters of this middle group, however, show a double attitude toward women and their bodies. In Letter 62, Zélis praises the custom of making women used to feeling subordinated to men's desires, and yet also alludes to a different kind of freedom: "Dans la prison même où tu me retiens, je suis plus libre que toi" (62: 130), and it may be that the man is not as free and independent as he seems: "tes soupçons, ta jalousie, tes chagrins sont autant de marques de ta dépendance" (62: 130). A similar ambivalence and questioning of the wives' total subservience to their husband is indicated by Letter 70, which focuses on the ill treatment of a young bride suspected or accused by her husband of not being a virgin and therefore not acceptable for marriage. Yet the letter ends in a curious reversal where Zélis casts doubt on the accusations against the girl, and expresses a woman's indignation: "Si ma fille recevait un pareil traitement, je crois que j'en mourrais de douleur" (70: 154). In both these letters, women are moving into a complicated relationship with their own subordination, not yet rebellious, even acquiescing to their own subordination, but also chafing under the restrictions imposed on them. This stage of the Persian women's self-reflection on their ambivalent imprisonment can be seen as exemplifying one aspect of women's situation, compared with the ambivalent freedom of the European women, to which I now turn.

The European Women's Ambivalent Freedom

Compared to the ambiguous situation of the Persian women, that of European women seems astonishingly free to the Persian men. Women are the first object of Usbek's comments upon his European landfall in Italy:

> Les femmes y jouissent d'une grande liberté. Elles peuvent voir les hommes à travers certaines fenêtres qu'on nomme *jalousies;* elles peuvent sortir tous les jours avec quelques vieilles qui les accompagnent; elles n'ont qu'un voile. Leurs

beaux-frères, leurs oncles, leurs neveux peuvent les voir sans que le mari s'en formalise presque jamais. (23: 53)

In Paris, further astonishing scenes await the Persians:

[. . .] dans ce pays-ci, [. . .] les femmes y ont perdu toute retenue; elles se présentent devant les hommes à visage découvert, comme si elles voulaient demander leur défaite; elles les cherchent de leurs regards; elles les voient dans les mosquées, les promenades, chez elles-mêmes; l'usage de se faire servir par des eunuques leur est inconnu. (26: 60)

They are mobile, not restricted to their houses, and when they circulate in the outside world, they are able both to see and be seen by others—reciprocity, rather than asymmetry seems to obtain here. What shocks Usbek so much is that women are not only objects of men's gaze, but also subjects that see and that seek others' seeing. This Usbek sums up as "une impudence brutale" (26: 60).

When the European women are initially the topic of discussion by the amazed Persians, it is significant that no mention is made of their bodies. When the women are considered as autonomous subjects, rather than as objects of men's desire, their bodies disappear too. However, the body reappears immediately in Letter 26, when Usbek remembers Roxane, her complexion, her perfume, her clothes, her voice, her blushing (60–61). The contrast between the imprisoned, subjugated Persian women and the liberated, autonomous European women seems, at this stage of the novel, quite sharp. However, when at least one of the Persians, Rica (significantly himself not the possessor of a harem), inspects society more closely and in detail, he finds that the situation of European women is not so free, and in fact, lacking in two important ways, one having to do with external appearances, and the other with intellectual capacities and social status. First, liberated though they are compared to Persian women, they are still disadvantaged compared to European men. Their very frequent and total changes in fashion seem to rob the European women of their individuality and identity: in Letter 99, Rica describes the "caprices de la mode" which completely change a woman's appearance every six months: the clothes, the hairdos, the "mouches," all of which change so much that "Une femme qui quitte Paris pour aller passer six mois à la campagne en revient aussi antique que si elle s'y était oubliée trente ans. Le fils méconnaît le portrait de sa mère tant l'habit avec lequel elle est peinte lui paraît étranger; il s'imagine que c'est quelque Américaine qui y est représentée [. . .]" (205–06).

A second and more important negative aspect of the European women's situation becomes apparent when the Persians go beyond appearances and investigate some of society's institutions—education, marriage, justice. In the often-quoted Letter 38, Rica quotes a "philosophe" (perhaps Fontenelle, according to a note of Vernière's) as saying that "L'empire que nous avons sur elles est une véritable tyrannie" (38: 82). Women are inferior, not by nature, but because they are given an inferior education: "Mais c'est une véritable injustice. Nous employons toutes sortes de moyens pour leur abattre le courage; les forces seraient égales si l'éducation l'était aussi" (38: 82)—a revolutionary suggestion in view of the separateness of education I mentioned earlier. This is mentioned just once in the novel, whereas later in the century, women's education became a focal point of discussion, and indeed Mary Wollstonecraft's entire *Vindication of the Rights of Woman* (1792) can be seen as a sustained tirade against what she calls the "tyranny of man" that does not allow women to have "sufficient strength of mind to acquire what really deserves the name of virtue" (88). The tribunals also offer a striking illustration of women's subordination and reduction. Rica goes to the Palace of Justice, and all he sees is justice dealing with women's bodies (Letter 86). There is quite a gallery of odd characters: the virgin who kept her virginity too long and wants to be married; the brazen woman who has cheated on her husband; the woman who, though married, is still a virgin and accuses her husband of impotence; the victim of seduction and rape who accuses the men and, Rica adds, makes them seem "plus mauvais qu'ils ne sont" (86: 182). Rica summarizes with heavy irony: "L'amour fait retentir ce tribunal. On n'y entend parler que de pères irrités, de filles abusées, d'amants infidèles et de maris chagrins" (86: 182). Not so much love as women's *bodies* fill this courtroom. When the women are seen as inferior beings within the male-dominated system of justice, they are again seen as mere bodies.[18]

Liberation?

Thus far, we have looked at two moments when women's bodies are of importance in the novel: the Persian women's letters at the beginning as well as a set of letters in the middle, which describe their separate existence as sexual beings, and the depiction by the Persian men of the ambivalent situation of women in European manners, culture, and institutions. Before analyzing the final episode of the women's revolt and their repression by the eunuchs, I would like to discuss briefly the three embedded stories in Letters 67, 125, and 141.

Though set in different places, these three stories all depict the women's happiness and their liberation from traditional marriage, and even their revenge upon past mistreatment by men. Letter 67 contains the story of Aphéridon and Astarté, a brother and a sister of the ancient Gabar people, who love each other and can, according to their laws (no problem with incest here), get married. At the end of their many adventures, they live happily ever after. In Letter 125, a Hindu widow refuses to throw herself on her husband's funeral pyre when she is told that she will be reunited in marriage with him after her death: "Me brûler pour lui?... Pas seulement le bout du doigt pour le retirer du fond des Enfers" (264). And she promptly converts to the Muslim faith. Both these stories are set not in long ago times, but in the present: Aphéridon relates his own story to Ibben, and the woman's story in Letter 125 is told to Rica by a traveler who was a witness. In a third story, set in ancient times, Zulema, the wise philosopher, reflects on men's degrading and insulting views of women and concludes that God will make up for this in the afterlife, in a mirror image of the situation on earth, rewarding the women with ecstasy: "elles seront enivrées d'un torrent de voluptés avec des hommes divins qui leur seront soumis: chacune d'elles aura un sérail dans lequel ils seront enfermés, et des eunuques encore plus fidèles que les nôtres, pour les garder" (141: 298). In this story is embedded yet another story, that of Ibrahim, the jealous husband who kills his wife Anaïs and is in turn punished by Anaïs when she gets to heaven: she dispatches a double of Ibrahim who is kind to his wives and expels the jealous husband from the home. However, this story, appearing so close to the final section of the novel, carries a not so euphoric message at its very end: for the jealous and mean Ibrahim does return after three years, and presumably undoes the new egalitarian society that the wives and the kind Ibrahim have set up. The political revolution has lasted only about three years.

Although one can discern a feminist aspect on Montesquieu's part, the overall message is more mixed. Embedding a story is open to two interpretations. One is more negative: by being embedded, it is as if the message of revolt and liberation is not appropriate for the main plot line, and has to be relegated to a level secondary to the main level of the narrative, the men's and the wives' stories. On the other hand, specific aspects of the framing of the stories can also mean that they are presented as examples, as models for women's happiness and even revenge on male oppressors. One needs to look at the precise nature of the embedding: the framing of the two most important intercalated stories indicates their exemplarity (Letter 125, which does show a woman's rejection of her religious tradition, is presented more as an anecdote). In Letter 67, both the narrator, Ibben, and his hero Aphéridon are clearly antitheses of Usbek, for Ibben finds happiness by integrating himself in whatever country he finds himself in, and he presents the Gabar whose tale he will tell as a model of honesty, generosity, and marital happiness—with only one wife. The story in Letter 141 is told to a woman of the court who was distressed about the seraglio and multiple wives: so Rica tells her a feminist story that could reassure her. But the message of this story remains mixed, not only because of the negative ending of the story, but because of the framing of the story by Rica: he calls his Persian tale "travesti" (296), a hint perhaps that this tale of a woman's subversion has been also transformed into a more suitable tale for the court lady to hear. In that case there is rather pointed irony on the part of Rica who says that Usbek will also delight in hearing the Persian tale in a feminist disguise.

In the fourth and final moment, Letters 147–161, the Persian wives do some extraordinary things. From an extreme lack of freedom at the beginning, to a grudging acceptance of their domination, they progress to an outright revolt: they drop their veils and allow themselves to see and be seen, just like the European women or the women liberated by the just Ibrahim at the end of Zulema's story; they sleep with female slaves; they write letters to unknown and presumably forbidden correspondents, and they even have male visitors, who in three letters are described as a "jeune garçon" (147: 324) or as a "jeune homme" (149: 325 and 159: 333). The women declare their freedom in the very place where that freedom has been denied and their identity repressed: their sexuality. They are sleeping with other women, and with young, uncastrated, presumably potent men. On the level of representation in the text, however, these women's bodies disappear completely from view. It is as if the woman's body, once no longer dominated by the man, no longer an object of pleasure for the man, is no longer visible. What is represented by the eunuchs are the facts of the women's illegitimate sexuality (both hetero and homo). The pleasures of the women are mentioned, but not described, by the eunuchs and servants in Letters 147, 149, and 151.

As for the women, they use a new kind of language, in two new and important ways. First, what they tell in Letters 156, 157, and 158, is not their newfound pleasures, but their indignation at the beatings and humiliating punishments they receive at the hands of the eunuchs: for example, Roxane complains about "un traitement indigne" (156: 330) and Zachi alludes to "ce châtiment qui ramène, pour ainsi dire, à l'enfance" as "un eunuque barbare porte sur moi ses viles mains" (158: 332). Second, and most significantly, they express in high moral terms their newfound philosophy of life, their liberation from tyranny and their desire for happiness. The tone becomes very lofty, even haughty: "Soyez sûr que vous n'êtes point heureux" (158: 332).

Do the Persian women find a final victory? Roxane's famous last letter affirms the woman's total unity and identity as a sexual and intellectual being, and shows her near death by suicide. She states that "j'ai su, de ton affreux sérail, faire un lieu de délices et de plaisirs" (161: 333), and that she has gained insight into what true knowledge and virtue really are: "Comment as-tu pensé que je fusse assez crédule pour m'imaginer que je ne fusse dans le Monde que pour adorer tes caprices?

Chapter Three

[. . .] Non! J'ai pu vivre dans la servitude, mais j'ai toujours été *libre*: j'ai réformé tes lois sur celles de la *Nature*, et mon esprit s'est toujours tenu dans *l'indépendance*" (161: 334).

The ending might seem satisfying: the plot ends on the women's revolt against injustice and tyranny; the women find the "right" values of freedom, independence, and courage, in a move that places them as equals to, if not higher than, the men who seem incapable of finding these values, especially Usbek, who is a ruthless despot; and suicide seems a noble gesture in the service of freedom and egalitarianism. As they liberate themselves from their master who is enjoying the luxury of meditating on the evils of despotism while being himself a despot, they seem to escape the particularism to which eighteenth-century society was confining them more and more. Indeed these women-philosophers seem to have found a noble role, as one present-day critic believes: "The final letter, the violent death of the women is in fact the greatest form of self-affirmation possible. What really dies here is not the women—her spirit is what infuses the "Réflexions"—what dies is the old order of slavery, the old language of blind power" (Newmark 25). I find it hard to agree with these statements. Even such an insightful writer as Aram Vartanian stated that "the sexual instinct becomes the source of a revolutionary energy that *threatens* to overthrow the entire system" (27). Women threaten the system but in vain, and they die—the consolation of having one's spirit live on after one's death seems meager indeed. Force wins out in the end, because though the women do revolt and question the system that oppresses them, the old order does live on, and the women do not. I would like to consider three interrelated aspects of the ending, the plot and the subplot, the philosophical values, and the meaning of the women's deaths.

The plot's ending seems satisfying because the women accomplish what the men were not able to do: they find truth and identity. As Peter Brooks has stated (297), there are two fears about plot endings: fear of an improper ending, and fear of endlessness. The men's plot threatens to fall into both traps: Usbek's story might have the wrong ending, as he falls into despair and feels "un accablement affreux: il me semble que je m'anéantis" (155: 329), and Rica's story does not end at all, as he becomes quite assimilated into French society. The women's plot brings the novel to a good, seemingly satisfying ending.

For the women, that is, literally, another story. Nancy Miller has proposed that there are two kinds of plots for women's stories (and probably for most stories as well): euphoric plots that end with integration into society, and dysphoric plots that end in death or nothingness (*Heroine's Text* xi). What is euphoric on the textual level, and allows the novel to have a dramatic finish, is dysphoric for the characters; and this fact, obscured by the apparently euphoric ending, takes place at the expense of the female characters.[19] Suicide, or rather execution—since Roxane poisons herself in a pre-emptive move to avoid being put to death by the eunuchs—hardly constitutes a positive ending.

Roxane's new knowledge is expressed in the most idealistic, abstract terms possible. It seems she acquired this knowledge of eternal ideals and the laws of Nature without books or external aid, without the benefit of travel, much less to foreign countries, apparently only by reflection and introspection, which suggests that these values are inherent in the mind, essentially human. At the same time, she is also discovering herself and her new sexual freedom. The appeal to universal truth and values certainly would seem like an irresistible solution for women, whose lives had been up till then confined, radically different from the men's public lives. Witness Wollstonecraft's statement toward the end of the century in the *Vindication of the Rights of Woman*:

> For man and woman, truth, if I understand the meaning of the word, must be the same; yet to the fanciful female character, so prettily drawn by poets and novelists, demanding the sacrifice of truth and sincerity, virtue becomes a relative idea, having no other foundation than utility, and of that utility men pretend arbitrarily to judge, shaping it to their own convenience.
>
> Women, I allow, may have different duties to fulfill; but they are *human* duties, and the principles that should regulate the discharge of them, I sturdily maintain, must be the same. (120; Wollstonecraft's emphasis)

Later in her treatise, she also demands:

> To render also the social compact truly equitable, and in order to spread those enlightening principles, which alone can meliorate the fate of man, women must be allowed to

> found their virtue on knowledge, which is scarcely possible unless they be educated by the same pursuits as men. (245)

However, what Roxane and Wollstonecraft are proclaiming is the integration of women into the "same pursuits as men," without understanding that this is precisely, and ironically, the very system based on a repressive series of dichotomies, such as mind/matter, man/woman, objective/subjective, reason/feeling, which, as I mentioned earlier in this chapter, represents a gendered system favorable to man and masculine reason. What Claudia Moscovici says about Wollstonecraft goes for Montesquieu: "Wollstonecraft's effort to make a space for gender-specific laws within otherwise unaltered masculine codes of citizenship proves a very difficult and self-undermining task" (87), because both retain an "androcentric framework" and because both are ultimately "less interested in ameliorating the status of women for themselves [. . .] as much as for the sake of men and for the good of a masculine society" (87).

Philosophically, then, the answer is an idealist one: in some distant time and place, in some utopia, all male and female beings would have stable, complete identities and live in a just and free society. The idealist position, which was critiqued during the rest of the novel, is recuperated at the end at the expense of the women. Indeed, the essentialist position which would fix an essence to men and women is, like biologism, naturalism, and other a-historical isms, antithetical to women and men's liberation from these fixed, predetermined essences (de Lauretis; Grosz; Moi; Brodzki and Schenk). As Toril Moi's analyses show, it is necessary to denounce the idea of woman, of essential femininity, and carry out "the programme of recognizing the multiplicity of women (rather than of 'woman')" (147). How hard this critical enterprise might be is suggested by Clément Rosset, whose history of anti-essentialist philosophies affirms that these are infrequent and short-lived in the history of Western philosophy: "l'histoire de la philosophie [. . .] se confond avec l'histoire du naturalisme," and hence only a crisis in the main tendency of philosophy can yield another, minority, viewpoint: "il faut une crise de la philosophie (impliquant que toutes les représentations de principe d'être, de cause, de nécessité, sont provisoirement écartées) pour que devienne possible une pensée artificialiste, assumant ses représentations de l'existence à partir de la seule idée de hasard" (127). He situates such crises in the pre-Socratic era, in the sixteenth century, and the pre-Cartesian seventeenth century, as well as later in the seventeenth century. I would submit that the later part of the seventeenth century was probably more imbued with naturalist thought than Rosset allows, but that lies beyond the scope of this book. In the age of Enlightenment, orthodoxies, both religious and political, were passing from the intellectual scene, but very slowly, not forming a crisis whereby artificialist thought might have re-emerged. As Toulmin says, "From 1750 on, the picture was at all stages open to revision," and the doctrines of the rationalist "cosmopolis" were not dismantled until the twentieth century (143). Montesquieu was certainly ahead of his time, as the demystification of ideals and essences is, I believe, one of the principal thrusts of his novel. By ending on a vigorous reaffirmation of idealist knowledge and the notion of a transcendental self, it turns out that the text is performing a remystification that is at odds with the rest of its message. This text is ambivalent, in the literal sense of the term of having two sets of values. Does one dominate, or are we left with an undecidable text?

Though the appeal to ideals may have positive value, it is effective and useful only in the short term, in a fight against inequality, particularism, exclusion, and separation of women from society. In the long term, the entire system must be rethought from the ground up in order to avoid falling into the trap of essentialism based on men's and women's functions. The problem must be insoluble, for both men and women are caught in social systems that are beyond individuals' capacity to modify, as Stewart suggests: "Ou le dilemme ne serait-il pas beaucoup plus profond, celui de l'*impossibilité foncière* de joindre comme de modifier ces deux univers [the West and Persia]? Le problème en Perse n'est ni une question de valeurs individuelles ni de *son* [Usbek's] despotisme personnel mais d'un *système* despotique qui obéit essentiellement [. . .] à d'autres que lui" ("Toujours Usbek" 149). Stewart's "essentiellement" points out the problem. The dilemma is insoluble within the framework of essentialist ideas and ideals, but could be envisaged on the political level by a realization that all systems are artificial and hence subject to modification, not by individuals but by political movements. Such an imagined idea might indeed make this text an undecidable one. However, Usbek does not ever raise the possibility of political action on this level, as Stewart says: "Usbek ne se pose jamais la question de savoir comment introduire en Orient les traits les plus positifs du libéralisme occidental" (149). Neither does the text; by reinforcing the existing systems' inevitability without the hint of any awareness that these systems might be modified, eventually it comes down on the side of conservatism and conservation of existing values.

But Usbek does take political action: the only political action that occurs in the novel is that the women are defeated and put to death by his orders. As Suzanne Pucci states, "this text recuperates [. . .] the same singular law of the father" ("Letters" 131).[20] There is no democracy at the end of the novel; on the contrary—the despot/husband is more dominating, and more cruel than ever. Virtue, truth, and freedom would demand a destruction of despotic power that does not happen in the novel, which emphasizes the cruelty of the despot and the inability of the dominated people to replace their masters, who exercise control through brute force. The final disaster—the execution of the women—is testimony to the fact that, however appealing demands for equality of treatment might be, these demands alone will not create conditions for freedom and democratic rule. Inasmuch as these ideals are presented as a goal and as a solution, this amounts to a remystification that the rest of the text had critiqued.

It is as if Montesquieu had dared to rethink radically the basis of society, philosophy, and sexuality,[21] then pulled back and established a foundational principle, precisely in sexual difference and the definition of sexual roles, transformed into essential definitions of masculinity and femininity. That is what is at stake here: nothing less than the possibility of boldly rethinking and restructuring society, in a novel which represents the crossroads of Western society as it was transforming itself from traditional and hierarchical to modern and democratic. And perhaps the failure of the revolution at the end forebodes, "in a glass, darkly," the necessity of a more violent and radical revolution yet to come.

Chapter Four

Who Are the Eunuchs?

> La coutume est une seconde nature, qui détruit la première. Mais qu'est-ce que nature? pourquoi la coutume n'est-elle pas naturelle?
>
> J'ai grand'peur que cette nature ne soit elle-même qu'une première coutume, comme la coutume est une seconde nature.
>
> Pascal
Pensées

Paul Valéry asks the question "Mais qui m'expliquera tous ces eunuques?" and speculates, "Je ne doute pas qu'il n'y ait une secrète et profonde raison de la présence presque obligée de ces personnages si cruellement séparés de bien des choses, et en quelque sorte d'eux-mêmes" (73). Ever since Valéry's time, critics have asked the same question about the meaning of the eunuchs in Montesquieu's novel and offered various answers.[1]

From the eighteenth-century travel accounts read by Montesquieu down to our own time, eunuchs and castrati have continued to be the object of curiosity and speculation.[2] Accounts of the eunuchs' role and significance show that many meanings can be attached to them: men may become eunuchs voluntarily out of a religious impulse to master one's desires, or to become ministers of a powerful ruler who will brook no equal man in his palace, or to become singers on the operatic stage.[3] Or men can become eunuchs quite involuntarily, out of punishment or revenge. And they have existed in such vastly different cultures as Persia, ancient China, Western Europe, and Russia from the Middle Ages to the nineteenth century and India in the twentieth century. Upon reading such accounts, one is struck by the divergence between the stark, apparently unambiguous nature

Chapter Four

of the physical operation and the variety of motives, means of operating, and consequences for the men involved.

Despite the fact that we no longer castrate men to create singers, ministers, or guardians of a harem, nor to punish criminals, the image persists in our time: for example, one thinks of Freud's "castration complex," of Zola's vivid scene of postmortem castration at the end of *Germinal*, of Barthes's use of Balzac's story "Sarrasine" in *S/Z* to illustrate the nature of a "texte scriptible." The very first words of Barthes's actual analysis of the text, "Le hasard (mais est-ce le hasard?)" (25), seem to suggest that something more than chance led him to study Balzac's story about a castrato.[4] The great variety of meanings attached to being a eunuch can only be enhanced by the absence of eunuchs in our time, and perhaps, after all, our minds are just as free to speculate now as in earlier times.

In this chapter, in answer to Valéry's question, I will focus on Montesquieu's eunuchs and situate them in the context of my interpretation of the novel's philosophical concerns. In the previous chapters, I have shown that the two principal male characters, Usbek and Rica, have opposite and complementary stances regarding the place and function of the self in society: Usbek wants to cling to his identity as permanent, unified in the face of a changeable, varied societal scene, while Rica allows himself to be dispersed and embraced by the various facets of society. The irony is that Usbek becomes isolated and unsure of who he is, both outwardly and inwardly, while the scattered Rica, losing his self, finds a happy mode of existence. To this impasse of "qui perd gagne," and the converse, "qui gagne perd," the women furnish an answer and rescue the novel (though not the men) from the skeptical crisis: the acquisition of transcendental values of courage, truth, and virtue, by deduction and introspection, and by affirming their personal independence from tyranny. However, the final answer lies on another, political, level, beyond the acquisition of eternal truths or values, for one of the men, Usbek, retains political power as ruler of a harem, and he uses it to punish the rebellious women.

Men and women, who together make up the human race, seem to constitute a natural diptych: as Chapters 2 and 3 showed, the men's plot and the women's dénouement are interdependent. This neat opposition and complementarity of the

Who Are the Eunuchs?

sexes is a false impression, for in the text's universe the eunuchs are present from the very beginning, and it was only my analysis that, by focusing on men and women, seemed to disregard them. The eunuchs are nothing if not the ultimate ambiguous human beings in this novel. It will be the goal of this chapter to reflect on their strange nature, and the crucial place they occupy in this novel. Both absent and present, a "third sex" which is not one (with apologies to Luce Irigaray), the eunuchs are a conundrum that makes them both apparently dispensable—not every critic who examines this novel discusses them—and yet indispensable to a full reading of the text. Though they never visit Europe, these strangers refract some of the most important philosophical and social issues that Montesquieu addresses in his novel.

The Text: Internal Clues

A close look at the text's organization furnishes a necessary and informative preamble to my subsequent analysis. For Montesquieu left little to chance in the structure of his novel: witness the clever rearrangement of the letters out of their strict chronological sequence in order to emphasize certain themes and questions, notably the regrouping of the seraglio letters at the end. To the question "Why so many eunuchs?" it can be noted that in the first version of the novel there did not seem to be so many. Out of the 29 letters that deal with eunuchs (by, to, or about eunuchs) in the final version of the novel,[5] 9 were added to the original version (which, I remind the reader, I consider to be the B edition, following the persuasive analyses of Edgar Mass): Letters 41, 42, 43, and 47 were not in the B edition, and Letters 15, 22, 157, 158, and 160 were additions in the C manuscript.

Some of these additional letters added by Montesquieu amplify the characterization of Usbek, adding to his complexity: Letters 41–43 show his clemency and kindness, while Letters 157, 158, and 160, by emphasizing the cruel and barbaric punishment the eunuchs carried out at Usbek's command, show him to be vengeful and harsh. Thus a change in Usbek occurs over time, indicating that Montesquieu wanted to emphasize the effect that staying away from his harem and remaining in

Chapter Four

Western society had on him. Neither Usbek nor Rica are meant to be mere mouthpieces for social satire; instead, they are to be taken as having their own internal dynamics as characters.

Three letters added by Montesquieu (15, 22, and 47) furnish an inside view of the harem environment. Letter 15, and Letter 22 which replies to it, are an addition in the C manuscript, both written by one eunuch to another, and emphasize the crucial theme of nature that I will analyze later. Letter 47 (analyzed in Chapter 3), which is lacking in the B edition, is written by Zachi who describes the problems women encounter while traveling to the countryside. Whatever Montesquieu wanted to say with these characters, he obviously wanted to emphasize and amplify even more as he reread his own text and added to it.

The 29 letters relating to eunuchs are in two groups, 16 letters in the first part of the novel (2–96) and 13 in the ending, and in the first group there are some subgroupings. Three groups of letters (2, 4, 7, and 9; 20, 21, and 22; 47 and 53) describe the situation in the seraglio in which eunuchs figure prominently as the wives' guardians, and Letters 41–43 form a minidrama where Usbek spares a terrified young slave from castration. Letters 64, 79, and 96 are written by eunuchs to Usbek. The last group of letters, 147–160, is interrupted by a single letter (155) only apparently not concerning the eunuchs: with 8 letters before and 5 letters after, placed at a kind of Golden Mean in the final tableau, it is deliberately out of chronological order, having been written in October 1719, and inserted in the dénouement which takes place in 1720. In this letter Usbek bemoans his condition as an exile in terms entirely reminiscent of the eunuchs' complaints in earlier letters, suggesting that as eunuchs acquire power to punish precisely through Usbek's order, Usbek himself has become a kind of eunuch. This is consistent with Montesquieu's view of nature as consisting of forces in equilibrium, in which an excess in one part causes a lack elsewhere in a reaction described by Josué Harari as mechanical: "for every action there should be an equal and opposite reaction [. . .] if one organ expands, another must shrink away" (95).[6] Later in the chapter, I will return to the connection between eunuchs, men and women, and power.

Although the letters regarding eunuchs are grouped, they are also scattered throughout the entire novel, so that never too many letters go by without the reader being reminded of the presence of these strange people. Even in the longer stretch of the novel when the eunuchs themselves are absent, between Letters 96 and 147, they are never totally absent, as they are evoked in Letters 114 and 117 in the section on depopulation (Letters 112–122). One might say that they constitute a thread that is constantly part of the fabric of the novel, just as the women are also present at various intervals in the novel. The nine additional letters also reinforce this interweaving, as they do not add so much as they highlight some characteristics belonging to the eunuchs, the women, and the men as they appear in the text.

Valéry's question, "Why so many eunuchs?" has now become: "Why so many more?" The eunuchs appear in Letter 2, just before the women, one of whom writes Letter 3. From the beginning men, eunuchs, and women form an inextricable structure that persists throughout the novel: and the fact that they appear before the women might be emblematic of their importance.

Natural Roles in Question

Letter 2 offers an apparently simple definition of the eunuch's role: "Tu es le gardien fidèle des plus belles femmes de Perse" (12), a sentence fraught with irony. The guardian will soon be called a monster (Letter 4), and not all the eunuchs are always faithful to their roles, judging from the confession made by the First Eunuch himself in Letter 9. There he admits to losing his self-control: "j'osai porter ma main dans un lieu redoutable" (24), whereupon the woman whom he is supposed to guard becomes his blackmailer. The word *gardien* is repeated several times as a definition of the eunuchs' role (Letters 22, 64, 114, 115), and, as the first noun associated with them in Letter 2, this word has implications that bear close examination. An excursus into family roles in Old Regime culture will serve to highlight their vicissitudes in Montesquieu's text.

In the domestic economy, the ones who are the custodians of the household's goods and wealth are the women who live within the house, while the men are the acquirers who go outside into the market place in order to bring the goods home. The man's task is to go out, travel, and acquire goods, while

Chapter Four

the woman's role is to guard them. This division of roles between men and women was generally the norm throughout the Old Regime: "Women for the most part lived in a world of their own but not cut off from the outside" (*A History of Private Life* 3: 412). Women were "guardians of the home and of family morality" (*History* 418) in the society of the Old Regime, until another model, that of companionate marriage based on personal aspirations of a couple to happiness, began to assert itself and take hold in the second half of the eighteenth century, when public and private spheres also became redefined away from the norms of court society.

As an example of such a statement of the separation of roles, I will refer to a text from that culture which is particularly eloquent in its overt apology for such separation, and insightful on the inner contradictions of such a separation. In *The Family in Renaissance Florence* [*I libri della famiglia*, Book 3], Leon Battista Alberti articulates the desire for "achievement of virtue and glory" to "the needs of contemporary civic life" defined by the city: and the city was "primarily a city of merchants rather than farmer-warriors" (Introduction 17–18). Alberti was in tune with the transformation of his society from one based on landed aristocracy to one based on exchange of goods, resulting in the rise of a patrician and merchant class that has a foot in the aristocracy, yet diverges from it by its source of wealth and its greater mobility. Such a continuing movement of wealth from land to commerce, is one of the long and slow transformations of Old Regime culture from the Renaissance on and throughout the eighteenth century.

In this evolving society, Alberti contrasts men with women by their respective functions as acquirer and guardian. He defines the man's role as dealing with "matters of wider consequence" and the woman's role as taking care of "all the smaller household affairs" (207). Alberti buttresses his definition by appealing to the laws of nature which institute a broad-ranging dichotomy between men and women, according to the authority of the ancients. The passage is worth quoting at length:

> They [the ancients] used to say that men are by nature of a more elevated mind than women. They are more suited to struggle with arms and with cunning against the misfortunes which afflict country, religion, and one's own children. The

character of men is stronger than that of women and can bear the attacks better, can stand strain longer, is more constant under stress. Therefore men have the freedom to travel with honor in foreign lands, acquiring and gathering the goods of fortune. Women, on the other hand, are almost all timid by nature, soft, slow, and therefore more useful when they sit still and watch over our things. It is as though nature thus provided for our well-being, arranging for men to bring things home and for women to guard them. (207)

This neat dichotomy is undermined, however, in two significant ways: when men become too involved in running the household economy, they are warned against becoming "idle creatures who stay all day among the little females" and against keeping their minds "occupied with little feminine trifles" that will make them "lack a masculine and glorious spirit" (208). The women's difficulty comes from the contradictory role they have to play: on the one hand they are excluded from going outside and are subordinated to the men, but on the other hand, inside the house they must not only guard the goods, but run the household as well. A wife must be obedient to her husband, and she must be "vigorous" and "wise" in her "rule of the household" (208). No wonder she needs long and detailed instructions by the husband if she is to become a "woman of authority" over the servants and children (220). Masculinity and femininity are defined as ideals existing in nature, yet in society, these ideals seem fragile, open to distortion or disintegration. A man finds the task of being "virile and a real man" (217) a "heavy task" (204): he must be constantly on guard and avoid "even the least bit of self-surrender in front of my wife" (217), and he can easily become like "little females" (208) if too closely involved in his own household. The strongest language is used by Alberti to drive home this lesson to the men: he castigates some men who "unwisely suppose that they can win obedience and respect from a wife to whom they openly and abjectly subject themselves" (216); and "I did not imagine for a moment that I could hope to win obedience from one to whom I had confessed myself a slave" (217).

If men are prone to slipping down from the high ideal of virile mastery, the women have an opposite difficulty: that of becoming rulers inside the household while remaining obedient to the master. (Apparently, Alberti does not consider the outright role reversals of disorderly women who try to become the "women on top" studied by Natalie Zemon Davis.) Women may succumb to two temptations that Alberti deals with at some length: "unchastity," which "angers God" and, in second place after that and in considerable detail, the temptation of putting on cosmetics: "you will disdain [. . .] those vanities which some females imagine will please men. All made up and plastered and painted and dressed in lascivious and improper clothing, they suppose they are more attractive to men than when adorned with pure simplicity and true virtue" (213). Women should "never anoint themselves with anything but river water" (215), a symbol of nature's purity that even the speaker's wife ignored on one occasion. That this occasion was Easter drives home the point that these ideals are hard to maintain, even on one of the most holy days of the Christian calendar. And the husband's deviousness in making his reprimand, "how did your face get dirty?" (216), undermines his own role as the stern teacher of his wife.

That there is a longer discussion of cosmetics than adultery might seem ironic, although one explanation might be that adultery is sufficiently condemned by religion and needs no further comment. Perhaps, however, the apparently frivolous issue of cosmetics carries more philosophical import than seems apparent at first blush. In her analysis of Alberti's text, Carla Freccero has stated exactly what is at stake here: "The invective against cosmetics is usually based on a nature-artifice opposition" (206) that is nevertheless fragile, subject to outward opposition and inner contradiction: "Patriarchy, like 'power' or hegemony, is never absolute." But contradictions are not sterile, they "are not necessarily less productive for being contradictions, whether on the material or cultural level" (207). Indeed, contradictions are a necessary condition of production of meaning, not just an inevitable weakness in the system. Cosmetics become meaningful only in opposition to river water, and vice versa; this opposition then is taken as evident, its own construction being repressed. Structured dichotomies such as male/female, master/slave, are no less constructed than the river-water/cosmetics one. The problem of advancing knowledge of the world by means of systematic oppositions is one

Who Are the Eunuchs?

that the entire eighteenth century struggled with; as Julie Hayes says, "knowledge suppresses consciousness of its own facticity, but at a price" (45). The price is that these dichotomies are taken for founded in a natural order, that they are abstract, impossible to realize and require devious accommodation to make them work, and that they are used to impose an order on subordinate groups—women, for example—that do not have access to the power necessary to escape from their domination.

The natural roles decreed for men and women are ideal, supposedly grounded in nature, and yet they are susceptible to distortion and transformation in Alberti's text. It was always possible for a man to become feminized, and for a woman not to live up to her role as guardian and as ruler. In Montesquieu's text, the eunuchs, themselves distorted human beings, become the guarantors of the natural roles of men and women: they are the intermediaries, the ironic enablers who allow the natural roles to continue existing. Through them Usbek (the husband) can rule over women without running the risk of becoming feminized, and the women are confined to playing one role only in their womanly sphere, that of subservient wife. The men and the women can fulfill their respective functions: the men can "travel with honor in foreign lands" and the women can "sit still" in the seraglio (Alberti 209).

The eunuchs represent yet another facet of human subjectivity different from the men and women, and yet necessary to both. Whereas the men split into two possibilities with Rica and Usbek, and the women furnish the solution to the men's dilemma, a resolution that seems very fitting, the eunuchs are different figures: they are split within themselves, and can never play a noble role. They form a contrast with both the men and the women, being an indispensable third term that never acquires a permanent, solid essence. They live in a slippery world of near-manhood, of persisting but vague sexual desires, in an alternation between mastery and slavery, glory and baseness, that seems uniquely theirs.

In other words, the internal slippage out of "natural" roles, such as those described by Alberti, is transferred, in Montesquieu's text, onto third parties, the eunuchs. They are the locus of doubleness and ambiguity. They are men who play women's roles by being guardians inside the house and they are both

Chapter Four

master and slave: slaves who play the master's role in the master's absence, masters who play the slave's role—and in addition, slaves and masters for each other, since there is a visible hierarchy in the harem. Through these characters, Montesquieu is free to explore nonnatural beings, and through them to address questions such as the contractual basis of society and the nature of power.

Nature/Artifice, or The Generalized Eunuch

Eunuchs, by their very nature, exemplify artificiality and contractuality. They are the result of a deliberate operation that removes them from "natural" genders: if today critics frequently discuss the "constructedness" of gender, then the eunuchs were an early and overt example of a construction of a third gender. And in Montesquieu's world, this manipulation was in the service of this contract between men: if you give up your manhood, I will give you power. In this section I will focus on the first part of the contract, the "giving up," and in the next section I will examine the compensatory acquisition of power.

Men, women, and eunuchs each write from their own perspective on the incomprehensible nature of the eunuch who gives up so much in order to have a privileged role in the harem. The husband stresses their artificiality and subservience, while the women stress their difference and strangeness, and the eunuchs themselves emphasize their suffering and their instability.

At the very beginning of the novel, Letter 2, written by Usbek, outlines the double and contradictory nature of the First Black Eunuch, who is both slave and master to the women. Logically enough, the master likes to remind his eunuch that he is a pure creation of the master who, godlike, made him *ex nihilo*: "Souviens-toi toujours du néant d'où je t'ai fait sortir" (13), perhaps implying that he might be plunged again into nothingness. In Letter 21, he insists heavily on the lowly nature of the eunuchs, calling them "vils instruments que je puis briser à ma fantaisie" and as insignificant as the "insectes que je trouve sous mes pieds" (51).

The First Eunuch expands on his master's perception from his own perspective, and describes his suffering in his "prison affreuse" (9: 23), his separation from himself, the compensations of having power, and the instability of being both a slave and a master. All these comments echo Letter 2, written by Usbek, stating in stronger terms the anguish of his constant anxiety and instability even within one day: "Combien de fois m'est-il arrivé de me coucher dans la faveur et de me lever dans la disgrâce?" (9: 26). Letter 9, however, yields another meaning if we read it in context of the letter preceding it. If Letter 8, which I analyzed at some length in Chapter 2, shows the inauthenticity of the men's supposed quest for knowledge that concealed a real fear for their lives, then Letter 9 shows the eunuchs to be just as embedded in lies. The eunuch himself is not always aware of this: although he says that there are compensations to having power that make him feel like a man again, and that old age has brought him some peace, he continues his letter with descriptions of the humiliations perpetrated on him by the women who perhaps sneak a young man into the seraglio and blackmail him into submission.

The women focus on the difference between the artificially created eunuch and the natural man and woman. These differences are rooted in the women's natural longing for their absent husband, in their very nature as bodily, erotic beings, and by the husband's insistence on his absolute mastery over both eunuchs and women. Zachi calls the Black Eunuch a monster (Letter 4), and Fatmé states that eunuchs are less than men in Letter 7. The most telling letter written by a woman is Letter 53, in which Zélis expresses her amazement at the eunuch Cosrou's passion for her slave girl, Zélide. Written for the most part in the interrogative, exclamatory mode, this letter asks: "Et quoi? être toujours dans les images et dans les fantômes! ne vivre que pour imaginer! se trouver toujours auprès des plaisirs, et jamais dans les plaisirs!" (112).

Perhaps this strange mode of existence betwixt and between is what appealed to the nineteenth-century painter Lecomte du Nouÿ, who painted *A Eunuch's Dream* (1874) showing a sleeping eunuch holding a still smoking pipe out of which arises a ghostlike beautiful naked woman who floats away wrapped in gauzy veils, while gazing longingly at the man (see fig. 1).[7] Next to the woman is an equally ghostlike putto holding a huge, glistening knife, also looking at the sleeping figure. The whole scene is set on a rooftop terrace, on which can be seen a stork,

Chapter Four

Fig. 1. Jean Lecomte du Nouÿ, French, 1842–1923. *A Eunuch's Dream*, 1874. Oil on wood panel, 54 x 75.5 cm. © The Cleveland Museum of Art, Seventy-fifth Anniversary Gift of Mrs. Noah L Butkin, 1991.173. Used by permission.

Who Are the Eunuchs?

with, in the background, several minarets and the domes of two mosques. Though the painting is said to be an example of "juste milieu" painting accessible to a wide audience, it also depicts the mystery of the eunuch's love which can be only imaginary, the inaccessibility of pleasures so near and yet out of reach, as well as the underlying menace represented by the huge knife. Zélis says it thus: "Je t'ai ouï dire mille fois que les eunuques goûtent avec les femmes une sorte de volupté qui nous est inconnue; que la nature se dédommage de ses pertes [. . .] et que, dans cet état, on est comme dans un troisième sens, où l'on ne fait, pour ainsi dire, que changer de plaisirs" (53: 113). Only in a dream is such a contradictory pleasure to be experienced.

The world in which the eunuch is necessary and possible is a world without originary presence, in which eunuchs exist as in a "third sense," in the logic of the "dangerous supplement." It is not intelligible to reason: "La raison est incapable de penser cette double infraction à la nature: qu'il y ait du *manque* dans la nature et que *par là même* quelque chose *s'ajoute* à elle. D'ailleurs on ne doit pas dire que la raison est *impuissante à penser cela*; elle est constituée par cette impuissance." The eunuch is a supplement to the two "natural" sexes, yet he is also indispensable to the master, to the sex in power, substituting for him in his absence, in a supplementarity that reason cannot account for: "[la raison] est la pensée de l'identité à soi de l'être naturel. [. . .] le supplément vient *naturellement* se mettre à la place de la nature" (Derrida, *Grammatologie* 214; Derrida's emphasis).

If on the one hand, eunuchs fascinate precisely because they are a supplement that reason is unable to understand, they are, on the other hand, not an extraordinary phenomenon: for both the men and the women partake of the economy of the supplement. Each is a dangerous supplement to the other. The husband is an apologist abroad for tolerance and a despot at home; absent, superfluous, he fears that upon his return there may well be no place for him (Letter 155). The women are reduced to being erotic objects suited only for the master's enjoyment, but they cannot be too stupid or they will be boring (cf. the double-bind noted in Chapter 3, p. 72). Intelligence and erotic sensibility are needed to supplement each other but always run the risk of being excessive. The notion of supplement is double-edged: it implies something it is supplement to, and it cannot exist without all the other components being themselves brought within the economy of supplement. The notion of separate and basic concepts, which can be supplemented, dissolves into a generalized supplementarity, where no term can dominate the other in the name of a fundamental "nature": there is no before and no after, nothing essential and nothing extra: "Aucun des termes de cette série ne peut, y étant compris, dominer l'économie de la différance ou de la supplémentarité"—Derrida claims that Rousseau's dream consisted in "faire entrer de force le supplément dans la métaphysique" (*Grammatologie* 444); on the contrary, Montesquieu has made the supplement enter the realm, not of the metaphysical, but of the fictional, populating the imagination of readers in the eighteenth century, and prompting Paul Valéry's question, the reason for all those eunuchs.

That Montesquieu envisages the similarity between eunuch and husband, slave and master, can be clearly seen in three letters that, though separated by large intervals in time and in the text, may be read together because of one significant detail: they are written to the same correspondent. Letters 6, 27, and 155 are written by Usbek to his friend Nessir, whose name has a somewhat negative connotation suggesting *nescire*, "to ignore or to not know," and who seems destined to receive melancholy outpourings from Usbek. In these letters, which span eight years, Usbek reveals himself in similar terms to be pervaded with doubts, negativity, and sadness. In Letter 6, he is unsure whether he can carry through with his trip: "une certaine inquiétude a achevé de me troubler et m'a fait connaître que, pour mon repos, j'avais trop entrepris"; in that same letter he reveals that he does not love his wives: "j'ai prévenu l'amour et l'ai détruit par lui-même; mais, de ma froideur même, il sort une jalousie secrète, qui me dévore" (18). Immediately upon crossing the Persian border into Turkey, he already fears the "tristes nouvelles" that might reach him from the seraglio, and he bemoans "l'état où je suis" (18), an incurable, hopeless ill that no friend can cure. Upon his arrival in Paris, in Letter 27 Usbek contrasts himself with Rica, and his complaints of feeling "triste," "abattu," and in feeble health foreshadow the much

Who Are the Eunuchs?

longer letter written 7 years later (62). Written perhaps when contemplating a return to Persia, Letter 155 is the culmination of this feeling, one long jeremiad that starts with his "tristesse sombre" (329) and that ends with his feeling of rejection from the human race just like his eunuchs: they are both a "rebut indigne de la Nature humaine" (330). Thus the master has become impotent, like a eunuch separated from himself, or rather he was always already impotent, from the moment he left his wives to flee to France nine years before his final cry of despair. Like his eunuchs who are separated from themselves, he feels separated from religion, home, country, and wives, but, unlike his eunuchs, he seems to have little compensatory satisfaction. Whether writing before his stay in Paris or at its conclusion, Usbek suffers from emptiness and loss: any state of natural superiority of master over servant has disintegrated into a state of emptiness for both: "For the despot shares, in a decisive sense, the impotence of his eunuchs" (Vartanian 30). However, the eunuch will have one superiority over his master: he will be able to mete out real punishment to the women. But before discussing the nature of the eunuchs' power, let us linger awhile longer on the question of Nature and its subversions.

In order to insist on these themes, Montesquieu adds two letters in which two eunuchs talk to each other and explore the aporia of nature. In Letter 15 (the first of the C supplement), the First Eunuch writes to a black eunuch, Jaron, who is accompanying Usbek on his travels to the West. The writer lingers on the question of nature in a sentence reminiscent of Pascal's fragment quoted at the head of this chapter: "Il s'en fallait bien que la nature eût encore parlé lorsque le fer te sépara de la nature" (38). What is this nature that has not yet spoken, yet from which he is already so far away? As if to drive this point home, he continues his paradoxical, Pascalian musings: "Je crus te voir prendre une seconde naissance et sortir d'une servitude où tu devais toujours obéir, pour entrer dans une servitude où tu devais commander" (38). The first natural birth into servitude is replaced by a second, unnatural birth into a more paradoxical state, into another type of servitude that includes the ability to command over women in the place of, and for, the master-husband. The first nature is erased, but not completely, since he remains a servant by birth, and replaced

Chapter Four

by a second nature that depends on an uneasy balance between "un flux et un reflux d'empire et de soumission" already described in Letter 9 (25).

In Letter 22, also added in the C supplement, Jaron, the black eunuch, writing to the First Eunuch, proposes an even more complex meditation on nature: "La Nature semblait avoir mis les femmes dans la dépendance et les en avoir retirées" (52). Is this a statement about nature's simultaneously placing and removing women from a natural state of dependence, or is there a chronological sequence at work here? Simultaneity is undone by chronology, chronology undone by something always already there. Note the inextricable interlacing of before and after, of order and disorder, in the eunuch's analysis: "Le désordre naissait entre les deux sexes, parce que leurs droits étaient réciproques. Nous sommes entrés dans le plan d'une nouvelle harmonie: nous avons mis entre les femmes et nous la haine, et entre les hommes et les femmes l'amour" (52). Equality breeds competition and disorder, and order is restored only through hate, itself a form of disorder. We have reached an aporia where equality is right, but impossible, and inequality a fact, but unliveable and wrong. There is no essential, natural ground for the relationship between men and women. And the love between men and women, which supposedly could end the disorder, is a sham, as we learned in Letter 6. It is not surprising that the eunuch who writes this continues with a description of his inner split: "Le dehors sera tranquille, et l'esprit, inquiet" (52). He and Usbek are not very different from each other, both unnatural wielders of despotic authority who destroy themselves before they kill others.

In his study of the structures of the seraglio, Alain Grosrichard begins by stating that in the eighteenth century despotism haunted Europe like a specter (7). He, as well as Vartanian, shows that in that century, despotism was a pervasive phantasm, which, being a phantasm, was able to contain the contradiction of being both contrary to human nature and inherent in it as a permanent possibility: a phantasm of pure power, that he says is woven into the chain of the novel: "Ce fantasme du pouvoir pur donnait consistance, déjà, à la trame des *Lettres persanes*" (66). This suggests one answer to what Montesquieu might have meant when he stated later that there is a secret chain in his novel. Power is the weft woven into the chain constituted by the men, the women, and the eunuchs. The power they represent and wield weaves all the components together into the novel's coherent fabric. Power is the weft that circulates between all the characters, with the eunuchs being the go-betweens, "the intermediary group [. . .] a 'party bureaucracy'" (Vartanian 28) that provides the chain of command back and forth between the husband and the wives.

What is significant in despotism, I believe, is that it is the locus of a reflection on human nature. For as Grosrichard shows, despotism is both possible within human nature and contrary to it: the question is how it can arise and endure, escaping "la contradiction entre nature du despotisme et nature humaine" (52). According to Grosrichard, Montesquieu will shift in his later work (*L'Esprit des lois*) the cause for despotism onto physical nature, especially in Asia where the physical elements of nature counteract human nature (53). Despotism, and the seraglio which best exemplifies it, haunt Europe in the Old Regime because it represents the ever-present possibility that something counter to "human nature" will arise and assert itself. The lack of natural basis for power, was, of course, Hobbes's position, and Montesquieu, in his distaste for the artificiality of the contract, looks to thinkers like Pufendorf to establish a foundation in nature for human society, and locates it in the concept of sociability and proximity that keeps families together and eventually brings together entire states.

Certainly Montesquieu himself is haunted by the possibility that despotism is part of human nature, but more disquieting is the fear that despotism is not inherent in nature because there is no such concept as nature.[8] In the fiction of *Lettres persanes*, before a theory of climate is fully worked out, both fears are given free rein. Indeed if one reads the work of fiction as exploring troubling social, philosophical, and existential possibilities, then the later work, *L'Esprit des lois*, can be taken as an attempt to make sense and establish firmer foundations for society. As Suzanne Gearhart has shown, Montesquieu's solution will be that "there is no concept of the state of nature that does not reflect the conditions existing in a particular form of government or society" (*Open Boundary* 157), and that solution will be to elaborate a particular concept of nature differing from the "state of nature" invoked by Hobbes and Rousseau which is prior to history. In the work of fiction, the contradictory hopes and fears, the impossibility of idealism and the desire for it, are more exposed, more troubling, and are left unresolved as only a work of fiction can allow. In that respect, his work of fiction is like the phantasm, or Freud's later dream-work which

> is not simply more careless, more irrational, more forgetful and more incomplete than waking thought; it is completely different from it qualitatively and for that reason not immediately comparable with it. It does not think, calculate or judge in any way at all; it restricts itself to giving things a new form. (545)

One might take exception to the diminution implied by "restricts itself," for is not giving a "new form" precisely the point of fiction?

The fear that there is no foundation upon which to found society or justice is manifest in the set of letters on depopulation (Letters 112–122), a fear that does not seem justified given the fecundity of the population in Old Regime France, which sought to control births rather than encourage fertility (*Histoire de la famille* 29). This set of letters starts out with a question, "Comment la nature a-t-elle pu perdre cette prodigieuse fécondité des premiers temps? Serait-elle déjà dans sa vieillesse, et tomberait-elle de langueur?" (112: 232). Like the initial question that provoked the Troglodytes' story, this question receives an answer by Usbek that evokes catastrophe upon catastrophe, but a strange, oxymoronic catastrophe that is not very catastrophic, because it is so long and drawn out as to be barely perceptible: "la plus terrible catastrophe qui soit jamais arrivée dans le Monde; mais à peine s'en est-on aperçu, parce qu'elle est arrivée insensiblement et dans le cours d'un grand nombre de siècles [. . .] une maladie de langueur qui afflige la Nature humaine" (112: 235–36). Letters 112 to 122 are a catalogue of historical facts that illustrate the vision of nature as ill and wasting away from internal weaknesses and terrible events: these include natural events such as the Flood, and human cruelty, which makes thousands perish in conquered and colonized lands, a theme already encountered in Montaigne's "Des

Who Are the Eunuchs?

Cannibales." Montesquieu also insists on the impact of moral and religious codes that encourage celibacy or discourage men and women's reproductive ability. He complains that Catholic Christianity has too many eunuchs, "Je parle des prêtres et des dervis de l'un et l'autre sexe, qui se vouent à une continence éternelle" (117: 246), and that by its stricture against divorce, it discourages men and women from forming productive unions, unlike Protestantism, where men and women, being freer to form or dissolve unions, are more fertile as a result. Nature is not necessarily explainable by rationality, for even the slightest cause can have huge effects: "La fécondité d'un peuple dépend quelquefois des plus petites circonstances du Monde" (119: 250).

The basic assumption concerning nature seems to be that it is, by itself, in a state of equilibrium: "La Nature agit toujours avec lenteur, et pour ainsi dire, avec épargne" (114: 240). Like the thrifty householder of Alberti's family, Nature acts with "règle et mesure" and if overtaxed "elle emploie toute la force qui lui reste à se conserver, perdant absolument sa vertu productrice et sa puissance générative" (240). But Nature is not defined as excess of vitality in production and destruction,[9] but rather as a state of very unstable equilibrium that is easily disturbed and diminished by undue human intervention, "si on la précipite" (240). The state of nature is also susceptible to being twisted out of its slow and deliberate functioning, just as a man is able to undergo a second birth that will make him into a eunuch and separate him from nature (Letter 15). What can happen on the scale of the individual can also happen on a generalized scale. It is as if the state of being a eunuch is more widespread than at first seemed possible: in addition to priests, nuns, and the seraglio's guardians, an entire country or race of people can be afflicted with infertility and the lack of will to reproduce. And, Montesquieu continues in an almost apocalyptic vein, "Le commerce ranime tout chez les uns [Protestant countries], et le monachisme porte la mort partout chez les autres" (117: 249).

If moral and religious codes can so easily corrupt nature's equilibrium, is there any hope for nature? Nature needs to be restored to its natural state, but how? By some supplement, some change in social codes: Montesquieu indeed suggests just

Chapter Four

that in Letter 122, affirming more optimistically that "La douceur du gouvernement contribue merveilleusement à la propagation de l'Espèce" (258). His solution suggests a management of individual sexuality at the political and religious levels of public policy, considering people as citizens first and foremost: "L'égalité même des citoyens, qui produit ordinairement de l'égalité dans les fortunes, porte l'abondance et la vie dans toutes les parties du corps politique et la répand partout" (258).

This text is significant because it constitutes an example of what Foucault describes as a shift in thinking concerning sexuality in the eighteenth century: "Une des grandes nouveautés dans les techniques de pouvoir, au XVIIIe siècle, ce fut l'apparition, comme problème économique et politique, de la 'population': la population-richesse, la population-main-d'œuvre ou capacité de travail, la population en équilibre entre sa croissance propre et les ressources dont elle dispose" (*Volonté* 35–36).

How hard this is to achieve is indicated by the remainder of that same Letter 122, which concludes darkly with the statement that even in France "la misère, la famine et les maladies" (259) make children die: "Que si, dans un ciel aussi heureux, dans un royaume aussi policé que la France, on fait de pareilles remarques, que sera-ce dans les autres états?" (259). Either Montesquieu is being highly ironic about the state of civilization in France, or he is being deadly serious: either way, the vision is that of a sick and decadent nature unable to sustain itself even in the best of circumstances, which are themselves so rare that they have existed in only a few places in the world. These include ancient Rome (Letter 115), the Jews, and China, and, in Europe, only two small Protestant countries, Switzerland and Holland, described as not being favored by nature: they are "les deux plus mauvais pays de l'Europe, si l'on considère la nature du terrain, et qui cependant sont les plus peuplés" (258). Writing in the early part of the century, Montesquieu was not aware as writers will be in the latter part of the century (say, Diderot) about the capacity for laws to remedy nature. Such organized interventions were not fully in place until the nineteenth century, according to Foucault, who states that in the eighteenth and nineteenth centuries, "le sexe devient une cible centrale pour un pouvoir qui s'organise autour de la gestion de la vie plutôt que de la menace de la mort" (*Volonté* 193). Perhaps Montesquieu, writing at the beginning of this shift in mentalities, is more aware of the pervasive threat of death, even as he considers the benefits of managing life more fruitfully through sensible, gentle government and tolerant religious codes.

Like the eunuch, like Usbek, indeed like most countries on the globe, nature is contradictory and susceptible to falling into a state of infertility, illness, and degeneracy. Far from being the exception, the eunuch's state is widespread. As Josué Harari says in one of the most complete studies of Montesquieu's eunuchs to date, "All the characters castrate and are castrated symbolically" and "The eunuch is at the center of the novel's system of meaning" (70). Perhaps that is why the eunuch is both omnipresent, pervasive, and yet invisible, like power itself. Who are the eunuchs? There are many, even more than Valéry thought.

To conclude this section, I will analyze an odd, short letter which has nothing to do with eunuchs, but which concerns Montesquieu's ambivalence about nature. In Letter 139, Rica describes the abdications of two queens of Sweden, one of whom (Ulrika) abdicated the regency because she wanted her husband to reign, and the other, Christina, who abdicated in order to study philosophy. One sacrifices power for the sake of personal happiness and her husband's superiority, the other sacrifices power for the sake of philosophy. Rica comments:

> Quoique j'approuve assez que chacun se tienne ferme dans le poste où la Nature l'a mis, et que je ne puissse louer la faiblesse de ceux qui, se trouvant au-dessous de leur état, le quittent comme par une espèce de désertion, je suis cependant frappé de la grandeur d'âme de ces deux princesses et de voir l'esprit de l'une et le cœur de l'autre supérieurs à leur fortune. (295)

One cannot be more ambivalent: Montesquieu reprimands the two princesses for their weakness and admires their courage. Total immobility of reason is achieved in the remainder of the commentary: "Christine a songé à connaître dans le temps que les autres ne songent qu'à jouir, et l'autre ne veut jouir que pour mettre tout son bonheur entre les mains de son auguste époux" (295). Montesquieu sets up a parallel structure of exchange, replacing "jouir" with "connaître" in the case of Queen Christina, and with "bonheur" in the case of Queen Ulrika. The object of this highly emotional, sexual verb "jouir" that is left unsaid has to be power for these sentences to make any sense. Giving up power, then, is the unnatural act that Rica both criticizes and admires, because, for these queens, enjoying power is natural, and knowledge and happiness are unnatural—an odd position perhaps for Rica to take, given his tendency to embrace a fragmented, variable sense of self. More in keeping with his viewpoint is his admiration for the two queens' turning away from their natural state in order to achieve more satisfying goals of personal happiness and knowledge. In the two queens' actions the situation of Usbek and his wives is mirrored, as Usbek gives up power to search for knowledge, and the wives give up their dictated roles to achieve knowledge and personal happiness (though not with their husband).

Thus Montesquieu sits on the fence, being both admiring and critical regarding turning away from natural roles. The two queens separate themselves from their inherent roles, just as the eunuchs are separated from themselves in order to gain something not belonging to their essence. Roger Kempf called Montesquieu's text "ce roman de la séparation, de toutes les séparations possibles" ("Les *Lettres persanes*" 84). Separation, yes, but gains too, and in the last analysis, an entangled coexistence of primary nature and secondary gain that might be secondary nature and primary gain. But this is not the last analysis, only the next-to-last, for the eunuchs have an advantage that no one else has in the novel, namely, the power to wield a sword. To the presence and absence of this advantageous asset we now turn, examining that supplementary object on which the conclusion of the novel depends.

Two Forms of Power: Surveillance and the Sword

The other half of the contract between the master and the eunuch concerns what the eunuch gains by giving up his manhood. Given the magnitude of the eunuch's sacrifice, this gain had better be good, and indeed it seems to be: it is the power to wield a sword, to punish by death, to rule in absolute fashion over women, other slaves, and other eunuchs in the case of the Chief Eunuch. This is the place where power is located: what the character of the eunuch enables Montesquieu to do is to meditate on the nature of power. It will not be surprising that this meditation reveals immense and unresolvable ambiguities. No one gender has complete power, but each has some: the master, who flees abroad, but passes it on to his eunuchs; the women, who are kept in a state of servitude, but rebel and liberate themselves only to be put to death; and the eunuchs, who reveal varying degrees of obedience and superiority among themselves and the women. In this last section, I will set this examination of power in the context of changing views about power, which in the early eighteenth century might have become all the more palpable when an absolute monarch's death gave way to the fairly free-wheeling period of the Regency. This was a time when the very foundations of society were beginning to be seriously questioned, not in the name of any democratic ideal, but tossed and turned in debates concerning the Roman or the Germanic origins of the nobility, the relations between monarchy and despotic rule, the origin of society in either a social contract or in natural law—with the ever present specter of Machiavelli who haunted the imagination of the Old Regime.

In a wider and very fruitful discussion, Foucault explains that a complex change occurred in the Old Regime, whereby the concept of power as emanating from the top down was slowly being replaced with a more pervasive and diffuse form of power that in the nineteenth century culminated with various forms of social organizations, such as schools, factories, and prisons. New forms of power that had hitherto existed only in particular environments, such as the convent, or the city at a time of crisis during a plague, became generalized and gradually took over social structures. Forms of power that seemed to come from one superior source, the monarch, were gradually replaced by forms of power that were not identifiable with one individual, or one class, but were everywhere. These new forms of power controlled space and time in a manner that seemed to be less arbitrary and willful, but they were actually much more efficient and more enveloping through the use of micro techniques for disciplining the body as well as the mind: "la technique disciplinaire, elle, a envahi insidieusement et comme par en bas, une justice pénale qui est encore, dans son principe, inquisitoire" (*Surveiller* 228).

Montesquieu, who was fascinated by the question of the legitimacy of power, asked himself the basic question "Who had the right to make law?" (Hulliung 60). Haunted as he was by the threat of despotism, his early text reveals a fascination with both forms of power, the old one that comes from the top down from a master or a monarch, and the bottom-up kind that micro-manages bodies and minds through various forms of disciplines and mind-control. In the *Lettres persanes*, both forms of power coexist, and do so in the persons of the eunuchs. The novel illustrates a fascinating example of the historical process described by Foucault, the gradual waning of power focused on the king's body and based on the use of predictable ritual: "une théorie politique de la monarchie, des mécanismes juridiques [. . .] liant à la fois la personne du roi et les exigences de la Couronne, et tout un rituel" (*Surveiller* 33). Over the seventeenth and eighteenth centuries, this form of power located in one individual (which, he says, made sense in the late Middle Ages when it replaced the contentious and individualist competition for power among lords) is now gradually replaced by a "nouvelle 'microphysique' du pouvoir" (*Surveiller* 140) that is not locatable in a person (the king) or a thing (the crown, the mace, the sacrament of coronation), and hence is not transferable as a commodity from one person to a successor. In the old form of power, "in the case of the classic, juridical theory, power is taken to be a right, which one is able to possess like a commodity, and which one can in consequence transfer or alienate [. . .] through a legal act" (*Power/Knowledge* 88), whereas the new form of power consists of "a whole series of power networks that invest the body, sexuality, the family, kinship, knowledge, technology, and so forth" (*Power/Knowledge* 122).

Both forms of power coexist in the *Lettres persanes*, as if in his fictional text Montesquieu were reflecting on the transformations of power in his era more than in his essays and polemical texts about, for example, the debates between Romanists and Germanists on the origin of nobility. There is

Who Are the Eunuchs?

an uneasy coexistence of both forms of power in the novel that link together the eunuchs, the women, the seraglio, and the husband-master. It is to this question that I return: What do the eunuchs gain by sacrificing their manhood? Power, but what kind?

The control of the eunuchs over the women is described in Letter 2 as a micro-management of the women's lives, making them feel "leur extrême dépendance" (13) as if they are in a prison. Both body and mind must be controlled with entertainment (music, dance, and drink), as well as with bodily hygiene through bathing (Letter 9), because "la propreté [. . .] est l'image de la netteté de l'âme" (13). The eunuchs also control every aspect of their travels, in which the women must remain invisible to any other man and are placed in movable prisons where the women can neither see or be seen (Letter 47). Eunuchs have minute control over the women as well as over the women's slaves, as they have the power to remove these slaves from the women who cannot even choose their servants.

In its absolute form, such a management of body and mind allows complete control. In a nostalgic vein, the Chief Black Eunuch recounts with great admiration and longing how the First Eunuch who had trained him in his youth used to rule over the women. The passage is worth quoting in full because it illustrates the perfection of a kind of utopian micro-management of the women's body and mind. This master eunuch

> avait non seulement de la fermeté, mais aussi de la pénétration: il lisait leurs pensées et leurs dissimulations; leurs gestes étudiés, leur visage feint, ne lui dérobaient rien; il savait toutes leurs actions les plus cachées et leurs paroles les plus secrètes; il se servait des unes pour connaître les autres, et il se plaisait à récompenser la moindre confidence. [. . .] Il avait persuadé son maître qu'il était du bon ordre qu'il lui laissât ce choix, afin de lui donner une autorité plus grande. Voilà comme on gouvernait, magnifique seigneur, dans un sérail qui était, je crois, le mieux réglé qu'il y eût en Perse. (64: 134–35)

This perfect knowledge, which the master had to be convinced about, is based on having a penetrating vision, a kind of panoptical seeing that is infinite both in quality as well as in

Chapter Four

quantity of control, for any number of women can be dominated thus: "Leur nombre ne m'embarrasse pas" (134). His all-seeing eyes are used to direct and control even his master's gaze upon the woman that would furnish him sexual pleasure: "l'eunuque y [to her husband] appelait qui il voulait, et tournait les yeux de son maître sur celle qu'il avait en vue" (134–35). But that was then, and now the seraglio has erupted in disorder: the all-penetrating eyes have to be replaced by another organ, the hands: "Laisse-moi les mains libres" (135). The eyes of surveillance are going to be replaced with the sword in the hand.

The reason that this form of surveillance through seeing and management of daily life has to be replaced is because this form of power is perceived as unstable. It is as if this form of power through minute control has not yet fulfilled its potential as a way of governing society. The utopian level of control achieved by the former master eunuch seems unattainable, for the women find ways to manipulate the eunuchs by demanding a high level of attention: "Souvent elles se plaisent à me faire redoubler de soins" (9: 25). The women, whose bodies are constantly under surveillance, use their very bodies to exert some control over the eunuchs: "elles savent feindre des maladies, des défaillances, des frayeurs" (25); they also know how to use their tears, sighs and charms. This form of control is best learned young and instilled by force of habit: Zélis wants to train her daughter at the age of seven to live in a state of subordination. In Letter 62, the paradox is that a natural state of liberty (in childhood) must be replaced by a state of subordination "où la Nature nous a mises" but which seems very unnatural indeed. But the first nature subject to erasure by a second nature (the liberty of childhood replaced by a state of submission), as stated by Pascal in the fragment quoted at the head of this chapter, undergoes a third reversal, for in her prison, and long before her final rebellion, Zélis has freedoms that her husband cannot imagine: "j'ai goûté ici mille plaisirs que tu ne connais pas [...]. Dans la prison même où tu me retiens, je suis plus libre que toi" (130). No wonder that in Letter 64, written five months after the disquieting Letter 62, the Chief of the Black Eunuchs sounds the alarm: "le sérail est dans un désordre et une confusion épouvantables; la guerre règne entre tes femmes; tes

Who Are the Eunuchs?

eunuques sont partagés" (132). And the remedy is clear: he wants his master to allow him to use not words, but strong, concrete "châtiments" (132) to keep the women in line.

The rule by surveillance and micro-management is unstable, susceptible to manipulation, breakdown, and abuse by the prisoners. It is ironic that the form of power which proved to be the way of the future was set by Montesquieu in the eunuch's youth, in a nostalgic past when this kind rule was perfect. In the present, the prison walls are penetrable, even though made of stone: one of the women's slaves has "fait cacher deux hommes dans un réduit de pierre qui est dans la muraille de la principale chambre, d'où ils sortaient le soir lorsque nous étions retirés" (151: 327). Only force can rule in an effective way, hence in 1719, Usbek declares, "Je te mets le fer à la main" (153: 328), thus answering the eunuch's call for such punishment already expressed several years before, in Letter 64, written in 1714. The women must obey "aveuglément," as if blinded by the lightning that is about to fall from above on their heads: "Puisse cette lettre être comme la foudre qui tombe au milieu des éclairs et des tempêtes!" (154: 328). The whole seraglio is plunged into darkness: "L'horreur, la nuit et l'épouvante règnent dans le sérail" (156: 330).

The mighty hand takes over, first as an indiscreet hand, then equipped with a sword placed there by Usbek. First Roxane complains that the sacrilegious eunuch has dared "porter sur elles [Zachi and Zélis] ses viles mains" and Zachi corroborates this in the following letter, stating that a "barbarous" eunuch has dared to punish her in a punishment fit only for children, "ce châtiment qui ramène, pour ainsi dire, à l'enfance" (presumably spanking) (157: 331). Then the final punishment is by the sword, as Solim himself kills the young man who had sneaked into the seraglio and causes a large amount of blood to flow with secret glee, "une joie secrète": the women will be "étonnées de tout le sang que j'y vais répandre" (160: 333). Thus only with power from the master is the Chief Eunuch able to rule effectively over the women and the servants. Replacing the newer form of power based on surveillance of bodies and control of minds, the form of direct control reverts to despotism, physical violence, blood and killing, what Zélis calls cruel tyranny (Letter 158).

Chapter Four

This reversion to an absolute, top-down, and violent form of power seems to suggest that the other form of domination is not (yet) efficacious, that it does not seem capable of sustaining itself over a long time nor in the absence of the ruler-husband. Power exercised in a network of surveillance that involves every aspect of daily life is replaced by a more familiar power identified with a single ruler, and present in and as an object—a commodity that can be given, taken away, and re-given to the eunuch by the master in the form of a sword and an authorization letter to carry out these punishments. The newer form of discipline, "un dispositif fonctionnel qui doit améliorer l'exercice du pouvoir en le rendant plus rapide, plus léger, plus efficace" (*Surveiller* 211) is replaced in the novel's ending by a "discipline-blocus, l'institution close [. . .] toute tournée vers des fonctions négatives: arrêter le mal, rompre les communications, suspendre le temps" (*Surveiller* 211). What Foucault calls "l'extension progressive des dispositifs de discipline au long des XVIIe et XVIIIe siècles" (*Surveiller* 211) seems instead to be going backward in the novel: it moves from a more "progressive" form of control to an older, more "authoritarian" form. Montesquieu depicted a more "progressive" form of discipline rooted in a form of control that was unable to sustain itself in the absence of the master: that is tantamount to saying that authority must always be exercised from above, and that substitutions in the form of pervasive control by the subordinates, whether they be the husband's eunuchs or the king's ministers, will ultimately be weak and ineffective. This point is made by the juxtaposition of Letter 146 on the corruption of ministers next to the dénouement of the novel, which starts with Letter 147.

The eunuch had always lived in a world defined by the supplement, in both senses of the word, as filling a lack or as an excess. When the master empowers the eunuch and orders him to mete out punishment, the eunuch thereby acquires an additional tool, the sword, which is also a replacement for the organ that was cut off to make him a eunuch. The "fer [qui] te sépara de la nature" (15: 38) comes back to him as a literal sword in the hand in Letter 153. Similarly, in the realm of sexuality, he was both deprived of himself, yet also endowed with a mysterious "troisième sens" that belongs to neither men nor women: thus "la nature se dédommage de ses pertes" (53: 113). In the realm of power, the eunuch is the replacement for the absent master, and lacks what the master has; yet by becoming the *de facto* master, he makes the master superfluous in his own household, as there can be only one master in the top-down model of authority.

The only solution to this conundrum is the one proposed by Rica in a letter close to the dénouement that acquires all the more meaning from that position. Letter 144, a C addition, is testimony that Montesquieu wrestled with the problem of the exercise of power as he reviewed his own text. In this letter, Rica praises the "hommes modestes" whom he prefers to the absolute rulers whom he wants to eliminate: "Et, quand je vous compare dans mon idée avec ces hommes absolus que je vois partout, je les précipite de leur tribunal, et je les mets à vos pieds" (317). Yet the modest men are out-numbered ("que je vois partout") by the absolute men. The "absolute men" who are everywhere are their own worst enemy, the instrument of their own doom, acting counter to their conservation: "la vanité sert mal ceux qui en ont une dose plus forte que celle qui est nécessaire pour la conservation de la nature. Ces gens-là veulent être admirés [. . .]. Ils cherchent à être supérieurs, et ils ne sont pas seulement égaux" (317). In the end there is a draw: Usbek prefers the authoritarian rule, Rica advocates for the "modest men," and while the two men are disagreeing, the eunuchs effectively seize power.

Thus ends Montesquieu's survey of humankind, men, women, and eunuchs: all are uprooted from an original nature, in which equilibrium and conservation should allow society to exist, the son next to the father, the modest men next to each other, men and women in a gentle relation of love. Instead there is a never-ending whirligig of absence, hate, deprivation, competition, and vengeance that seems perilously close to Thomas Hobbes's famous description of the natural state of life as "nasty, brutish and short" (*Leviathan* 100). The recuperation of Enlightenment values at the end is also coexistent with death, in which the only survivors are the absent master, the sword-wielding eunuch, and the cowardly women who do not have Roxane's courage to commit suicide. It seems that an Enlightened conscience cannot live fully, or even just survive, and that

Chapter Four

bloodthirsty rulers or cowards are the ones who remain standing. Just as the Troglodytes' story ended in an infinite cyclical regression of domination and rebellion, so does the entire novel end in a cycle of disorder and brutally restored order that can only be repeated without end. The women's stories end in rebellion, submission, or death, and the master's life ends in impotence, while the eunuchs alone remain in their ruling position. And yet the novel ends in a powerful affirmation of eternal values amidst the carnage, not livable in the novel itself, but making an impression on the reader: Roxane's legacy lives on after her death, beyond the grave, in a time outside life, outside fiction.

Montesquieu, Naturalist or Artificialist?

By this question, I mean to conclude by surveying the ambivalence which I had suggested subtends the whole novel. I earlier suggested that Montesquieu is tempted to view the world through the eyes of a person disabused and disappointed in nature, but who cannot bring himself to make a complete break with the notion of a foundation, and who makes an effort to find a principle that organizes human life and society. The *Lettres persanes* is the text where this anxiety is given a voice, but is also refuted. Clément Rosset says this about philosophy: "la philosophie est d'abord médecine, moyen parmi d'autres de se guérir contre l'angoisse" (72). The two alternatives are: "rassurer en redonnant le sens, ou rassurer en en privant complètement" (72). Can one say the same about this text of literature? I suggest that this text at least is more ambivalent: it does not eliminate meaning completely, but comes close. At the same time it presents a modified meaning that is not completely "natural" either.

One can argue, as Mark Hulliung does, that the skeptical crisis seems to have won out, and the idea of "nature" is no longer dominant in Montesquieu's thought at this time. As he observes, in the *Lettres persanes* Montesquieu conducted a "remarkably daring experiment in (human) nature and made his mythical Persians vehicles for the dissemination of unthinkable thoughts" (110). In his view, "skepticism, relativism, and toleration [...] uprooted the side of natural law that sought universally valid norms" (111). Though this opinion pulls Montesquieu in the direction of artificialism, making him a follower of Lucretius ("a favorite of Montesquieu," says Hulliung [115]), I believe that the novel is more complex and less resolvable into a final "message." Hulliung himself concludes his analysis with the idea that

> between "is" and "ought" there are vital passageways [. . .]. The function of reason is to discover them [. . .]. Natural law philosophy, with its emphasis on a rationally discernible connection between "is" and "ought," is acceptable after the emendation that the "nature" in question is not physical nature but the nature of socio-political systems. (139)

Montesquieu's dilemma was the following: face the abyss of the absence of "natural law," unthinkable but true, or find a "natural law" that is thinkable but illusory. One passage in the novel gives a crucial insight into Montesquieu's dilemma. He never ceases to hope for a natural form of society, where the son lives next to the father: "ils naissent tous liés les uns aux autres; un fils est né auprès de son père, *et il s'y tient*: voilà la société et la cause de la société" (94: 193–94). No elaborate explanation is necessary, and people are in their proper place. Yet the apparently insignificant clause "et il s'y tient" adds a nuance, a reservation, which is actually of immense importance, for it introduces a gap in nature's plenitude. Society is founded on both birth *and* an act of will that is necessary for this presence of father and son to be sustained, implying that the son does not have to stay next to the father. That the structure of patriarchy is both a model for society and not transferable to the structure of society has been discussed by Pucci: "Comment les propriétés du patriarcat ou de la filiation pourraient-elles être investies par quelqu'un d'autre?" ("Patriarcat" 299). But even the family's links depend on a decision to make consanguinity and proximity coincide, for the son to stay close to his father. As Pascal said, the first nature of love between parent and child is easily abolished, to be replaced by a second nature that becomes a habitual "first" nature, assuming that the word *nature* still has a meaning.

This sentence is indicative of Montesquieu's stance in this novel: nature is there, but it has to be supplemented, not so

Chapter Four

much by an act of reason, as Hulliung has it, but by an act of will, perhaps based on reason. A supplementary decision is necessary for nature to function, but this act may not take place. A son can leave his father and become, say, a eunuch; a wife can leave her husband, and become a rebellious wife; a man can leave his mother or his fatherland. Quite a few forms of government can be detrimental to the natural growth of population. This ambivalence seems, to me, to constitute Montesquieu's stance: an inclusion, in that both nature and artifice coexist and need each other. Artifice is "founded" on an underlying nature, and nature needs human assistance to continue being nature. Nature needs the additional gesture of the human will, and the human will is based on a state given in nature. Modifying Hulliung's analysis: "physical nature" (birth and family life) does not become, nor is it replaced by, "the nature of socio-political systems" (society is built on the son's decision to stay near his father). The complex structure of the novel bears out the inclusion and the interdependency of both nature and system.

The eunuchs, supplementary and necessary to the novel's economy of the two "natural" genders, enable Montesquieu to explore some very disquieting ideas indeed. But, in a countermove, the very oppression by the husband and the eunuchs leads the women to assert the "natural law," allowing some positive concepts to be affirmed in the novel's ending, as Roxane and some other wives find transcendental, eternal values that the men are unable to find. Montesquieu is haunted by an underlying pessimism, which he overcomes by a belief in foundational ideals and human nature. In this aspect the novel is decidedly not postmodern, but, as Toulmin suggests, exemplifies the position of the Enlighteners who want to reform the "cosmopolis" without overturning its foundations wholesale. The eunuchs make it possible for Montesquieu to explore some uncomfortable artificialist ideas, to conduct a complex meditation on the pervasive artificiality of human organization, on the manmade dangers threatening society with extinction and depopulation. The novel is pessimistic through the cruelty of the eunuchs and the masters, and yet it is also hopeful, as it shows how the possibility of resistance to absolute power lies in absolute ideals. Like dreamwork, the work of fiction enables both visions of society to coexist without finding a resolution. Like the eunuchs themselves, the novel's meaning is ambiguous—while we postmodern readers can appreciate the insights, the subtlety, and the boldness of the questions raised by the novel, ultimately we can see also the hesitations and limitations. Perhaps we might have wished for a more generalized eunuchdom.

Chapter Five

Montesquieu's "Introduction" and "Réflexions," and the Question of the "Secret Chain"

To bring this analysis of the novel to a close, I would like to consider two texts that surround the *Lettres persanes*: the "Introduction" (7–9), which accompanied the novel in 1721, and the well-known retrospective statement, the "Quelques Réflexions sur les *Lettres persanes*" (3–5) published in 1754.

The importance of preliminary texts is no longer to be ignored especially after Gérard Genette's monumental study *Seuils*, although Genette limits himself to a taxonomy, albeit thorough and detailed, of all the possible types of accompanying texts, titles, postfaces, notes, etc. But, as Lorraine Piroux has demonstrated in her study that goes far beyond Genette's taxonomy, the situation of dedications is one of complex hybridity. Piroux states that the dedicatory epistles lie on several frontiers: between the main text and the reader, between the world and the book, between literature and culture: "l'étude d'une dédicace doit nécessairement passer par la singularité du texte auquel elle se rapporte et du milieu culturel qui l'a produit" (29). The preface also involves an address by the author to his or her readers, at a time when authors thought much more about who their readers were or should be: in the Old Regime, "la question de l'adresse faisait partie intégrale du projet de l'écriture [. . .]. Décider de ceux pour qui l'on écrivait consistait alors à décider de la visibilité et de la portée que l'on voulait attribuer à son écriture" (20). Despite the dedications' apparent marginal status and conventional content, they set up a circulation of meaning and interplay that, properly interpreted, can renew the interpretation of the texts in an original way.

By Montesquieu's time, the traditional practice of an author's dedicating a book to a powerful and distinguished protector was starting to fade, as authors acquired more independence and status as writers, and depended less on patronage from aristocrats and monarchs. Indeed, in his study of French dedicatory letters, Wolfgang Leiner cites Montesquieu's "Introduction" to the *Lettres persanes* as explicitly rejecting the practice of dedication in its first paragraph, stating bluntly that a work must stand on its own merit (309). However, if dedications were passing from the scene, the practice of prefacing texts was still current, and perhaps because prefaces displaced dedications, they still carried a certain weight. While authors were no longer searching for attention from higher personages, they were still dependent on a reading public, perhaps more than in our time where large commercial entities like bookselling chains and publishing house conglomerates remove the author from his or her audience—book tours and signings in bookstores are an attempt to overcome this distance. Apart from press reviews and word of mouth, such aids to develop readership did not exist in the Old Regime, but the situation was different. As one writer describing the situation in Elizabethan England says, aside from the author the bookmaking process consisted of only three functions: "that of the capitalist who owns the manuscript and finances the enterprise, that of the craftsman who prints the book, and that of the merchant who sells it to the public" (Gebert 22). In France, the "libraire" was frequently the purchaser of the manuscript and the seller of the book as well, thus reducing even further the number of entities between the author and his public. (On the other hand, the production of "contrefaçons" unauthorized by the bookseller-publisher and the author lay beyond the author's and the bookseller's control in the days before copyright of intellectual property; and other factors such as growing literacy rates and lending libraries contributed to a wider readership.) Despite these factors, and despite the passing of personal patronage, prefaces and introductions could still be written and read as more personal statements from an author to his or her audience than in the following century.

Therefore, it would have been logical to look at Montesquieu's "Introduction" before analyzing the novel itself, but I depart from that sequence because of a peculiar circumstance connected with Montesquieu's novel, the existence of a text that Montesquieu wrote much later about the novel: his

"Quelques Réflexions" which were written to defend his novel against a clergyman's accusation of impiety.[1] These remarks have caused much debate among his readers, especially one sentence in which he made the famous claim that a "secret and unknown chain" linked together the various aspects of the novel:

> Mais dans la forme de lettres, où les acteurs ne sont pas choisis, et où les sujets qu'on traite ne sont dépendants d'aucun dessein ou d'aucun plan déjà formé, l'auteur s'est donné l'avantage de pouvoir joindre de la philosophie, de la politique et de la morale à un roman, et de lier le tout par une chaîne secrète et, en quelque façon, inconnue. (3–4)

Little did Montesquieu suspect that he was sending future critics on a detective hunt for this secret chain. After discussing the 1721 "Introduction," I will re-examine the matter of the secret chain, in order to understand Montesquieu's statement in the later "Quelques Réflexions" and then show its congruence with the earlier "Introduction."

The "Introduction," or The Author's False Modesty

Although Montesquieu does not write a true dedication, he reminds the reader at the beginning of the "Introduction" that there is such a genre by saying that he is not writing an "Epître dédicatoire"; he does not specify until the last word what he has been writing, a "préface," while at the same denying that he has just written a preface. What these negatives indicate is that something else is being presented here.

The initial allusion to the dedication genre, which reminds the reader of it and rejects it at the same time, is a double gesture that is only one of the many moves which this short text performs. Let us first note that traditional dedications had three principal rhetorical components, as Leiner explains: an *exordium*, a *narratio*, and a *conclusio*. The first and last parts were usually rather brief, while the narration was longer, usually more ornate, and designed to please and convince the dedicatee in a *captatio benevolentiae* that would result in pleasure and success for all persons concerned and for the book. And the "Introduction" follows exactly that pattern: the first and last paragraphs are an *exordium* and a conclusion, and the middle seven paragraphs form a narration, telling a story, or actually several stories. Within the form of the traditional dedication, however, the text also subverts its usual content. The *exordium*, rather than asking for the reader's favorable attention, emphasizes the distance between the author, his text, and his readers, showing some contempt for the whole process ("je ne me soucie pas qu'on le lise"), and of course, nothing could be further from the truth: obviously Montesquieu cared very much whether or not his novel was read. At the very least, the reader is warned of much irony to follow. The last paragraph also creates distance, not between the writer and the reader, but between the writer and his text; and by stating that the writer has not written a boring preface, it contains an oblique appeal to the readers, who have not been bored by a usual preface praising the work they are about to read. "False modesty," says Vernière in a note (9); but more is going on here than irony of pride disguised as false modesty. For while seeming to create distances between reader, writer, and text, the author is also close to his text, praising it, and exercising control over the readers, who are not distanced at all, but mightily "interpellés" by this text.

The middle part of the narration, traditionally designed to capture the good will of the reader or the dedicatee, seems to have nothing to do with the readers, but everything to do with the author, or rather the author masquerading as an editor. The first story it tells is of the editor's many activities, beginning with the general statement "j'ai détaché ces premières lettres pour essayer le goût du public" (7). The first function that Montesquieu the editor assumes is that of having "détaché" a few letters: in French, the word *détacher* also has the meaning of sending a representative ("faire partir quelqu'un pour faire quelque chose" says the 1986 Larousse entry)—Montesquieu sends these letters as ambassadors to represent him in public, to do something, namely, to summon the reader to read.

In the fictions of editors used by eighteenth-century writers (studied by Bongjie Lee), editors assumed many roles in order to buttress the illusion of having found a real manuscript: Lee lists those of copyist, discoverer, translator, publisher (in the sense of taking care to see the work published), corrector,

Chapter Five

annotator, commentator, furnisher of necessary information, organizer, writer of titles, and even sometimes intervener in the story itself. With the exception of the last, Montesquieu's "editor" assumes all of the above roles in the *Lettres persanes*. He mentions several in the "Introduction" (copying, translation, corrector of style, commentary) and does others in the book itself, adding information or comments in footnotes, organizing them not always according to chronological sequence, and of course adding titles and dates and places for each letter. Montesquieu has attributed to himself every possible role taken by fictive editors, emphasizing his very active role in preparing the supposedly found letters for the public. All these roles of the editor are of course easily replaced by one principal role that surpasses them all, that of writer. Does not the act of writing contain all those roles anyway?

But there is another story in this middle section, also concerning the very active editor: his relations with his Persian guests. If the author retreated behind the mask of the multi-talented editor, and behind the mask of anonymity, he also foregrounds himself all the more. Like Descartes, Montesquieu advances masked—"Larvatus prodeo" could have been the subtitle of this "Introduction." The more one is masked, the more one can move forward. These Persians lived with their editor, spending their lives with him, telling him everything they saw without reserve, and leaving him their entire correspondence. At the same time, "ils me regardaient comme un homme d'un autre monde" (7). There could be no better statement of the ambiguity of the stranger, who is both intimate and distant, and who makes everything intimate become distant, and everything distant intimate. The stranger becomes more familiar to me than myself: "des gens transplantés de si loin ne pouvaient plus avoir de secrets," and suddenly I become strange, I am the one who seems to be from another world. And being from another world enables rather than restrains communication, for, as Simmel pointed out, the stranger is less menacing, less involved in the culture he is visiting, and hence the locals can open up more to him without fear of judgment.

The stranger, of course, is none other than Montesquieu, who alludes to this later in the "Introduction": "Il y a une chose qui m'a souvent étonné: c'est de voir ces Persans quelquefois aussi instruits *que moi-même* des mœurs et des manières de la Nation" (8). In the same paragraph, the writer wonders why Asians can learn more about the French than the French about Asians, even more than Germans about the French, in a sentence that may be deliberately ambiguous: "il est plus facile à un Asiatique de s'instruire des mœurs des Français dans un an, qu'il ne l'est à un Français de s'instruire des mœurs des Asiatiques dans quatre, parce que les uns se livrent autant que les autres se communiquent peu" (8). The subtle interplay of nouns, and of singulars and plurals, does not make it all that clear who exactly is "les uns" and who is "les autres." Ultimately, of course, they are all one and the same, the writer.

Behind the ironies and false modesties, beyond the apparent disdain for his work, there is a writer who fills all the roles, pulls all the strings, who, as he gives his work to the reader, reveals his power and his control over all his creatures, including his readers. A writer who not only does all this, but who could do more, as is implied in the second paragraph: there is a large reserve of letters, "un grand nombre" (7), in the "portefeuille" that he is ready to "lui donner dans la suite" (7). His portfolio, his bag of tricks, is by no means exhausted, we are warned. What is presented as a sheaf of letters, incomplete, corrected, and with Asiatic pomposity removed, is, the readers are also warned, a more substantial work than many other such collections of letters: "Si la plupart de ceux qui nous ont donné des recueils de lettres avaient fait de même, ils auraient vu leurs ouvrages s'évanouir" (8). With this irony, Montesquieu gives a clear hint: my work has more substance than anyone else's. And you, the reader, will have to look for it. For I, Montesquieu, am not going to tell you: I am not going to comment or adorn my work, not going to point out its usefulness, its merit, and its excellence, even though I (could) have. You, readers, are on your own. But if you don't find what I want you to find, you will be deluded. Not by me, but by yourselves. And so the "Introduction" joins with the end of the "Quelques Réflexions," which reads: "elles [the *Lettres persanes*] ne tromperont jamais que ceux qui voudront se tromper eux-mêmes" (5).

Laurent Versini calls his prose style "la phrase miroitante"; moreover, not only is Montesquieu's sentence style "miroitant," so is his "Introduction," and so is his entire book. All present

Chapter Five

many facets, but underneath the seemingly endless variety of aspects, there is substance to be found, a "substantifique moëlle" to use Rabelais's famous phrase. Underneath the attractive, ever-changing exterior, there is a serious purpose and meaning, and the reader is alternately enticed and controlled, charmed and obligated. Under the infinity and complexity of surface phenomena, there is the certainty, the regularity of laws of nature. In this new form of dedication, the book is not dedicated to an important personnage by a humble author, but given to the humble readers by a proud author who is never more French than when he pretends to be Persian, never more sure of his game as when he pretends to play.

When Montesquieu looked back at his phenomenally successful novel over three decades later with his life's work behind him, he could not but be satisfied by what he had achieved in his younger years. Truly, Rodrigue's statement applied to him: "aux âmes bien nées / La valeur n'attend pas le nombre des années" (Corneille, *Le Cid* II.2.405–06). Yet, he was also being attacked, accused of impiety, and so there was still something to say, a supplement to what needed (no) supplement.

The Question of the "Secret Chain"

In a useful and judicious review of the writing on the "secret chain" question, Theodore Braun analyzes the attempts of critics, especially from 1960 onward, to identify and explain the "chain." According to Braun, critics have concentrated their analyses on three principal areas, listed in the first three paragraphs of the "Réflexions": in the first paragraph, the structural or formal characteristics of the novel; in the second, the allegorical content of the novel viewed as a *roman à clé;* in the third, the advantage of the epistolary form over ordinary novels (278–79).

Critics have proposed diverse and often ingenious solutions to the riddle of the chain. For those considering the structure, and they are in the majority, this structure can be dual—novel and treatise (Dauphiné); for some, it is triple—social, moral, political (Crumpacker, Laufer); or in six parts (Kra); or there is a causal chain (Raymond).[2] Recent analyses focus on the tension between the invisible chain (for Usbek) and the visible relation of the personal to the political, visible only for the reader (Strong); or a tension between the individualist esthetics conveyed by the fictional characters and the search for universal principles (Miething). Braun suggests, rightly, that the one interpretation relating to the *roman à clé* principle is unconvincing and incomplete. He finds the discussions of the relation of content to epistolary form only partially successful because they "correspond to only one of the several possibilities suggested by Montesquieu" (288). I do not believe that considering the epistolary form alone can yield an answer because this form was put to very different uses and can have very different meanings. In Montesquieu's time, the letter novel could be, like the *Lettres d'une religieuse portugaise*, as tightly organized as a five-act Racinian tragedy, or it was capable of infinite expansion, like the direct model for the *Lettres persanes*, Marana's *Lettres d'un espion turc*, which had no plot structure or organizing principle other than the quantity of the Turkish spy's observations.

Whether based on the structure of the content or the form, these analyses, while insightful, have not yielded a definitive answer. The secret chain has remained hidden, present enough to provoke critics into searching for it, yet elusive enough to escape perception—no single explanation has obtained a consensus. Braun summarizes, "we may not have crossed the finishing line yet" (290), and the impression remains that there is still something to be discovered, just out of reach, yet almost palpable.

I would like to suggest that the hunt for the hidden chain has not yielded a definitive answer because probably there is no chain to be found in the literal sense, and that the question *What is the secret chain?* is misguided. Although Montesquieu's own intentions cannot be known, I believe that his remarks can bear some reexamination and be better understood; then I will propose two different approaches, one based on the esthetic context in which he made these remarks and one based on the overall philosophical stance of the novel as I have interpreted it in this study.

At the outset, let us reflect on the exact nuances of the words *inconnu* and *secret* in the early eighteenth century. In his

Chapter Five

Dictionnaire (1690), Furetière defines *inconnu* as "qui ne veut point se faire connaître ou qui ne peut l'être en effet," "qui n'est su que de peu de personnes," or "anonyme, sans réputation." The modern *Larousse* definitions (1986) are starker: "qui n'est pas connu," "qui n'est pas célèbre." Although the difference of meaning can seem slight, it is not insignificant: it is worth noting that the word *inconnu* in the late seventeenth century implied more something that is not easily known or recognized than something that is simply unknowable. Similarly, *secret* was something "connu de peu ou point de personnes," "ce qu'on tient caché, qu'on ne veut pas découvrir pour quelques causes particulières" (Furetière); again, compare this to the simpler *Larousse* definitions: "ce qui doit être caché," "ce qu'il ne faut pas dire." The words had a subtler meaning in the late seventeenth and early eighteenth centuries than in our own, with *secret* perhaps closer to our modern *discret*, and *inconnu* closer to a meaning of not too obvious, very subtle. A "secret chain" does not mean so much a completely hidden chain that no one can ever know, but rather a subtle, discreet connection between the various parts of the text, not evident, but not unknowable either. This understanding of the earlier meanings of the key words suggests that subtlety of reading is important here. Rather than look for a real, but hidden chain, better to look for hints of a chain that may be elusive and subtle, but perhaps knowable.

Montesquieu himself invites his readers to consider the novel's elusive nature in the very first sentence of his "Réflexions": "Rien *n'a plu* davantage, dans les *Lettres persanes*, que d'y trouver, sans y penser, une espèce de roman" (3). The impersonal construction "rien n'a plu" rather than the more expected "rien ne m'a plu," continued in the rest of the paragraph by the impersonal pronoun *on*, indicates the author's distance from his own creation and the readers' delight, and even surprise, at finding a kind of novel, almost by chance, "trouver, sans y penser, une espèce de roman." But what the readers stumbled upon was not just any novel, but a highly organized, chronologically coherent plot that had a double development in opposite directions: all the while that, "à mesure que," the Persians were becoming knowledgeable about Europe and prolonging their stay there, back home in Persia disorder and fury were increasing in their private household. All the while that their intellectual understanding about Europe was becoming more organized, their private world in Asia was disintegrating with the wives' unexpected rebellion. The chiasmic structure of the double movement in space and time, from intellectual astonishment to understanding in Europe, from political order to disorder in Persia, leads to a contradiction between intellect and passion—a contradiction that the readers can feel strongly, "ce qui fait plus sentir les passions que tous les récits qu'on en pourrait faire" (3).

However elusive self-knowledge and knowledge of the world were for the characters, those are the questions posed for the readers, as they compare themselves with the characters, "l'on se rend compte soi-même de sa situation actuelle." And, Montesquieu says, such realization is best achieved not by "récits" but by "romans" (3). The old opposition between showing and telling is at work here: showing the characters' contradictory feelings in a novel, rather than telling through an account, a "récit," removes the text from the obligation to furnish an example, and, in a move reminiscent of Descartes's in the *Discours de la méthode*,[3] removes the author's responsibility for what readers might conclude or feel, while exerting at the same time a greater impact on the readers through an appeal to their imagination and passions. This is in accord with J. Robert Loy's interpretation highlighted by Braun: "the 'chaîne secrète' lies in the juxtaposition not of various letters dealing with like topics, but of reality and the perception of reality [. . .] the readers are made to re-examine their beliefs and perceptions of reality" (qtd. by Braun 283).

But this interpretation is only half of the story: the author does not place complete trust in the readers. Like Descartes, Montesquieu does not want to leave the interpretation entirely up to the readers' feelings. Descartes employed overt authorial telling in the *Discours*, for example: "Et je pense pouvoir dire sans vanité que s'il y a quelqu'un qui en [la communication de mes pensées] soit capable, ce doit être plutôt moi qu'aucun autre" (173). With a lighter hand, Montesquieu also claims an active role as an author: "l'auteur s'est donné l'avantage de pouvoir joindre de la philosophie, de la politique et de la morale à un roman, et de lier le tout par une chaîne secrète et, en

Chapter Five

quelque façon, inconnue" (3–4). In this paragraph, however, Montesquieu does not come back to the "récit," but in a more complex move, he explains that the *Lettres* are both less than and more than a "récit": they are less than a "récit," being disjointed, digressive, lacking a rigorous plan or framework—"aucun dessein ou plan déjà formé"—and they are more than a "récit," consisting of philosophical, political and moral reasonings, "raisonnements." These diverse reasonings are bound to the plot line and become even more persuasive through the novel's impact on the readers' emotions. Therefore the chain is not a chain among abstract "raisonnements," but between those "raisonnements" and the novel: Montesquieu's enterprise was to "joindre de la philosophie [. . .] à un roman." Cleverly, Montesquieu conducts a kind of writing that is the literary equivalent of having your cake and eating it too, leaving the interpretive work to the reader through identification with the situations and emotions of the characters, while assuring himself of a strong impact on the reader.

The novel's plot evolves over time in differing directions that lead to strong feelings within the readers, and embeds throughout the text a potentially infinite number of digressions on a variety of topics, philosophical, moral and political. Given the complex nature of the overall text, it might in fact seem surprising to see Montesquieu claim that he wanted to bind all these aspects in a whole, "lier le tout par une chaîne." Indeed, it is the evident complexity that makes any underlying unifying principle so hard to discern and frustratingly elusive for literary detectives. I suggest refining the question *What* is the chain?, to: *Why* did Montesquieu write about a chain? Why did Montesquieu feel compelled, thirty years later, to point out the unity and wholeness of a work that was so obviously diverse and whose philosophical and political letters were potentially infinite in number?

One answer is that Montesquieu's retrospective reflection must be situated in the esthetic context in which he wrote it, and contrasted with the earlier context in which he wrote his novel. The three decades intervening between the novel and his discussion brought about a sea change in taste that I would describe briefly, using vocabulary familiar in art history, as a change from a rococo sensibility to a neoclassical esthetic. I use these terms to suggest certain types of tastes, guarding against specific analogies or point by point comparisons between literature and the arts of decoration or painting. Patrick Brady, who has written extensively on the rococo in both literature and the arts, warns against making specific analogies, "highly specific analogies should remain suspect unless and until validated by recourse to deeper laws and drives they allegedly externalize" ("Are Digression" 38). However, analogies and similarities can be useful, and awareness of esthetic climates or "esthetic horizons" (Blanchard 25) will be pertinent to our understanding of the different esthetic contexts in which both the novel and the "Réflexions" were written.

Montesquieu wrote his "Réflexions" in the 1750s, the age of a neoclassical reaction against the earlier rococo taste, which Brady sums up as having "the elegance and exquisite taste of Watteau, Boucher, Lancret or Pater, the artistocratic refinement and true delicacy of Fontenelle and Marivaux, the pure ludic and relatively gentle and sophisticated mockery of that most quintessentially rococo poem, Pope's *The Rape of the Lock*" ("Are Digression" 38). Gita May (181) and Brady (*Rococo Style* 44–46, and "The Present State" 105–14) have described this change as a move from the freedom of expression through ornamental, sinuous shapes, color, and movement to the neoclassical revival of austere form and controlled, unified, hierarchical organization. As Weisgerber points out in his detailed study of the rococo period, already in the late 1730s and in the 1740s attacks became more frequent against the rococo style. I propose that the claim of a unifying chain constitutes an attempt on the part of Montesquieu to describe his novel, which was loosely structured in keeping with the rococo esthetic, in terms of the new esthetic which emphasized unity and coherence. The "new or bizarre" manner is certainly descriptive of the rococo taste for newness, for its consciousness of being playful, asymmetrical, open-ended, oblique, in short turning its back on the Louis XIV age of grandeur, order, and symmetry. In the search for "beautés nouvelles" (Weisgerber 111) and desiring more freedom, the rococo dared much, rebelling against the preceding era's classicism and search for unity and purity; this corresponds to the bold religious and political critiques that Montesquieu set forth through his Persians' unique

Chapter Five

perspective on society and religion. The rococo was an auspicious climate for imagining some ambiguous, perplexing strangers whose perceptions were startling and bizarre, and at the same ultimately profound and reassuring.

If the "secret chain" statement is an argument made in the 1750s about a 1720s work, there is probably little purpose in looking for an actual unifying chain among the various parts of the work, which was not written with such an overall unity in mind. By contextualizing the "Réflexions" as well as the novel, a better understanding of the novel can be looked for elsewhere than in a hunt for the identity of the chain. In the swing away from the rococo to the neoclassical, Montesquieu, looking back at the novel of his youth, was no doubt pleasantly surprised that an argument could be made that his text was nevertheless not incompatible with the new taste. Perhaps the initial sentence, "Rien n'a plu davantage, dans les *Lettres persanes*, que d'y trouver, sans y penser, une espèce de roman" (3), has an omitted first-person pronoun after all: the most pleased person of all was in fact the aging Montesquieu, who realized that his text satisfies both the earlier and the later esthetic tastes.

There is a strong sense of the author's presence as he looks back with great satisfaction at his work in the short fourth and fifth paragraphs of the "Réflexions." The fourth paragraph, written in the past tense (passé simple), marvels at the sudden success the novel enjoyed and mocks the search for imitations, while the fifth confirms that on the contrary the *Lettres persanes* are unique and can have no sequel, "elles ne sont susceptibles d'aucune suite." It is surely no accident that the latter paragraph is in the present tense and shows "je" appearing for the first time and claiming his uniqueness. Replying to the accusations of impiety, he must have felt all the more convinced of the worth of his novel, and of the naiveté of at least one reader, the abbé Gaultier.

In the remainder of the "Réflexions" the proud author comes to the crux of the matter, the defense of the heart of his novel, saying that the critique of religion through naive characters was necessary in the beginning, "il y avait un temps où il fallait nécessairement les [les Persans] représenter pleins d'ignorance et de préjugés" (4). Arguing that it was not so much the substance of the religious critique but the manner in which it was carried out that seemed shocking, Montesquieu concludes: "Il [le lecteur] est prié de faire attention que tout l'agrément consistait dans le contraste éternel entre les choses réelles et la manière singulière, neuve ou bizarre, dont elles étaient aperçues" (5). In these last paragraphs, Montesquieu drives home his most important point, which has to do with the overall philosophical stance of the novel. For Montesquieu wishes, through his naive, uninformed Persian strangers, to confirm that some things are real underneath the puzzling exterior of social customs. Like the naive abbé, the reader who is not perceptive enough to understand the contrast between "les choses réelles" and their perception in a manner that is "singulière, neuve, ou bizarre" and who is taken in by the latter, is simply deluded: "Certainement la nature et le dessein des *Lettres persanes* sont si à découvert qu'elles ne tromperont jamais que ceux qui voudront se tromper eux-mêmes" (5). If there is any kind of chain, it is the connection that is made between the novel's critiques and the knowledge and self-knowledge the text produces for the reader, that I take to be the sense of that sentence that concludes the "Réflexions."

Finally, the image of the chain, used by Montesquieu to evoke the novel's philosophical sense, is also grounded in an ancient association with the power of eloquence dating back to the Renaissance and antiquity.[4] In the Renaissance emblem books, as John Steadman has shown in his *Hill and Labyrinth*, the chain was used to represent the power of Eloquence as it pulled the listeners in its wake: a gold or silver chain linked the ears of the audience irresistibly to the tongue of the majestic Herculean figure of Eloquence. The chain of Eloquence cheerfully and powerfully binding together listeners and author-speaker by the sheer force of imaginative language has an ancient lineage, for it is Socrates who in Plato's *Ion* describes the link between divine inspiration, poetic expression, and audience fascination as a chain that transmits inspiration to human beings:

> sometimes there is formed quite a long chain of bits of iron and rings, suspended one from another [. . .]. In the same manner also the Muse inspires men herself, and then by means of these inspired persons the inspiration spreads to others, and holds them in a connected chain. (*Ion* 421)

Chapter Five

What Socrates is describing, the divine inspiration of poets, and even of critics like Ion who can understand only one author (Homer), can be considered as analogous to the power of the literary work pulling its audience toward its meaning. I am not claiming that Montesquieu had any acquaintance with these images, but I find a convergence worth noting between the power represented in these chains and the ability of the novel to pull the readers into its world better than any "récit" could—there is, after all, a long and venerable tradition of wisdom reposing in these emblems and images that stayed alive for centuries. The seductive power of the fictional creations of eloquence, as opposed to the difficult recognition of naked moral truth, resulted in the famous dilemma, first analyzed by Georges May, of the novel that was caught between the desire to amuse and the need to show reality and virtue. It seems fitting to conclude the analysis of this enigmatic and prophetic novel by evoking an image of divine power. Not only in the eighteenth century, but also in later centuries do readers find themselves still caught in the wake of the novel, pulled along by this text of immeasurable and elusive power.

Part 3
Graffigny's Elusive Peruvian

Chapter Six

Graffigny's *Lettres d'une Péruvienne*
Giving (and) Reading

> And does not everything that we take *seriously* betray us? It always shows what has weight for us and what does not.
>
> Nietzsche
> *The Gay Science*

The Preliminary Texts and Their Mandate

Françoise de Graffigny's epistolary novel begins with two important preliminary texts, an "Avertissement" and an "Introduction historique aux *Lettres Péruviennes*," which are an integral part of the novel and as such merit a more prolonged look than the usual quick reading accorded to such paratexts. In both these texts, Graffigny foregrounds the role of the reader. In the first prefatory text, she emphasizes the importance of active reading, the intervention of the reader, without which the text's meaning cannot come into being. In the second, however, she puts the reader in the role of resisting the dominant Western European culture, while speaking as a European herself praising the Peruvian culture. Does this overt, even blatant stance not stifle the reader's capacity for interpretation? While in the first text she leaves the reader free but obliged to interpret the coming text, in the second, she seems to dictate the correct moral and historical stance in a moralizing discourse that leaves little room for irony or distance. It will take the third text, the novel, to balance and carry out the enterprise announced in the first two pieces. The critique occurs as a function of the relation of these three texts together, obliquely as it were, in the spaces in between these texts that the reader will create in the course of reading and interpreting.

Chapter Six

Read without its two prefaces, the novel falls into two familiar categories: the story of an unhappy, virtuous heroine, and a cultural critique from the viewpoint of an outsider. The Peruvian woman of the title, Zilia, is abducted from her land and torn away from the man she loves. She writes letters to Aza, her fiancé, about her experiences in her new surroundings while expressing her undying love and her hope to marry her beloved; in the end, she does not marry anyone, neither Aza nor her French suitor, Déterville. During the course of her letters written first to Aza and then to Déterville, as she becomes more and more acquainted with French society, she becomes a bolder and more impassioned critic of that society, especially of its treatment of women. Her economic wealth deriving from the gold treasures that belonged to her in Peru enables her to settle into an independent life of leisure and learning suitable for a distinguished woman of her times.

This story is told without much deviation from the timeline save for a few flashbacks to Zilia's life before her capture recounting her falling in love with Aza. It also proceeds, as a close reading of the novel suggests, in a classically structured manner.[1] There is an exposition, in which Zilia is kidnapped and travels to Europe, and a dénouement in which she renounces marriage with Déterville. After the exposition's first nine letters, the letters continue to be grouped by nines. In Letter 10, Zilia begins recounting her French experience. In Letter 19, she tells of her life in a convent, where she spends six months learning to write in the French language while Déterville is off to an unnamed war. In Letter 28, she moves in with Déterville's sister, Céline, who has just married and moved into a new house. In Letter 37, the first letter of the final part of the novel, she writes not to Aza, as was the case with her previous letters, but to Déterville, who is now in Malta. The last section has five letters, the number of acts in a classical tragedy. In Letters 37 and 38, Zilia describes Aza's brief visit to France when he informed her that he has converted to Catholicism and is engaged to a Spanish woman. Letter 39 shows her plunging into anger and despair, and Letters 40 and 41 bring Zilia to a new life of independence and learning. Thus the letters are marked by new places, and for the last act, by a drastic change in correspondent, so that the novel has a five-act structure.

Lettres d'une Péruvienne

Act I is Zilia's voyage; Act II, her life in France; Act III, her life in the convent; Act IV, her life with Céline; and Act V, both the ending of her relationship with Aza and her refusal to marry Déterville. Whether this structuring was conscious on the part of Graffigny is of course impossible to tell, but she was a successful playwright at the time she was writing the novel, and there is nothing to prevent supposing that she was shaping her materials in forms reminiscent of a drama.

At the juncture between each group of letters, there is a transition that marks a new stage in her apprenticeship in French language and society. In Letter 9 she learns her first French words, and in Letter 10, the first letter of Act II, she experiences seeing herself in a mirror for the first time. Letters 17 and 18, which conclude Act II and mark the end of her stay in Déterville's Parisian house, also show Zilia coming to the end of her Peruvian system of writing with the knotted threads called *quipus* and learning how to write with pen and paper. Letters 26 and 27 have Zilia returning to her *quipus* and confronting the gifts made to her by Déterville and Céline. In Letters 35 and 36, the last ones of Act IV, Zilia is given a new house by her benefactors, and she writes her last letter to Aza. Act V consists entirely of letters to Déterville. Thus new places, new systems of writing, new ways of living in French society, and new relationships manifest a clear progression in Zilia's deeper understanding of herself and of society, and also guarantee that Zilia remains an outsider as she confronts new demands placed on her. To sum up, Zilia moves from ignorance of French society in Act I, to an apprenticeship in language and mores in Act II, a critique of French society in Act III, a confrontation with the situation of women and with love relationships in Act IV, and a final resolution in Act V.

Read with the two prefaces, however, the novel is transformed by the preliminary texts that frame it, the "Avertissement" and the "Introduction historique," from a love story and a critique of cultural mores into an indictment of European civilization's propensity for conquest, cruelty, and injustice that move the novel into the realm of philosophical oppositional writing. As I hope to show, the two prefaces also transform the reader from a consumer of a love story and cultural critique to an interpreter of all three texts. In my reading of Graffigny's

Chapter Six

novel I will suggest that by the use of her two prefatory texts, her novel carries out together with them an enterprise of critical fiction, indeed an oppositional fiction in Ross Chambers's sense of the word.

Drawing on Michel de Certeau's profound distinction between strategy and tactics, Chambers focuses on narrative literature's special position as a critique of culture within the boundaries of the dominant culture, as a practice of tactical opposition. Chambers especially likes to focus on texts that "advertise their oppositional status, in part through self-reflexivity, in ways that make them designated objects for an investigation into the oppositional working of narrative authority" (13). As a woman writing in an age where women were visible in the culture but not dominant, and as an author deliberately replying to one of the most famous texts of the period, the *Lettres persanes*, which has a rather misogynist stance, Graffigny is not in a position of power that would enable her to have a strategy. A strategy demands having one's own proper place which one can inhabit and from which one can go out to master other places: it is "le lieu du pouvoir et du vouloir propres" (Certeau, *L'invention* 59). She is, however, able to act using tactics: "Aussi doit-elle jouer avec le terrain qui lui est imposé tel que l'organise la loi d'une force étrangère. Elle n'a pas le moyen de *se tenir* en elle-même, à distance, dans une position de retrait [...]: elle est mouvement 'à l'intérieur du champ de vision de l'ennemi,' comme le disait von Bülow, et dans l'espace contrôlé par lui" (60–61; Certeau's emphasis). Quite deliberately I have quoted the text without specifying who "elle" is: in Certeau's text, it refers to "la tactique" but, in a happy accident of French gender, I propose that it can refer as well to our woman author who makes sure that she is seen as circulating within an unfamiliar and often dangerous field.

In describing the functioning of tactical opposition in narrative, Chambers draws the distinction between two primary aspects of storytelling texts, the narrative function, present in classical texts, and the textual function, more present in modern texts, which overshadows the narrative aspect: "an important difference between ancien régime oppositional narrative and nouveau régime oppositional writing" (45) lies in the modern, "new foregrounding of self-reflexivity" "in which the 'textual function' tends to submerge or devalue [...] the 'narrative function'" (44–45). In ancien régime oppositional texts, the reader is invited to partake of the story and to take an ironic opposition to it, which corresponds to a social situation where power is centralized and easily identifiable in the élites and in the figure of the king. In the nouveau régime obtaining after the eighteenth century, power is more diffuse, pervasive, and enveloping, and in oppositional texts there is a "diffuseness of identity mirroring the new diffuseness of power" that "shifts the responsibility for the production of the text's oppositional identity even more heavily than in classical irony onto the act of reading for (and to) which the text 'appeals'" (15). In the post-Revolutionary era, Chambers maintains, the subject is more uncertain of his/her position, more alienated from any secure understanding—hence the author's seeking to seduce and win over the reader, "turning the alienating other from attitudes that are oppressive [...] to a more sympathetic 'understanding'" (17). In this new world, there is a second kind of opposition, a textual opposition that Chambers calls "melancholy" writing: in the nineteenth century, the opposition in a "kingless world" must take other forms, such as melancholy. The new authority is so diffuse that it cannot be attacked directly and must be countered only by one's conscious rejection of it, and by subtracting oneself from the milieu by isolation or even by suicide— an extreme solution made attractive to the reader by seducing the reader into agreement with this reaction to the new but just as repressive authority.

I want to suggest that Graffigny's novel, while engaged in the ancien régime's mode of ironic opposition to power, also turns to the textual mode, but with a difference. The ironic opposition is carried out not by the novel, but by the two prefatory texts, which do not belong to the novelistic discourse, but rather tell a story of colonization and Peru's pre-colonial history. The seductive, "textual" opposition is produced by the novel proper read in this particular context, where, however, the narrative element of the love story is less important than the social critique and is used as a "hook" (to use Chambers's word [46]) to seduce the reader. Her opposition, unlike that of the later Romantics, turns out to be anything but melancholy.

I have just suggested how interconnected the two prefatory texts are to the novel framed by them—the framing texts and framed text depend on each other to carry out the total work of

Chapter Six

opposition. In the following two sections, I will concentrate my analysis on each prefatory text in turn, posing the questions Who is Graffigny's stranger and What is she up to? In so doing, I will also discuss the connections between the "Avertissement" and the "Introduction historique," and the relation of these two short texts with this ironic and seductive novel.

The "Avertissement"'s Gifts

The "Avertissement" Graffigny puts at the start of her novel jumps immediately into a discussion of truth, verisimilitude, and prejudice, in contrast to the *Introduction* Montesquieu had written, which made reference to the Old Regime custom of authors' dedicating their works to powerful people. While Montesquieu seemed to have somewhat distanced himself from the customary request for protection from the dedicatee by denying that his text was an "Epître dédicatoire," nevertheless he was linking himself subtly to that practice by the very use of the word *dédicatoire*. On the contrary, Graffigny's word, *avertissement*, is free from allusions to earlier customs of authorial obeisance to protectors, and illustrates Genette's thesis that there is a gradual waning of the practice of dedicating one's works to a noble personage during the course of the eighteenth century (*Seuils* 114).

What exactly is an *avertissement*? It is one of many terms used for signifying a prefatory text, though, as Genette points out (*Seuils* 150–51), various terms can convey subtle connotations and nuances. In French, the word contains the meanings of warning, of informing, and of imparting knowledge. As a kind of preface, Graffigny's "Avertissement" lays out a multilayered discussion of concepts and gestures that will play themselves out in the rest of the novel. This apparently rather simple text pleads in favor of a better appreciation of Peruvians and tells about the text's transmission to the French reader. Moving easily from one paragraph to the next, it is a well-organized, logical argumentation that is worth following from beginning to end. Lest we be accused of misreading, we must pay our tribute to this rich text by reading it in detail, being duly forewarned and informed.

The text can be divided into two principal sections, the first seven paragraphs dealing with the subject matter, the Peruvians, and the last four paragraphs (starting with "Il semble inutile") with the medium, the letters themselves. This seems to separate the substance (the Peruvians) from the literary artifact we are about to read (the letters), but the substance has a message, and the medium has a substance.

The first paragraph's opposition between reason and prejudice identifies the problem we encounter when we are faced with something unlikely: "Si la vérité, qui s'écarte du vraisemblable, perd ordinairement son crédit aux yeux de la raison, ce n'est pas sans retour; mais pour peu qu'elle contrarie le préjugé, rarement elle trouve grâce devant son tribunal" (3). If something unlikely but true collides with reason, reason can be persuaded to accept the unlikely; but if it collides with prejudice, prejudice usually wins and we refuse to accept the unlikely as true; we believe something false. Why is the "tribunal" of reason more able to accept implausibility, while prejudice is so obstinate? And, by implication, why is reason so unable to rescue us from prejudice? One must examine what "raison" is in order to answer these questions.

The second paragraph furnishes the transition between that general premise and the particular application of the first paragraph's pronouncement. A young Peruvian woman enters the scene, sliding into view without fanfare, timidly introduced by her editor: "Que ne doit donc pas craindre l'éditeur de cet ouvrage, en présentant au public les lettres d'une jeune Péruvienne" (3). And with her enters an entire nation—and the prejudice we have of this nation. This Peruvian woman will expose what is meant by "reason" as well as our prejudices, in one blow. The third paragraph addresses the question posed by the first, why reason is weak and unable to overcome prejudice. It does not state its topic as clearly as the first two—certainly not as clearly as the fourth paragraph, which with its first words, "Mais toujours prévenus en notre faveur," clearly announces the topic of prejudice, the opposite of reason. The topic of this third paragraph is indeed reason, but it does not *name* reason, which oddly disappears in the very place where it should be, and indeed is, discussed.

Along with others who viewed the Peruvians favorably in the eighteenth century, such as Voltaire, Graffigny makes the reasonable argument in favor of the Peruvians: that since we have profited so much from their wealth, we should respect

Chapter Six

them because it is reasonable to acknowledge riches and respect the people who give them. Reason entails the recognition of a debt, "re-connaissance," knowledge and acknowledgment. An even and proportional exchange, a quid pro quo, seems reasonable: you give me something, therefore I give you respect, and if that something is very valuable, my respect will be all the greater. Reason defines the structure of the exchange of material goods for moral approval.

This form of exchange is one of the three basic forms of exchange as defined by Marshall Sahlins: a balanced reciprocity consisting of "transactions which stipulate returns of commensurate worth or utility within a finite and narrow period" (194–95). Although intended to describe nonmonetary transactions, Sahlins's concepts can furnish insights on societies with money economies. This is a kind of exchange that necessitates calculation of value in order to assure the commensurability and the utility of the terms of the exchange, and it is the form that, according to historians of mentalities, came to dominate Western European economies in the Renaissance. Balanced reciprocity is a kind of exchange where a quid pro quo is expected and mediated by the quantification of value. Exchange value replaces use value in the new commercial world of the Renaissance, displacing previous concepts of use value, and of relations between people based not on commerce but on inherited, traditional, and unquantifiable characteristics. As Philippe Desan explains, even though capital had existed long before the Renaissance, the period constitutes

> un moment historique où le modèle économique devient si prépondérant qu'il empiète sur les autres domaines et modifie irrémédiablement non seulement les rapports de production, mais aussi les rapports humains [. . .] durant la seconde moitié du XVIe siècle, le marchand et le commerçant imposent leur langue et donc l'idéologie véhiculée par celle-ci. (21)

The tension between two mentalities among the dominant classes—the noble and the merchant—which historians such as Ellery Schalk and Desan locate in the sixteenth century—was vividly perceived as a felt change at that time. However, the tension was perhaps not entirely limited to that period, and I would suggest that it persists, albeit in less urgent modes, throughout the Old Regime until the principle of qualitative hierarchy was irrevocably challenged during the French Revolution.[2] The nobility was by now a complex group consisting of the traditional and new nobility arising out of the enriched merchant class, as these orders gradually grew more intertwined over the course of the next two centuries. However, this growing rapprochement did not erase all the distinctions between the two: in the eighteenth century, thick volumes were still being produced enumerating all the dangerous possibilities for the famous "dérogeance" that could come about through, among other things, engaging in commerce—the noble's fall from rank that continued to threaten the nobility of whatever provenance, either of the sword or of the robe.

The quantified, even exchange that seems very reasonable is occulted by something much more troubling: "Enrichis par les précieuses dépouilles du Pérou, nous devrions au moins regarder les habitants de cette partie du monde comme un peuple magnifique" (3), says Graffigny. As the words "nous devrions au moins" suggest, this debt of respect was not paid. What occurred between us and the Peruvians turns out to be not an exchange at all, but thievery and killing, both of which are connoted by the word *dépouilles*, a term associated in French with death or with leaving behind something that is no longer valuable or alive. These particular "dépouilles," however, have enriched us: they constitute another sort of economic exchange, an uneven one that leaves the Peruvians despoiled and the colonizers richer. This is what Sahlins calls negative reciprocity, which is "an attempt to get something for nothing with impunity," and "ranges through various degrees of cunning, guile, stealth, and violence to the finesse of a well-conducted horse raid" (195). No wonder reason could not be mentioned in such an uneven, irrational, and murderous transfer of wealth. Reason, which at least should have made us acknowledge our debt to the Peruvians, is in fact completely absent, obliterated by the colonizer's violent appropriation.[3]

What does dare show its head in this unseemly context of thievery, because it seems more fitting, is prejudice, the topic of the fourth paragraph: "Mais toujours *prévenus* en notre faveur, nous n'accordons du mérite aux autres nations qu'autant que leurs mœurs *imitent* les nôtres, que leur langue *se rapproche* de notre idiome" (3). Our prejudice comes from a

Chapter Six

narrowness of the intellect: we can appreciate only customs, ways of living ("mœurs"), and language that are close to our own. The customs have to mirror our own, and language can differ a little, but not too much, because the slightest difference is cause for misunderstanding. Thus, ironically, we are ruthless in obliterating a nation and despoiling it under the guise of a rational exchange, and then we become delicate and can understand its foreignness only if it is not *too* foreign.

As if to underline the problem of knowing the other, which is either foreign and unintelligible, as was the case with Montaigne, or intelligible and no longer foreign, as was the case with Montesquieu, Graffigny quotes the famous, unanswerable question, "Comment peut-on être Persan?" and takes pain in the later edition of 1752 to add the words, "*Lettres persanes*," in a footnote (3).[4] I would like to suggest that it is the aporia of foreign/unknowable and same/knowable that Graffigny will break open in her novel. She inserts the question of "being" Persian/Peruvian/French at the very beginning of her novel in the context of a discussion of our overwhelming prejudice, suggesting the European haughtiness that lurks behind the expression of amazement. I will return to this question and her answer at the end of this chapter.

The next three paragraphs of the "Avertissement" continue the descent into blind ignorance. We despise ("méprisons") other peoples despite the availability of their history, which is "entre les mains de tout le monde" (3), and despite the efforts of a great poet (Voltaire's *Alzire*, quoted in a footnote [4])—despite so much "lumières répandues"—we are still blinded by our own prejudices: "mais le préjugé a-t-il des yeux?" (4). The situation seems blocked, except for the hint of a tiny opening: "si son empire était sans bornes" (4). The countrary-to-fact "était" suggests that there are limits to our prejudices, and that we can learn something in some manner that has only been hinted at. We are ready for something to move us beyond the discourse of reason and prejudice, for an event, in short, for the young Peruvian woman's re-entry, which takes place in the second part of this text. Another discourse, that of experience, is ushered in.

This time, the woman's entrance is marked as different from her previous modest entrance as a generic "young Peruvian woman," for now she has a name: Zilia—another name of a woman beginning in Z—but how different her life and fate will be from those of Zélis and Zachi. In the first half of the "Avertissement" she had brought in her country, Peru, and now she brings in herself, and furthermore she appears as a doubly remarkable person, named twice, whereas her correspondent, Déterville, is named only once and not further described except for his noble rank. She is remarkable in that she is bestowing on us an exceptional gift for which we are to be grateful, because without her intervention it would not have reached us at all. First, we are to be grateful for her being a writer, a role itself divided into the two functions of author and translator; second, we are to be grateful for her being a donor who is so obliging ("complaisance") as to give her letters to Déterville, and for giving him permission to give those letters to us. It is not he who allows the letters to be published, because he must ask her permission merely to keep them: "la permission qu'il obtint de les garder les a fait passer jusqu'à nous" (4). Zilia is foregrounded as the writer, the translator, and a generous donor, while Déterville and we are the mute grantees of her permission. In short, she is a loquacious gift-giver, a generous one who seeks nothing in return, no simple quid pro quo. Her gift is part of a generous, open-ended code of exchange: this is the third form of exchange, which Sahlins calls a generalized reciprocity, consisting of "transactions that are putatively altruistic" (193), examples being "'sharing,' 'hospitality,' 'generosity' [. . .] and *'noblesse oblige'*" (194; Sahlins's emphasis). That is not to say that reciprocity is excluded: but "the material side of the transaction is repressed" and "the counter is not stipulated by time, quantity, or quality" (194). The gift's value lies not in a quantifiable, exchange value, but in its use value, and its use will be that of effecting a change in how we perceive supposed inferiors of the world, colonized peoples and women, in opposition to the conventional valuation. As recipients of Zilia's gift, we have an obligation, and that obligation is to read and so put an end to prejudice. We have now been forewarned of our role, which is the topic of the remaining paragraphs of this "kind of preface."

Into the tiny opening in our prejudices, Zilia has bounded and she has magnanimously bestowed her letters on Déterville

Chapter Six

and on us, her grateful readers. The one remaining difficulty, which had already been indicated in the fourth paragraph, is that of language—a language so different that only one person can bridge the gap, Zilia herself, who must be the translator. Zilia not only bestows the gift of her letters, she also give us the translation, re-emphasizing her generosity and the immeasurable nature of her gift.

After Zilia's first anonymous and silent entrance and after her second, more triumphal entrance, there is one more authorial presence that appears silently, without a name, yet ever present and active: "on" (4–5). The anonymous nature of the "on" belies its powerful presence, so overwhelming that the "nous," which had been indicated several times in the two previous paragraphs as receiver of Zilia, disappears entirely or almost so: one oblique mention of the first person remains in "notre style." Clearly "nous"/we have been pushed aside by Zilia and by "on." We are in such a position of subservience that we disappear entirely. But what of "on"? "On" has been hard at work as an unseen editor: "on" left in some grammar mistakes as well as mistakes in style to preserve the "ingénuité" of the original, and "on" eliminated some outdated figures of speech, while leaving in a few to give us a flavor of the original. "On" has also been a re-writer of philosophical texts, that most noble branch of knowledge, in order to "donner une tournure plus intelligible à de certains traits métaphysiques, qui auraient pu paraître obscurs" (5). The appearance of a young Peruvian woman named Zilia puts a human face on our colonization and its underappreciated effects on the colonized; the anonymous editor assures us that the text will be easy to read. While Zilia confronts us with the distance between us and them, the anonymous editor does her best to reduce the distance and remain invisible behind Zilia. The reader is thus beholden to a very clearly named writer, Zilia, and an unnamed but most active editor, incurring a debt to two people which asks for double attention, as a compensation for the despoiling of Peruvian riches mentioned earlier. The result is that Graffigny, never speaking in her own voice, but present both as Zilia and as "on," puts the reader into a position of having to read for moral reasons, to make up for past European excesses, and also for literary reasons, in appreciation for the extraordinary writerly gift made available.

Lettres d'une Péruvienne

Thus Graffigny contests both the negative reciprocity exchange and the even, quid pro quo forms of exchange, replacing them with a "noblesse oblige" transaction where we readers must play the role of indebted recipient to several noble givers. In my analysis of the novel, I will suggest that even this latter form of exchange, while preferable to the other two, may itself be challenged and replaced by a fourth, new form of exchange.

In the face of this "singulier ouvrage"—the last words of the "Avertissement"—the reader's task is clear. The most singular work of all is the complex circuit into which Graffigny has inexorably placed the reader, a textual economy of exchange as singular as the text itself. In one blow, she has included in this circuit the reduction of reason to the shameful violence of colonization, the slim possibility of knowing a truly foreign culture through the text of a young woman and its reworking by an anonymous editor. The reader's part in this circuit is, simply, to read well. Reading well will atone for the horrendous violence done to the culture that we are about to encounter, thus making the act of reading a literary work into an effective compensation for multiple criminal acts that took place in history.

The "Introduction historique aux *Lettres Péruviennes*": The Stranger's Gaze

While the dynamic between the "Avertissement" and the rest of the novel clearly sets up the reader as an obligated person, whose act of reading will compensate for past excesses, there is a second prefatory text, the "Introduction historique," a second frame that the reader must penetrate before proceeding to the narrative. Why did Graffigny, upon reflection, add this second text (written with possible collaborators[5]) to the single preface of the first edition? While the first text indicated *why* we must read, the second framing text will say *how* we should read, positioning the reader in an unavoidable perspective that will reinforce the impact and importance of the first text. After the general imperative: read well, Graffigny adds the specific, Peruvian substance: read from this point of view. The anonymous editor "on" reappears briefly in the "Introduction" to state the necessity of understanding various aspects of Peruvian culture for reading the letters to follow. Though these descriptions

Chapter Six

seem deceptively straightforward, they set up complex interplays between the gifts of the "Avertissement," the perspective of the "Introduction," and our position as readers/interpreters of these three texts.

The second prefatory text, narrated in an impersonal voice, can also be divided into two main parts. The first part announces that it will go beyond the history of a mere "quatre siècles" told by the ancient Peruvians' "annales" (7) and treat their earliest origins and ancient history. Beginning with "Une analyse aussi courte des mœurs" (10), the second part describes the mores of the people—their beliefs, customs, the organization of their society, their arts, and their education. The first part begins innocently enough with an evocation of the first legislator and ruler, the first "Inca," Mancocapac, who gave the Peruvians all their laws and culture. But the situation is not so simple. One complication is that the first ruler's society is not the first state of the Peruvian people. Much as the virtuous Troglodytes had a previous history of nonvirtuousness that could threaten to repeat itself, so too the Peruvians were something else before their first ruler. The "first" state is already an "afterward" state. Before, there was anarchy, and a long-lasting one at that, "la barbarie dans laquelle ils vivaient depuis longtemps" (7). The first ruler comes after a long and unhappy prehistory, but he alone is not a foundational ruler.[6]

The other and more striking complication is that there is not a single original ruler but two. The Sun places a woman alongside the founding father of the kingdom. Mancocapac is joined by his wife, Coya-Mama-Oello-Huaco, the length of whose name might suggest that she is at least as important as her husband. If one remembers that both Mancocapac and Coya-Mama-Oello-Huaco are children of the Sun, then the brother is also a husband and the sister a wife, a case of incest not denied by the text itself: "Le Soleil, disait-il [the first Inca], qu'ils [the Peruvians] appellaient leur père" (7). But in contrast to what might be expected, such a new and possibly immoral beginning actually leads to the founding of a beneficial and productive society, for this brother-sister/husband-wife couple establishes the most content, moral, and civilized society imaginable. A society with complex and problematic origins, with a short written history but a long, unremembered previous history, and a moral society founded by incestuous founders, such are some of the paradoxical (for non-Peruvians) aspects that Graffigny highlights in the first part of her "Introduction historique." The beginning of society, which is not an absolute and single originating point, is located in a brother-sister/husband-wife couple, a structure of doubleness that will be repeated with variations at key points in the novel.

Into the tableau of a virtuous society, enter the invaders who sow disorder and death among the Peruvians, whose very contentment and virtue are not as advantageous as they seem. Their history undergoes a third stage, that of being colonized by invaders whose shameful barbarism threatens to send the Peruvians back to their initial, uncivilized state. On this moment of conquest Graffigny spends considerable time, for she explains how it is possible that such civilized peoples fell victim to the Spanish conquistadors without realizing what was happening to them. The explanations focus on the Peruvians' belief in astrological forecasting, which seems to have announced the coming of extraordinary men who would invade their kingdom and destroy their religion; on the Peruvians' ignorance of astronomy, which makes them misunderstand celestial phenomena; and a prophetic vision, given to the son of the reigning Inca, of a strange animal and a differently dressed man who claims to be the son of the Sun. Within the contented society of "hommes raisonnables" (7), there was a fatal flaw, that of ignorance without which they could not have been conquered and destroyed.

This means that the Peruvians were an easy prey for the Spaniards who do not so much conquer as seduce their victims because of "la crédulité des habitants du Pérou, et la facilité que trouvèrent les Espagnols à les séduire" (9). Graffigny emphasizes the visual aspect of seduction, prepared by the ghostly vision, and the brevity of the conquest: "dès qu'ils [the Peruvians] virent les Espagnols avec de grandes barbes, les jambes couvertes et montés sur des animaux dont ils n'avaient jamais connu l'espèce, ils crurent voir en eux les fils de ce Viracocha [. . .] tout fléchit devant eux" (8). In turn the Spaniards are enticed by what they see, because the Peruvians "avaient trop laissé voir leurs immenses richesses" (9), thus offering a spectacle of extraordinary wealth that dazzles the

Chapter Six

conquerors: "Quel spectacle pour les Espagnols, que les jardins du temple du Soleil, où les arbres, les fruits et les fleurs étaient d'or, travaillés avec un art inconnu en Europe!" (10). But underneath the apparently mutual seduction lies another entirely different attitude: that of cruelty, rape, and massacre, "Tous les droits de l'humanité violés" (9), so that the invader gains the upper hand by sheer strength and killing. The seduced is now a victim: "L'ignorance de nos vices et la naïveté de leurs mœurs les jetèrent dans les bras de leurs lâches ennemis" (10). The previously mutual seduction is obliterated by the brutality of the conquest, which has sexual overtones: "jetèrent dans les bras" suggests an erotic embrace while the very opposite is taking place. As in the "Avertissement," where reason occulted prejudice, what seems appealing actually hides shameful acts of killing and despoiling. The didactic tale of seduction followed by killing foreshadows the novel's story, also a story of kidnapping and seduction that, however, does not end in killing—hence the novel will offer a modified schema of seduction and conquest that will balance the account of horror given in the history.

Thus the first part of the "Introduction historique" is a didactic text that leaves little room for the reader to interpret it except as a condemnation of colonization—a historical tale of seduction that is anything but seductive. The second part retreats from this overtly polemical stance, leaving much more "room for maneuvering" for the reader—an account of the society before the conquest that seems objective but is a technique of seduction introduced, significantly, by that hidden but active editor "on," who reappears here: "Une analyse aussi courte des mœurs de ces peuples malheureux [...] terminera l'introduction qu'on a crue nécessaire aux Lettres qui vont suivre" (10).[7]

The second part of the "Introduction" seems to be a straightforward and objective description of the Peruvians' character, religion, learning, and arts before the conquest. Their religious beliefs in the Sun as a god to be worshiped is accompanied by a belief in another, higher god whose name is rarely evoked, as well as a belief in a Moon goddess, mother of all things, reflecting the dual origin in the first brother-sister/husband-wife lawgivers. After the description of temples, festivals, and the education of youth in the principles of modesty and obedience, Graffigny sums up their exemplary morality with the affirmation that "il passait pour constant qu'un Péruvien n'avait jamais menti" (13), an echo of Montaigne's description of the Cannibals as a people whose vocabulary did not include such concepts as "la mensonge, la trahison, la dissimulation" (204). After this summation, Graffigny describes the Peruvians' learning. One could almost say that this description constitutes a third section, but in reality the type of learning shows their morality in action and constitutes the climax of this second preface.

Indeed, Graffigny makes the link between morality and education by explaining that "la modestie et les égards mutuels étaient les premiers fondements de l'éducation des enfants" (12). The entire education in the sciences which is pervaded by the moral principle of modesty at the personal level translates into self-sufficiency at the cultural level: "Les Péruviens avaient moins de lumières, moins de connaissances, moins d'arts que nous, et cependant ils en avaient assez pour ne manquer d'aucune chose nécessaire" (13). The Peruvians have just enough knowledge of geometry to measure land, just enough medical knowledge to treat specific accidents, and generally just enough not to want for anything, and they even cultivate their land with the strength of their arms, not needing tools made of steel or iron. This means that they have less knowledge than do we Europeans, but if they have enough to live well, does that not suggest that we have too much? Even their music and theater are subordinated to a goal of religious celebration. No knowledge is gained for its own sake, no art is practiced for art's sake, nothing is developed in excess of a specific use. As Graffigny summarizes it, "La morale et la science des lois utiles au bien de la société étaient donc les seules choses que les Péruviens eussent apprises avec quelque succès" (15).

Self-sufficiency, strict limitation of art, science, and learning to immediate use, obedience to religious and moral authority, absence of need and vice, and yet the ability to build superb roads and aqueducts (14), such are the characteristics of the society from which Zilia will emerge. This way of life seems different from both the uncivilized state of nature characterized by barbarism and the contemporary cultures characterized by excesses. Nor is it a far-off and irretrievable golden age, where no work is needed and nature provides abundant sustenance and shelter. It is utopian in being a nonmercantile society that produces goods and learning, but where only use value, not exchange value, governs the production of goods and knowledge.

What Graffigny does here is to sketch her version of utopia, neither entirely natural nor excessively civilized, which is why she leaves out aspects of the Peruvians' character that do not concord with it.[8] This second part develops the critique of European society in a more subtle way by suggesting that, to quote a modern phrase, "less is more," which is the theme of her citation of Puffendorf at the end: "'Il faut avouer [. . .] qu'ils ont fait de si grandes choses'" (15). After the hard-hitting critique, her utopia accomplishes, in the same understated manner as the society depicted in it, a subtle critique of European society's excesses, which are unnamed—the sole exceptions might be the mention of "fer" and "acier" (14), materials not known in Peru, which I find only reinforce the absence of any mention of European technology. Hence the reader is presented with a society that was organized otherwise, with economy of means, adequacy of resources, and manpower to the task, and with admirable results.

Although Zilia is not mentioned in the second prefatory text, her background is directly linked to this complex history: being betrothed to the son of the Sun, she participates in her people's history, religion, and culture at its very heart. And she is also the most prominent victim of the Spanish invaders, along with her fiancé, Aza, both destined to occupy the central position in the kingdom. The rest of the text will reflect this double heritage of Zilia, the product of a contented, virtuous people and the victim of an unbelievably cruel invader. At the same time, Zilia's personal destiny is to compensate for the brutal history of her people and to show a different outcome than destruction. That this exists only in the imagination accounts for the anachronism—the strange timelessness and the conflation of the sixteenth-century invasion and the eighteenth-century life of the heroine analyzed by Julia Douthwaite—though I part company with her conclusion that Graffigny presents a "utopian solution for the future" (*Exotic Women* 112).[9] The compensation exists not in the future, but in the imagination of the reader of the novel, who, previously obligated to read well, now has been made to read against him or herself as a member of the colonizer group. For if the French readers can distance themselves from the barbarity of the Spaniards, Graffigny does not let non-Spaniards off the hook, as the conquerors are introduced as coming from "un monde dont ils ne soupçonnaient pas même l'existence" (7), which is of course the Western European world. While in the bulk of her account of the conquest Graffigny opposes Peruvians and Spaniards, toward the end of the account she again opposes generally them and us, "nos vices et la naïveté de leurs mœurs" (10). Any difference between the Spanish conquistadors and their French counterparts will be erased in Letter 3, when the French takeover of the Spanish ship is described in terms of blood, horror, and violent savagery that equal or surpass the terms used to describe the Spanish kidnapping (30–31).

Far from being a mere name or a position from which to observe our society, Zilia, whom we remember from the first text, is now understood as representing another society that has its own history, morality, and culture. While the "Avertissement" had obligated the readers to read well, the "Introduction" obligates the readers in another way: to read from a point of view informed by the very description we have just read, which, as we saw, critiqued openly the immorality, excesses, and violence of the readers' own society, and criticized covertly other excesses of European society. The two prefaces together obligate the Western European readers to read against themselves: this is an "oppositional reading" (Chambers 16) of another kind, not aimed at the text but at the readers' own culture. In that sense it is closer to the modern "seductive reading" whereby the readers are encouraged to feel a "more sympathetic 'understanding'" of the alienated heroine (Chambers 17).

Unlike twentieth-century Hollywood films that forced women to view themselves through the culturally dominant male gaze,[10] Graffigny's novel forces French readers to view themselves through positions that are culturally "inferior": through the gaze of the colonized, and through a female gaze, both inferior even if the reader is an enlightened man or woman

Chapter Six

and a hater of the violent colonization of far away lands. As Janet Altman says, "the place of the female in Graffigny's fiction is also [. . .] the space (to be) occupied by peoples who have experienced colonization and cultural expropriation" ("Graffigny's Epistemology" 177). But the difference here is that Zilia never sees herself as inferior; indeed, she retains her sense not only of distinctness but of superiority. Together with Zilia, we will circulate within our own culture, adopting her point of view during the course of the narrative.[11]

Graffigny's textual machine is set into motion with remarkable efficiency to carry out its work of critique. Framed by the two prefaces, the novel can now be read as oppositional, indeed must be read in such a way. The novel's specific critiques of eighteenth-century society are a form of tactical opposition framed by the writer's enterprise of focusing on much larger topics: immorality, prejudice, cruelty, as exemplified by conquest and colonization, some of the West's most egregious acts of injustice and despoiling. Graffigny's aims are multiple and enfold each other: critiquing society under the guise of a sentimental novel, the overriding aim, and using the sentimental novel and the social critique to attack colonization. Thus both the prefaces and the novel are tactics to one another. Our woman author, circulating under the guise of a sentimental story teller, sends Zilia, circulating as a vanquished heroine into the reader's world. This is what her stranger is up to: no less than questioning the very bases of a society that can conquer other continents and dominate its own female citizens.

Zilia's Play: Place, Language, and Exchange: The Acts of Discovery and Self-discovery

1. Act I: Exposition—The Voyage

The first act is crucial not only in launching the plot and explaining the characters to the reader, but also in inaugurating certain preoccupations and modes of description that will be continued throughout the novel. In this way, the entire novel is dependent on the initial wrenching experience of Zilia, as she is not only colonized, but enslaved. Thus to the anticolonial thrust of Graffigny's prefaces is added an antislavery motif: in the very first sentence of the novel, Zilia cries out for Aza to break "les chaînes de mon esclavage" (1: 17). The sentimental aspect of the novel, expressed in her continuing to write to Aza and her hopes of marrying him, guarantees that the reader will never forget what she never forgets, that she is removed from her legitimate place against her will, no matter how respectfully she is treated.

In the very first pages of the novel, Graffigny initiates a mode of description and perception that could be called phenomenological, so closely does it resemble what Merleau-Ponty will call by that name two centuries later: "une philosophie phénoménologique ou existentielle se donne pour tâche, non pas d'expliquer le monde ... mais de formuler une expérience du monde, un contact avec le monde qui précède toute pensée *sur* le monde" (48; Merleau-Ponty's emphasis).[12] The kidnapping of Zilia by Spanish, then French captors, leaves her unable to understand what is happening around her, a situation that is heightened by the extremely elevated and privileged life she had led as a princess. Not unlike Montesquieu's Persians, Zilia is amazed by everything she sees and experiences, but unlike them, she is and remains in a state of incomprehension about the conditions in which she finds herself, such as being on a ship, looking through a telescope, and traveling in a carriage. This leads to some amusing de-familiarizing descriptions of familiar objects that are part of the "naive outsider" genre.

What is extraordinary is the consistency with which Graffigny reminds the readers of this kind of phenomenological description unaccompanied by interpretive understanding not only in this first act, but throughout the novel's first four acts. In these sections, Zilia learns much, but she remains a perpetual traveler who never quite knows where she is and who struggles to make sense of the simplest facts of life. Even in Letter 35, the second-to-last letter of the fourth act, Zilia seems not to understand what she is signing and why, and takes the whole episode as a joke: "ah! volontiers, lui dis-je en me prêtant à la plaisanterie" (147)—a joke that is nothing less than the gift of the completely furnished house given to her by Céline.

The gradual habituation of Zilia to her French surroundings never erases completely her feeling of puzzlement, her sense of being an outsider. Though Graffigny shows her being more

Chapter Six

and more understanding and critical of her surroundings—a novel written entirely from the point of view of a completely ignorant and surprised outsider would be tedious—she is able to convey that Zilia never leaves entirely the level of phenomenological observation. This enables Graffigny's novel to have a more thoroughgoing critical stance than Montesquieu's, because her heroine is never fully absorbed into French society, never completely settled into a stable identity, never confident of understanding all the signs around her. Her various locations during the entire novel emphasize her dislocation in the mental and personal aspects of her life. There is a balance between amazement, which enables Zilia to see society differently, and knowledge, which enables her to make cogent critiques—a balance that Graffigny strives to keep throughout the novel and that gives it its unique force.

What Graffigny's imagination does in the first part of the novel is to carry out a kind of thought experiment that was fashionable in the middle of the eighteenth century, but different from imagining a statue deprived of its senses and restored to its senses systematically one by one (Condillac), or imagining a person deprived of only one sense (Diderot's *Lettre sur les aveugles*). Her view of a human being is a more holistic one. Not only are the senses, language, perceptions, and thoughts intertwined and interdependent, but a human being has a given place in the spatial and temporal universe, so that one exists in a continuum that includes what is inside and outside one's self. Graffigny imagines that a rupture occurs in this continuum and emphasizes it by describing the kidnapping as a moment that should be torn out of the universe: "le moment terrible (qui aurait dû être arraché de la chaîne du temps, et replongé dans les idées éternelles)" (1: 17). Zilia is not deprived of any of her senses, nor is she deprived of language or thought. In the first few pages Zilia is crying out and calling out, and she is all too aware of painful sensations, suffering to the depths of her being. Yet a moment of rupture occurring anywhere in this continuum brings disorder to the entire human being. Hence her summing up of her amazement in the following terms that emphasize her new situation in the universe: "la place que j'occupe dans l'univers est bornée à l'étendue de mon être" (21). Such a rupture is so contrary to the holistic aspect of each human being's experience in the world that it is felt by Zilia as a moment of horror: "Le temps s'écoule, les ténèbres succèdent à la lumière; aucun dérangement ne s'aperçoit dans la nature; et moi, du suprême bonheur, je suis tombée dans l'horreur du désespoir, sans qu'aucun intervalle m'ait préparée à cet affreux passage" (18).

The reference to "nature" that is unaware of this violent event happening to Zilia inaugurates a complex appeal to nature throughout the novel. Here nature is used to criticize the violent human event to which it is oblivious and which therefore should not occur. However, it is also something that is known and embodied personally by the Peruvian nation. This ambivalence of nature is represented by the use of the pronoun *nous* in such phrases as the following: "le penchant naturel qui nous porte durant la vie à pénétrer dans l'avenir" (3: 32) or: "cette heureuse liberté que la nature nous a donnée de rendre nos sentiments impénétrables" (5: 37). Does "nous" refer to the Peruvians with whom Zilia identifies as she is in the process of being captured by the Spanish and the French, or does it refer to humanity generally? At times nature seems to be an impersonal force that could be intuited by any human being, impelling in her "un mouvement naturel et presque involontaire" (1: 20). At other times it is personalized; for example, it is associated with Aza, through whom nature speaks to give her a desire to live: "la timide nature [. . .] emprunte ta voix plus puissante que la sienne pour retarder une fin toujours redoutable pour elle" (6: 41). Or it is described as being particularly well known and represented by the Peruvian nation as she compares it with the French: "La nôtre, plus favorisée de la nature" (16: 74). This is an ambivalence that will remain throughout the novel, and that will receive a unique solution only at the very end.

Neither strictly materialist or sensualist, Graffigny stresses the relations between one's body, thoughts, and language, and the feeling of powerlessness in adjusting perceptions and communication: "Entourée d'objets importuns, leurs regards attentifs troublent la solitude de mon âme, contraignent les attitudes de mon corps, et portent la gêne jusque dans mes pensées" (5: 37). Throughout this early part of the novel, Graffigny stresses the interrelation of the material and the abstract. Turning around Milan Kundera's title, one could say that she writes about the "unbearable heaviness of being": "je crains que mon corps n'occupe trop de place" (7: 42).

This moment of rupture in the universe, in Zilia's universe, is also the one moment of rupture of the chronological timeline in the entire novel: it is here that we have flashbacks to the pre-conquest lives of Zilia and Aza that emphasize the wholeness and connectedness between them. After all, it was on the very day of their wedding, called "union" (18), that the Spaniards broke into the temple. And the relationship between Aza and Zilia is described as a merging of feelings and intellects, where Aza wants to remove barriers between him and her, to elevate her to his level of learning: "ton âme, supérieure aux coutumes, ne les a regardées que comme des abus; tu en as franchi les barrières pour m'élever jusqu'à toi" (2: 23). With the added comment that this will be beneficial to their posterity (23), the utopian nature of the relation between the two lovers, transcending gender differences, is emphasized, connecting this brief evocation of past happiness in the flashback to the longer depictions of pre-colonial Peru of the "Introduction historique."

When her sea voyage comes to an end in Letter 9 and she starts to acquire a few words of French, another voyage through France and through language begins. The scene is set for a more complete exploration of the twin processes of learning language and social mores in the second part of the novel. Unlike Condillac's statue, which is deprived of senses at the beginning and is given back one sense at a time, Graffigny's Zilia has all of hers, and unlike the statue, she is not informed by her senses: "Je savais que la privation d'un sens peut tromper [. . .], et je vois avec surprise que l'usage des miens m'entraîne d'erreurs en erreurs" (9: 48–49). For Condillac, the information given by the senses seems to flow immediately into information about what is seen: "La plus légère attention doit nous faire connoître que, quand nous apercevons de la lumière, des couleurs, de la solidité, ces sensations, et autres semblables, sont plus que suffisantes pour nous donner toutes les idées qu'on a communément des corps" (16). But for Zilia, her senses leave her only in the dark, in "ténèbres," for a reason indicated in her crucial question, "L'intelligence des langues serait-elle celle de l'âme?" (49), a question that indicates that body, mind, thought, and soul are inseparable and accessible only inasmuch as language gives them shape; deprived of language, she is deprived of access even to the most intimate part of herself, her soul.

Going beyond the imaginative descriptions of physical sensations, Graffigny explores the relation between sensations and thought and language, none of which seem to have priority. This illustrates Graffigny's holistic view of human beings, where sometimes objects and men's gazes impinge on Zilia's thoughts, and at other times she needs the material substance of her knotted *quipus* to express her thoughts: "ces nœuds qui frappent mes sens, semblent donner plus de réalité à mes pensées" (4: 36). Matter and thought seem not only interrelated, but inextricable. The phenomenological exploration of the totality and simultaneity of human experience is paralleled by the sentimental aspect of the novel, where Zilia's anguish at her immediate situation is repeated in her relation between herself and Aza: "tu ignoreras toujours où je suis, si je t'aime, si j'existe; la destruction de mon être ne paraîtra pas même un événement assez considérable pour être porté jusqu'à toi" (6: 41). As I already said, reliance on nature and feelings of love for Aza are put on a par when she debates whether to commit suicide: "la timide nature [. . .] emprunte ta voix plus puissante que la sienne pour retarder une fin toujours redoutable" (6: 41), but Zilia's determination is stronger than both nature and Aza: "mais, c'en est fait, le moyen le plus prompt me délivrera de ses regrets..." (41). Only her "surveillants" (7: 42) are able to restrain her by physical force from carrying out her suicide. This sense of uncertainty regarding Aza as well as her own existence is resolved only at the end of the novel, in her final statement, "*je suis, je vis, j'existe*" (41: 168; emphasis in the original), which must be read in this context, as an answer to her initial confusion. Rather than analyzing the various components of human experience, she will conclude with that statement of synthesis, a simple affirmation of being alive.

2. Act II: Self and Language

The first act has several functions: besides launching the sentimental plot—a heroine torn away from her intended husband/lover—on the philosophical level it depicts the unique act of

Chapter Six

Zilia being wrenched away from her place in the universe, and it initiates the phenomenological mode of description that will recur throughout the novel. Both the wrenching and the mode of description allow Graffigny to explore the nature of subjectivity, the manner in which a subject is constituted. What happens to Zilia as a kidnapped woman is the passive equivalent of Descartes's own rejection of his personal past and his traditional learning in one radical gesture at the beginning of the *Discours de la Méthode*: "mais sitôt que j'eus achevé tout ce cours d'études [. . .] je changeai entièrement d'opinion" (128). This decision leads him to undertake a voyage and to study "le grand livre du monde": "j'employai le reste de ma jeunesse à voyager" (131).

Not unlike her philosophical predecessor, Zilia is engulfed in doubt: "je demeure incertaine, je doute presque de ce que je vois" (10: 49), but this quasi-Cartesian doubt does not lead her to any foundational Cartesian intuition such as "I think." Descartes's doubt had led to a radical separation of sensing self from thinking self, to "a disembodiment of the subject and to its isolation and autonomous constitution as an entity independent of historical or social context" (Judovitz 87). At the opposite end of the philosophical spectrum, Condillac expresses the view that the sensory experiences are immediately clear, using the well-known Cartesian terms *clair* and *distinct* while rebutting the Cartesian philosophy: "Il est d'abord bien certain que rien n'est plus clair et plus distinct que notre perception, quand nous éprouvons quelques sensations. Quoi de plus clair que les perceptions de son et de couleur! Quoi de plus distinct!" (17). Instead, Zilia obtains little certain information, especially in the experience of seeing herself in a mirror for the first time, in which she learns nothing, remaining in a "mer d'incertitudes" (10: 51). This crucial mirror experience is Graffigny's fiction of the construction of the self, not as a Cartesian "theoretical construct, not to be confused with [. . .] the historical, psychological individual" (Judovitz 183), but on the contrary as a historical and contextualized person. But Graffigny's refusal to ground her subject in rational, Cartesian subjectivity does not automatically make her into a non-Cartesian, "postmodern" subject. I would like to show how this episode gives us an insight into the formation of the subject of Old Regime culture, a subject that is neither abstract and rationalist, nor fragmented in a postmodern manner, nor constituted according to psychoanalytic concepts which were the first, historically, to challenge the idealist, autonomous subject in control of its own processes and actions.

It is worth quoting the passage in full when Zilia cries out upon seeing herself:

> En entrant dans la chambre où Déterville m'a logée, mon cœur a tressailli; j'ai vu dans l'enfoncement une jeune personne habillée comme une Vierge du Soleil; j'ai couru à elle les bras ouverts. Quelle surprise, mon cher Aza, quelle surprise extrême, de ne trouver qu'une résistance impénétrable où je voyais une figure humaine se mouvoir dans un espace fort étendu! (10: 49–50)

The experience continues to expand when Déterville makes her see his own image beside hers in the mirror:

> L'étonnement me tenait immobile, les yeux attachés sur cette ombre, quand Déterville m'a fait remarquer sa propre figure à côté de celle qui occupait toute mon attention: je le touchais, je lui parlais, et je le voyais en même temps fort près et fort loin de moi. (50)

This episode gives us contemporary readers a unique glimpse into the formation of subjectivity in Old Regime culture, a view different from the post-psychoanalytic view that is more habitual to us. The difficulty of imagining other forms of subjectivity is described as a major hurdle by Judovitz at the beginning of her *Subjectivity and Representation*: "It is as if once [the Cartesian] subjectivity comes into being, no other ways of defining being human can continue to exist" (1). And, I would add, after psychoanalysis and especially after Jacques Lacan's *Ecrits* (1966), it is difficult to resist reading in a contemporary manner the mirror episode in which Zilia apparently has her first ever encounter with that object and hence with her image—Douthwaite's book conveniently has a 1797 illustration of this moment (117). It is tempting for us to read Zilia's experience as an example of the mirror stage in the formation of the subject, but Graffigny's episode shows precisely the

Chapter Six

opposite, the nonformation of the subject here and its formation elsewhere.

According to Lacan, the mirror stage involves the baby's recognition of itself, more precisely the baby's recognition of its image as an image, "son image dans le miroir *comme telle*" (93). The understanding of the image as an image enables the subject's later socialization, the subject's entry in the dialectics of the relation with the other, which will then make him/her a full-fledged subject: "l'assomption jubilatoire de son image spéculaire par l'être encore plongé dans l'impuissance motrice et la dépendance du nourrissage" (94). The mirror stage prefigures and enables the formation of the self, both as an entity unto itself, and as socially determined: "la permanence mentale du *je* en même temps qu'elle préfigure sa destination aliénante" (95; Lacan's emphasis).

As various historians have explained (Elias, Chartier, Greenblatt, Laqueur), notions of the subject, of gender, and of the body have a history. Modern concepts cannot be read back into periods where completely different concepts of the subject existed. Norbert Elias was particularly conscious of this, as Roger Chartier explains: "A la psychanalyse, et à Freud jamais nommé, il [Elias] reproche de constituer un inconscient 'sans histoire' comme instance dominante et invariante de la structure psychique" (xxvi). Enough warning indeed against reading Zilia's experience in a modern manner, as a mirror stage in the constitution of the self. It is not surprising that the mirror experience teaches her nothing about a concept of the subject that is not of her period. For in her time, the subject was defined not by one's personal unconscious or conscious, but much more by interrelation with others, in which the subject is defined by self-representation to others, by one's role played in social rituals, and by others' opinions of the subject's self-presentation: in ancien régime society, "la construction de l'identité de chaque individu est toujours au croisement de la représentation qu'il donne de lui-même et du crédit accordé ou refusé par les autres à cette représentation" (Chartier xxi). In the aristocratic society that Graffigny inhabits and describes in her novel, prestige defines the individual aristocrat's worth: such recognition is verified and shown through visible expressions of clothing, residence, language, etiquette, and especially the ability to support oneself through one's wealth without work. In the ancien régime society, it was necessary and important to cultivate certain specific and useful qualities: "l'art d'observer, les autres et soi-même, la censure des sentiments, la maîtrise des passions, l'incorporation des disciplines qui règlent la civilité" (Chartier xxii).

After the Revolution, society is radically different, and much more familiar to us: "une société marquée par l'obligation générale du travail, une stricte séparation entre le for privé et la vie publique, une hiérarchie des valeurs qui donne le primat à la réussite économique" (Chartier xxvi). In this society dominated not by the aristocracy but by the more egalitarian-minded middle classes, the self is structured differently: it is a self with depth, i.e., with an ego and a superego, a preconscious and an unconscious, and with a personal history firmly rooted in the nuclear, private, restricted family. In both types of societies, the subject exists within a surrounding social configuration, so that what changes after the Revolution is both the social configuration and the concept of the subject. To sum up, there is a contrast between a self previously defined more in relation to external hierarchies existing in society at large, and a self now structured by internal layers and defined more by its immediate family structures.

Zilia's experience before the mirror gives her no epiphany, and brings her no understanding whatsoever about her self. She will learn much more as she enters the world of hierarchical social relations, as indicated in the very next paragraph when she acquires a maid and finds consolation in having women around her and being served by them. In the following letter, she enters the world of the aristocracy when she is introduced to the "Pallas," a woman remaining otherwise unidentified to the reader, who can suppose she must be a ruling aristocratic lady of the area. From this lady, Zilia learns what to do and what not to do in the presence of a hierarchically superior person. During these various social interactions, she is illuminated about herself, as others mirror her back to herself. Despite the linguistic difficulties, she understands that her clothes excite curiosity, and by her behavior she tries to communicate to the persons around her that she is not at all different from them: "je ne pensai plus qu'à leur persuader par ma contenance que mon âme ne différait pas tant de la leur que mes habillements de leurs parures" (11: 53). In a society that classified individuals by the place and rank of their birth, i.e., by orders rather than by economic classes, there is more difference between ranks than between people of the same rank, and less difference between people within the same rank, whereas in our modern era, it is different: not having the concept of orders and ranks, we prize individuals for their distinctness and we consider them equal in having the same rights.[13]

It is only after being thus formed as a subject that Zilia is free to ask herself questions about her new surroundings, and specifically to ask what her fate might be (Letter 11). She can now turn her attention to language. During this second act, Zilia's being an outsider to the French language enables Graffigny to describe various aspects of the communication of messages, i.e., semiotics. Having no ability to understand the language and most of the actions surrounding her, Zilia is forced to invent a set of signs that she and Déterville can use to communicate: "les signes du *Cacique* me sont quelquefois plus utiles. L'habitude nous en a fait une espèce de langage, qui nous sert au moins à exprimer nos volontés" (11: 52; emphasis in the original). These signs, which are never specified, could be possibly gestures, which are not a language in the usual sense of the word. But, as Umberto Eco has shown, even kinesic indices do indeed form a type of semiotic code, as long as "a convention exists which correlates a given expression to a given content, irrespective of the way in which the correlation is posited and accepted" (121). Thus Zilia's and Déterville's private "kind of language" is appropriately so named, semiotically speaking.

When not communicating with Déterville through their mutually understandable signs, she has to decipher signs without knowing the code. As she observes people speaking and gesturing, laughing, bowing, kissing each other, she tries to interpret their behavior and sometimes she succeeds, sometimes she fails. She is reassured by demonstrations of kindness and gifts, but these convince her (erroneously) that Déterville must know that she will be queen of Peru: "Cette conviction me rassure et calme une partie de mes inquiétudes; je comprends qu'il ne me manque que la liberté de m'exprimer [. . .]

mais jusque-là j'aurai encore bien des peines à souffrir" (15: 70–71). On the other hand she deciphers correctly the coldness of Déterville's mother, whom she would not have taken for his mother had she not been told who the woman was, presumably by means of their kind of language (11: 52). At other times, she goes straight to the correct connotation: for example, without understanding words, she grasps that the relations between Déterville and his sister are "fondés sur la confiance et l'amitié" (13: 65).

Throughout this section of the book, in which Zilia is the most bewildered, Graffigny goes beyond Zilia's difficulty of communicating through the use of the French language, and explores the more profound question of the connection between language and thought. Zilia is bemoaning the fact that she is unable to express her puzzlement and her worries, suggesting that there is thought prior to language. Derrida describes this as the traditional metaphysical view founded on the belief in plenitude and presence of thought as prior to instituted language: "la parole étant naturelle ou du moins l'expression naturelle de la pensée, la forme d'institution ou de convention la plus naturelle pour signifier la pensée, l'écriture s'y ajoute" (*Grammatologie* 207). For example, she is unable to explain to Aza what she sees because "je ne trouve dans notre langue aucuns termes qui puissent t'en donner l'idée" (15: 70). She has feelings and ideas that she would like to remember, organize, and express later: "conserver le souvenir des plus secrets mouvements de mon cœur [. . .] pour amuser ton loisir dans des jours plus heureux" (16: 72).

Yet other passages suggest that language does not come after thought but constitutes it. In the following passage, Graffigny brings both together in such a way that it is difficult to determine which view has precedence, thus figuring at the textual level precisely the conundrum she is exploring: "Si je trouve à présent tant de difficultés à mettre de l'ordre dans mes idées, comment pourrai-je dans la suite me les rappeler sans un secours étranger?" (16: 72). Language is both "étranger" and necessary, and its absence leads to a loss of her thoughts. Precisely in the next paragraph Graffigny evokes the new language in terms that are again ambivalent, as someone comes to give Zilia "des leçons de sa langue, et de la méthode dont on se sert

Chapter Six

ici pour donner une sorte d'existence aux pensées" (16: 72). Language is described in all its materiality so that it seems diametrically opposed to abstract thought, with its new instruments of pen and paper, sounds and words, replacing the knotted cords of the *quipus,* which are running out at this time in the novel.

The loss of the materials to make her *quipus*, at a moment when she does not yet possess the French language and the Western writing system, leads to a loss of her self, a sinking into nothingness, and a loss of her connection to Aza. Again, the phenomenological, sentimental, and linguistic strands of Graffigny's text all come together at the moment when Zilia feels she is losing simultaneously her language, her mind, and her beloved:

> je vois la fin de mes cordons [. . .] ces nœuds, qui me semblaient être une chaîne de communication de mon cœur au tien, ne sont déjà plus que les tristes objets de mes regrets. [. . .] mes pensées errantes, égarées dans le vide immense de l'absence, s'anéantiront désormais avec la même rapidité que le temps. (17: 77)

After spending six months learning a new language, she feels that she has regained her self and her love and her capacity to speak: "Rendue à moi-même, je crois recommencer à vivre. Aza, que tu m'es cher, que j'ai de joie à te le dire" (18: 78). And she wishes she had more languages at her command, in order to express her love all the better, "dans toutes les langues" (78): the more languages, the more love she could feel and express. Rather than being a "dangerous supplement" that threatens plenitude, as was the case for Rousseau (abundantly analyzed by Derrida), language for Graffigny is more ambivalent: coming after thought, yet indispensible to it. Language, an arbitrary human invention (Letter 17), is inherent to thought which then inherits this arbitrariness.

When Graffigny seeks to locate something prior to the arbitrariness of both thought and language, it is in nature. After going to the opera, Zilia reflects: "des sons aigus expriment mieux le besoin de secours dans une crainte violente ou dans une douleur vive, que des paroles entendues dans une partie du monde, et qui n'ont aucune signification dans l'autre" (17: 75).

Nature is beyond imitation: "il faut [. . .] que la nature ait placé dans ses ouvrages un attrait inconnu que l'art le plus adroit ne peut imiter" (12: 58). At the most nature is successfully imitated by songs and dance in a limited way: "La nature, plus puissante et plus attentive aux besoins et aux plaisirs de ses créatures, leur a donné des moyens généraux de les exprimer, qui sont fort bien imités par les chants que j'ai entendus" (17: 75). The most natural phenomenon is the playfulness of animals, "les jeux naïfs des animaux," in turn imitated by the dances that "inspirent [. . .] à peu près le même sentiment" (17: 76). There is some slippage in the imitation, which is general, imperfect, and approximative, thus guaranteeing that something beyond imitation by human invention will remain. At the same time that nature is this inimitable state, it is also an informative one, since it reveals to Zilia, for example, the coldness of Déterville's mother while at the same time it seems erased by her very coldness: "je n'aurais pas reconnu les sentiments de la nature dans les caresses de cette mère" (13: 62). I think that we are not far from Pascal's famous question about nature's capacity for being so easily erased, quoted as the beginning of Chapter 4.

Letter 18, the concluding letter of the second act, faces both backward and forward, and Zilia is both newly empowered and demystified. After six months of language learning, Zilia is happy at being reborn upon learning to communicate in a new language, and she has new knowledge about her new circumstances, but she is now disabused of any belief in the superior glory of her native land and bereft of the basis of her former identity. The words describing her correspondence with Aza are highly ironic, testifying to the nonnatural situation in which she henceforth finds herself: "j'ai joui du bonheur artificiel que je me faisais en croyant m'entretenir avec toi" (18: 78). The very words "artificiel" and "croyais," which show awareness of delusion, are prophetic of even greater delusions to come. This letter also marks the transition to social criticism that will dominate in the third and fourth acts—a critique directed not only at the greedy Spanish colonizers, but also at Peru, for she finds that the Sun does not shine only on Peru, but on the whole world. Thus demystified, she has to face a new reality: "un nouvel univers s'est offert à mes yeux. Les objets ont pris une

Chapter Six

autre forme, chaque éclaircissement m'a découvert un nouveau malheur" (18: 78).

Like those who felt lost and diminished when a geocentric universe was replaced by a heliocentric one, Zilia feels the void and anguish of belonging in a new, infinite, and decentered world, where the far away Aza represents her last and only support in facing the new hardships to come—a loss of illusion that for the moment moves her forward to face her new surroundings, and which foreshadows the later loss of Aza himself to the Spanish (woman and religion). The reference to the "cupidité des Espagnols" (79) at the end of the letter reminds the reader of the initial framing of the novel, the condemnation of the colonizers who are responsible for this decentering, brought on not by exploration of cosmic space but by the conquest of remote and unknown regions of the Earth.

3. Acts III and IV: Society's Contradictions

The bulk of Graffigny's social critique occurs in Acts III and IV, which focus on Zilia's life in French society, first when she is in the convent (Letters 19–27), then when she is living with Céline (Letters 28–36). These Letters concern such topics as religion, government, social hypocrisy, ostentatious spending, and the situation of women, to which she pays particular and detailed attention. Less satirical and comic than the Persians' letters, Graffigny's observations center around a few recurring themes. Zilia is particularly attentive to inner contradictions and reversals of what she knew in Peru. For example, in Letter 20, she observes that in France the subjects give their wealth to the king, whereas in Peru the reverse takes place and kings give their wealth to their subjects, which seems more logical to her since kings have more wealth. She notes the contradiction in the religious man who tries to convert her to Christianity but has no regard for any religion but his own (Letter 21) and becomes deceitful (Letter 22); she fails to see any connection between the nuns' religious life and the ignorance required of them (Letter 19).[14] Her most detailed critiques of French society focus on another theme, the emptiness of their behavior, rules, and attitudes: words without meaning, superficial shows of respect, caring without true affection, having one's social duties carried out by servants, superfluous compliments, ostentatious spending for its own sake (Letter 29). In short, her puzzlement, which could at first be ascribed to her foreignness, remains constant: society has rules and codes, but these do not make any more sense when she is finally able to decode them. She performs on French society an operation that can be called a kind of denaturalization, in the sense of Roland Barthes who deconstructs the tendency of society to view its concepts as natural. For Zilia, as for Barthes, but not for her French counterparts, "la Nature dans laquelle on les [people] enferme sous prétexte de les éterniser, n'est qu'un Usage" (*Mythologies* 244), and usage is itself unexplainable, arbitrary, and irrational. As Barthes says in his 1970 foreword to *Mythologies*, "pas de dénonciation sans son instrument d'analyse fine, pas de sémiologie qui finalement ne s'assume comme une *sémioclastie*" (8; Barthes's emphasis). The revelation of artificiality lies at the heart of her view of society, and for Zilia, the stranger ever attentive to her spatial situation, this is emphasized by her descriptions of both indoor and outdoor living spaces.

She notes the tumultuous amount of useless and superfluous ornamentation of clothes, houses, and gardens. This leads her to the observation that the superfluous has become the object of a quasi religious cult: "les Français ont choisi le superflu pour l'objet de leur culte: on lui consacre les arts, qui sont ici tant au-dessus de la nature" (28: 117). The next paragraphs describe how, in an almost baroque frame of mind, people overturn nature's elements so that earth is surprised by plants from foreign climates, water is made to gush upward into the air instead of flowing down, and fire, deprived of its destructive power, is channeled and used to illuminate and dazzle: "Quel art, mon cher Aza! Quels hommes! Quel génie!" (118). In short, Zilia is surprised, even dismayed, by these spectacles, which wrench natural elements out of their usual purpose and make them perform a kind of seductive dance for human entertainment. The critique of superfluity and distortion reappears in Letter 29, where the excesses and defects of French society are attacked as depravation and deliberate deception in very strong terms worthy of La Bruyère or Rousseau: "ce qu'ils appellent politesse leur tient lieu de sentiment: elle consiste dans une infinité de paroles sans signification, d'égards sans

Chapter Six

estime, et de soins sans affection" (122). In this letter, added in the 1752 edition, Graffigny emphasizes the unreality of a society so exclusively focused on appearances that nothing of value can be discerned. Her bitter denunciation of an artificial society is summed up at the end of the letter: "le superflu domine si souverainement en France, que [. . .] qui n'a que du bon sens est sot" (125).

After Zilia moves in with the now married Céline, she also moves into a more personal critique. The tension between respect and contempt, politeness and betrayal occurring between men and women, which is discussed in Letter 33, culminates in a full discussion of the particular situation of women in Letter 34, which was also added in the 1752 edition and written in the same scathing tone as Letter 33. This Letter focuses on the plight of women who are trapped in a discordant situation of unreality, "le peu de rapport qu'il y a entre ce qu'elles sont et ce que l'on s'imagine qu'elles devraient être" (34: 137). Their education does not make sense, as they are educated in a convent and then asked to live in the world; they are asked to exist only for show, taught only how to put on a good face, and not taught anything of substance. They are expected to be virtuous without being taught or shown what virtue is; they are not even properly instructed in their native language, so that, in an ironic reversal, the Peruvian princess who had to learn language from the ground up knows French better than they do: "je ne m'aperçois pas sans une extrême surprise que je suis à présent plus savante qu'elles à cet égard" (141).

Graffigny's long indictment of the education given to women and the behavior expected of them continues the theme of ornamentation which we had seen regarding the treatment of nature and spaces: women are only a "figure d'ornement" and they exist only "par la représentation" (142). They are taught how to construct themselves artificially: "Régler les mouvements du corps, arranger ceux du visage, composer l'extérieur, sont les points essentiels de l'éducation" (139). Thus fashioned, they are objectified and reduced to being mere possessions, even less prized than furniture or jewelry, yet they are also blamed for being flighty and inferior to men. Graffigny's language becomes indignant as she heaps condemnation upon condemnation. She asserts that women are subject to "l'espèce d'anéantissement qu'on lui présente sous toutes sortes de formes" and they are subject to unfair demands: "sur quel fondement on exige d'elle la pratique des vertus, dont les hommes se dispensent en lui refusant les lumières et les principes nécessaires pour les pratiquer" (145). This discussion goes beyond the brief and matter-of-fact observation of Letter 38 of the *Lettres persanes*, that if education were equal, the sexes would be equal too; the tone and style betray Graffigny's anger at the unbelievable double bind in which women of all ages are placed by men, not only in marriage but in the family: "Mais ce qui se conçoit encore moins, c'est que les parents et les maris se plaignent réciproquement du mépris que l'on a pour leurs femmes et leurs filles, et qu'ils en perpétuent la cause de race en race avec l'ignorance, l'incapacité et la mauvaise éducation" (145–46).

This is a crucial sentence by its position as the last sentence of the last letter of social critique, coming in the next-to-last letter of the fourth section. Reading well, the task that lay before the reader as mandated in the "Avertissement," has led us to this impassioned critique of the impossible situation of women, one of the main themes of the novel. Reading well, which had been asked of us as a compensation for the violence and destruction of European colonizers in the New World, leads to the implied comparison between the situation of women in the Old World and the colonized people of the New World. Both the colonized and women are threatened with a kind of annihilation. And if justice is asked regarding the others in the New World, the same must be demanded for the colonized others existing within the Old one.

Thus the women of the Old World are in the ambiguous position of both belonging to their society, and being excluded from fully partaking in all its activities. In this sense, the women are both insiders and outsiders, evoking simultaneously reactions of respect and contempt by the men who are not outsiders, but full citizens of this world. In her study of this period, Sarah Kofman describes cogently this double attitude toward women: "Cette idéalisation des femmes, leur métamorphose en êtres sublimes, ne peut pas ne pas être suspecte car elle a toujours été au cours de l'histoire l'envers de leur rabaissement: les hommes respectent les femmes certes, mais ils cherchent toujours aussi à les tenir en respect" (13). In the eighteenth century, as Dena Goodman points out (especially chapter 3), it was especially the *salonnières*, women like Zilia with intellectual and social ambitions, who suffered from being neither fully integrated nor completely excluded—which put them in the position of having to use tactics, like interlopers on someone else's territory.

The solution stated by Zilia at the end of Letter 34 is the imitation of the model of virtue represented by Aza and the naive simplicity of Peruvian mores, but this is impossible. Graffigny bemoans the fact that French women are placed in the uncomfortable position of being constructed for social intercourse and men's enjoyment, and she also laments that nature is not powerful enough to instruct women, or that it cannot because the instruction society furnishes is completely contrary to nature: "Mais il faudrait que la nature les fît ainsi; car l'éducation qu'on leur donne est si opposée à la fin qu'on se propose, qu'elle me paraît être le chef-d'œuvre de l'inconséquence française" (34: 137–38). But the solution, a return to "la naïve simplicité de nos mœurs," is also impossible because any such place where life according to nature would be possible is out of reach since the society has been destroyed by colonization. The eloquent wish expressed by Zilia is both ardent and completely unrealizable by either the Peruvians or the Europeans: "Heureuse la nation qui n'a que la nature pour guide, la vérité pour principe, et la vertu pour mobile" (32: 134). It is time to turn to the resolution that Graffigny's women—Zilia as well as Céline, whose role increases in importance in the novel—envisage as acceptable modes of existence in this foreign world.

Before considering the final act of the novel (Letters 37–41) when Zilia realizes the impossibility of marrying Aza and decides not to marry Déterville, I will consider the complex question of gift-giving, which is treated in some detail. I will suggest that there is a link between the problematic and the significance of the gift and the ending of the novel, Zilia's final choice of friendship over marriage. Finally, all these considerations take up again in a fuller way the bestowing of gifts by the authors of the *Lettres d'une Péruvienne*—Zilia, the anonymous "on," and Graffigny—upon the readers of the novel.

4. A New Kind of Exchange

Among Zilia's major difficulties in learning the codes of society were the acts of gift-giving and gift-receiving. In Letter 27, the last letter of Act III, Zilia is both the subject and the object of gift-giving lessons. At the beginning of the letter, exchanges seem to flow smoothly: the judges have returned to Céline, who had been disinherited by her own mother, what rightly belongs to her; Céline in turn becomes kinder to Zilia, and Zilia is grateful, remarking that "nous sommes toujours redevables à ceux qui nous font éprouver un sentiment doux" (109). But some kinds of indebtedness are not so easy to accept or to acknowledge, as the rest of the letter will show: Zilia has to go through a moment of "trouble fâcheux" (109) in order to learn this lesson.

The problems arise for Zilia when she is given generous gifts by Céline that she cannot reciprocate equally and immediately, the kind of gifts that involve a "vagueness of the obligation to reciprocate" (Sahlins 194). Hence at first she refuses Céline's generous gifts of clothes, jewels, and housing, feeling them to be humiliating. Later in the letter, when Déterville gives Zilia the treasures that belonged to the Peruvian temple from which she was abducted, Zilia, still in a reciprocating frame of mind, wants to give him a generous gift that is also refused at first. Céline upbraids her very logically: "Quoi! vous voulez faire accepter des richesses immenses à mon frère, vous que l'offre d'une bagatelle offense; rappelez votre équité, si vous voulez en inspirer aux autres" (113). Although this might seem to make sense as a version of the golden rule, this is not the final message regarding gifts in the novel. Remembering that the act of bestowing gifts without expecting a quid pro quo was so positively portrayed in the "Avertissement," we might be cautious about seeing this episode as endorsing an even kind of exchange.

Zilia must first learn a lesson: how to accept a generous gift. And the French culture possesses rules for such "diffuse obligation to reciprocate" (Sahlins 194), which Céline promptly teaches her. Like any child, Zilia has to be taught when and how to write a thank-you letter: "Ecrivez-lui donc, me dit-elle en souriant; sans une lettre de votre part, les présents seraient

Chapter Six

mal reçus" (114). Only after Zilia has accomplished this social ritual can she experience the pleasure of giving without offending. There was no way for her to know the rules intuitively, for these are not given in nature and are extremely difficult to discern: I believe that this is the sense of her exclamation, "Que les vices sont près des vertus!" (113). So close that there is no difference except the one that society ascribes to any given action. Without rules that are different from culture to culture, virtues and vices are indistinguishable from each other. A similar proximity of the permissible and the impermissible will be evoked by Graffigny in those most fundamental structures of society, incest and marriage rules: Zilia and Aza's marriage, allowed in Peru, becomes a crime under Catholic law, while breaking the engagement is a crime in Zilia's eyes (Letter 38).

Gift-giving is fraught with difficulties, whether the generous kind or the balanced reciprocal kind. Another episode of gift-giving goes beyond these two types of gifts, which seems even more outrageous: it is the gift of the furnished house, complete with gardens, linens, servants, and money, that Céline and Déterville give to Zilia in Letter 35. At first Zilia is taken aback, not knowing whether to be offended or amused: "'Vous poussez trop loin l'outrage, ou la plaisanterie'" (150). But then she is told something that changes everything: that all these belongings are the result of the sale of her temple's treasures, so that they already belong to her. The gift turns out be not a gift at all, but a reverse magical transmutation, not into gold but from gold, of what already belonged to her in Peru into material goods and servants, into a usable form in French society. This is a kind of transformation of her own possessions, that, to use a medical analogy, is like an autologous transplant: "derived from the same individual." No rejection by the hostess is possible. This could represent a fourth kind of exchange, in addition to Sahlins's three: a paradoxical one, for an exchange does take place—Peruvian treasure into French palace—and yet no exchange takes place, since the gold was already hers. Just as the Peruvians were self-sufficient in their pre-colonial land, so Zilia will also be self-giving, receiving what is already hers. This transmutation is not like any other kind of exchange, not even like the potlatch "giveaways between chiefs and in the internal relations of chiefs and their respective followers" where goods "move one way, in favor of the have-not, for a very long period" (Sahlins 260, 194). It is unique, unrepeatable, so that Graffigny thereby re-creates another utopia, like the life that obtained before Western intervention into foreign lands, but now on French soil.[15]

There is a sleight-of-hand, however, which Zilia must forgive her donors: getting her to sign unawares the document making the ownership legal. Even in the most utopian gift transaction, there is a slight remainder of trickery, a supplement that subtracts from its purity without threatening it, as Derrida explains: "Le supplément transgresse et à la fois respecte l'interdit" (*Grammatologie* 223). The same structure of supplementarity that Graffigny had detected in the relation between language and thought is there too, but lessened by two factors: the fact that it is a woman, Céline, who does the gift-giving, thus reinforcing the womanly aspect of this unusual gift—Déterville had worked behind the scenes, but it is Céline who performs the actual transaction. The second factor is Zilia's own affirmations, at the end of the Letter, that she indeed owns her gift: "des domestiques que je savais être à moi," and her "palais enchanté" is truly hers (154). Nevertheless it is tainted by another supplementary emotion, a brief and inexplicable melancholy mood that Zilia notices overcoming Déterville and Céline at the very conclusion of the episode. They hide it so well that Zilia wonders if she saw it at all: "mais l'un et l'autre reprenaient si promptement un air serein, que je crus m'être trompée" (154). Thus there remains a bare trace of the price Céline and Déterville have to pay, confirmed by their refusal to stay with Zilia in her new palace. Even this gift which is not really a gift, since it is a retaking and transformation of objects already rightly possessed, is tainted by a trace of something that exceeds it: and that excess is displaced onto the agents of the transformation and gift givers, leaving Zilia as untouched by it as possible. For Zilia, this event is perfection, and out of this perfection will come the conclusion, and ultimately Zilia's generous bestowing of her letters on Déterville and on us, her readers.

Chapter Six

5. Act V: The Dénouement—Zilia's Way, Imitable or Inimitable?

It is the autologous nature of the transmutation that points to the novel's dénouement, when Zilia refuses to marry Déterville after Aza has come to France and informed her that he has become a Catholic and will marry a Spanish woman. Thus Aza has accumulated betrayal upon betrayal by abandoning her, treating her coldly, and going over to the former conquerors of Peru. Such extreme suffering does Zilia feel that even the memory of the shadow cast by Aza on a wall where this encounter took place—in Céline's house—is painful, in a poignant example of a "lieu de mémoire": "jusqu'à son ombre effacée d'un lambris où je l'avais vue se former, tout faisait chaque jour de nouvelles plaies à mon cœur" (40: 164). After this painful memory, she swears off dependence on another human being, asserting that only objects have a power over her (163), and determines to live in her "locus amoenus" where Aza has never been; in Céline's house, she sees the objects that "me retraçaient sans cesse la perfidie d'Aza" (164).

After this rejection by Aza, which she turns around into a rejection of everything that might remind her of her dependence on him, she becomes dedicated to living in freedom, independence, solitude, and self-sufficiency, values already achieved on the material level in her new house and domain. On the moral and philosophical level, she uses strong words to express her certainty that she has reached a final, irrevocable rule: "Ce n'est point au simulacre de la vertu que je rends hommage, c'est à la vertu même. Je la prendrai toujours pour juge et pour guide de mes actions" (165).

Letter 41 spells out what this true virtue consists of, in a reply to the last letter of the *Lettres persanes* and in an echo of the last page of Madame de Lafayette's *La Princesse de Clèves*, another novel of renunciation of love by a woman. Unlike the women of the *Lettres persanes*. who are killed or commit suicide, and unlike the Princess of Clèves, who dies at the novel's end, Zilia lives on, in her oft-quoted, triumphant statement, "cette pensée si douce, ce bonheur si pur, *je suis, je vis, j'existe*" (168; emphasis in the original). Her virtue, she suggests, can be and should be imitated, unlike that of the Princess of Clèves, whose short life leaves behind "des exemples de vertu inimitables" (416). By putting the plural on "inimitables," Lafayette suggests that it is not the virtue that cannot be imitated, but the examples, which therefore turn out not to be examples at all, reinforcing the negativity of the novel.[16] What does Zilia's virtue consist of, exactly? Not only in appreciating life, but in living it well, in an independent manner that spares the soul of the "nouvelles chaînes" of love (166). "Venez, Déterville, venez apprendre de moi à économiser les ressources de notre âme" (168), she urges Déterville in a richly significant sentence. It is she who is now the teacher ("venez apprendre"), and what she teaches is the proper husbanding (I cannot resist the use of this word) of one's finite resources ("économiser les ressources"), so that one can have a durable knowledge of oneself and as much knowledge of the universe as is possible in a lifetime, what she calls modestly "une connaissance légère, mais intéressante, de l'univers" (167).[17] Her independent mode of existence is what she sets forth as an example, but one that can be shared, as she insists that Déterville join her. Unlike the Persian women, who are married, Zilia remains unmarried and a virgin, emphasizing the autonomy of the woman who, by force of history, never married Aza, and by choice does not marry. And unlike the Persian women, who have found the profound laws of nature and knowledge, Zilia renounces any such pretension by emphasizing that she is not seeking any knowledge of nature, "sans approfondir les secrets de la nature" (167), because her independence is more important than penetrating the secrets of nature. Thus comes the resolution, as unique as the end of the novel itself, of the complex interrogation of nature that Graffigny had pursed in her novel. For Montaigne and for Graffigny, the wisest course is not to interrogate nature—the suspicion being that there is no nature that could divulge any secrets.

As the (nearly) perfect gift was autologous, so the (nearly) perfect existence is independent, self-sufficient. But just as there was a trace of something foreign in the perfection of the autologous gift, so too there are traces of imperfection in this existence: a supplement consisting of Déterville himself, whom she implores to come and learn from her. This is underlined by the positioning of the word *amour* as the last word of the novel, not by accident, I believe: for even in the most free and calm life, filled only with innocent and lasting friendship, a trace of love is never completely absent. Indeed love had to exist so that it could be supplanted by friendship; friendship is thus a double supplement, one that fills the void of love, and one that remains in excess of a love persisting, after all, as the last word. Once the Peruvian utopia is undone and left behind, a new utopia can be created, but never without a slight excess or imperfection. Nancy Miller sums it up as follows: her life "remains unfigured by plot, and historically unfinishable" (*Subject* 153).

The new utopia with the asexual relationship between Zilia and Déterville (who could have married but did not—a potential husband and wife who relate as brother and sister) reproduces, in a slightly different way, the situation of Zilia and Aza, a brother and sister who were engaged and should have married,[18] itself a reproduction of the historical founders of the Peruvian culture, brother-sister/husband-wife Mancocapac and Coya-Mama-Oello-Huaco, who did marry and had descendants. A foundational historical event relies not on a single point of origin, but on a dual one, of which the original incestuous Incan rulers are the fullest example. Both contemporary couples are foundational, whether incestuous or platonic, not unlike the other brother-sister couple in the story, Céline and Déterville, who also enable Zilia's new life. By contrast, the only sexual union occurring and legitimated during the novel, that between Céline and the shadowy figure of her fiancé,[19] has no role to play in the text other than providing a place for Zilia to live for one of the acts. Reversing the categorical affirmation by Lévi-Strauss, who seeks to demonstrate "l'existence universelle de la prohibition de l'inceste" (56) as the one foundational law of human nature, Graffigny envisages another possibility, different from Lévi-Strauss's patriarchal view that "dans la société humaine, ce sont les hommes qui échangent les femmes, non le contraire" (57). In her universe, men do not exchange women, nor do women exchange men, but women and men live in various configurations that include incest, indeed where incest is the most productive of relationships, but where it can be modified, allowed, or rejected. Not being a simple reversal of the incest taboo, Graffigny's anthropology imagines more possibilities to exist for human relationships, and, more daringly, it allows the possibility of the prohibited relationship to be the most productive.

The final situation of Zilia in the last three paragraphs of the text has been the object of much critical attention, because Zilia does not marry, die, or enter into a religious order, the usual means of providing closure to heroines.[20] Rather than considering what the ending is not, I would like to focus on what the ending is, and what it conveys to the reader.

First, it should be noted that the novel almost comes to a conventional end in Letter 39, when Zilia, in despair after seeing Aza for the last time, is ready to die. Indeed "mourir" is the last word of this Letter, and the beginning of Letter 40 emphasizes Zilia's illness, which had threatened her life. The difference of the more unusual ending in Letters 40 and 41 is highlighted by the proper ending that almost took place. But Zilia does not die. So the ending is euphoric for the heroine, but puzzling, maybe even dysphoric for the reader, while the Persian women's ending was certainly dysphoric for the women, but euphoric for the reader.[21] Graffigny's text shows that Zilia is very aware that she is going counter to the convention, as is Céline, who apparently tries to persuade her otherwise, in terms that are left vague: "Peut-être la fastueuse décence de votre nation ne permet-elle pas à mon âge l'indépendance et la solitude où je vis; du moins, toutes les fois que Céline me vient voir, veut-elle me le persuader; mais elle ne m'a pas encore donné d'assez fortes raisons pour m'en convaincre" (40: 165).

Independence, freedom, "les douceurs de la liberté" (164), and solitude are certainly positive goals, and already constitute a marked departure from either a wedding or death. But there is something more to Zilia's final attitude that contributes to the exceptional nature of the ending: it is that Zilia not only practices a new lifestyle, but she also tries to convince Déterville of its value. In short, Zilia tries to win over and seduce the man who had tried to seduce her—and Graffigny attempts to seduce her readers as well. I would like to examine this seduction specifically in the context of the other seductions that occur in the novel.

A seducer is by definition an active figure who tries to win over someone on whom seduction is being exercised; another activity for winning someone over, but a violent one, is capturing and kidnapping. Both seduction and capture are active, while the captured/seduced persons are on the passive side.

Chapter Six

Both seduction and capture occur in the novel; indeed, they set it into motion and conclude it.

In the beginning of the novel, the Spanish capture Peru and kidnap Aza and Zilia (Letter 1); the French capture the Spanish ship and Zilia (Letter 3); beforehand, Aza had seduced Zilia and persuaded her to elevate herself to his level of education (Letter 2); Déterville starts trying to seduce Zilia by taking her hand (Letter 4), and in Letter 5, he almost worships her. Finally, in Letter 36, a young Spanish woman has seduced Aza, who will marry her. While Zilia, as a woman, is the conventional object of efforts of seduction as well as the unfortunate victim of two successive acts of capture, the man Aza is also taken by force and seduced, placed in a position of weakness, and thereby feminized. This is further highlighted in the text by the suggestion that Aza is not only captured forcibly by the Spaniards, but also seduced by them, which brings a clear-sighted, sharp rebuke by Zilia:

> Non, mon cher Aza, ces peuples féroces, que tu nommes Espagnols, ne te laissent pas aussi libre que tu crois l'être. Je vois autant de signes d'esclavage dans les honneurs qu'ils te rendent que dans la captivité où ils me retiennent.
> Ta bonté te séduit [...] mais moi qui n'entends pas leur langage, moi qu'ils ne trouvent pas digne d'être trompée, je vois leurs actions. (2: 24)

At the end of the novel, Aza is again clearly shown in a position of passivity, as he has been "séduit par les charmes d'une jeune Espagnole" (38: 160), and also convinced to convert to Roman Catholicism. The weak Aza is contrasted to Zilia, who resists Déterville's advances and never converts to Christianity.

The opposition weak man/strong woman (and the oppositional woman) is fully realized in the last two letters, when Zilia acquires agency and full subjecthood and now attempts to be a seducer of Déterville, who still hopes to convince Zilia of his love. She tries to convince him of his error: "un faux espoir vous séduit" (41: 166), and in order to win him over to the delicate joys of friendship, she makes him imagine a life of tender sharing, mutual learning and the pleasure of being alive together. The last paragraph culminates in repeated, imperative, impassioned pleas, "Venez, Déterville, venez apprendre [...]

Renoncez aux sentiments tumultueux [. . .] venez apprendre à connaître les plaisirs innocents et durables, venez en jouir avec moi," ending with phrases indicating that Zilia will give abode to him inside her very own self: "dans mon cœur, dans mon amitié, dans mes sentiments" (41: 168).

While we see Zilia's attempt to seduce Déterville, we readers also experience our own seduction. We had read her letters addressed to Aza, over his shoulder, so to speak, like a voyeur; but Aza was unfaithful, and easy to castigate, to be ironic about. Now we are reading over the shoulder of another man, who is more likely to be seduced, and it is not so easy to dismiss him ironically. Neither is it possible to dismiss Zilia ironically, for we are with her in her pleading for friendship, just as we were with her in her criticism of the impossible and detrimental situation women find themselves in society. Thus out of this text arises an oppositional stance that is neither ironic nor melancholy, the two types that Chambers had singled out in his reading of ancien régime literature and romantic literature. It is a third kind of opposition; let us say that it is a woman's way, a gentle but impassioned co-opting of the reader.[22]

Feminist moves do not mean overturning or inverting the male/female hierarchy, and they involve acceptance of ambiguity and otherness. Zilia's solution involves neither ironic opposition, nor madness or suicide, but cheerfulness, pleasure in living without tumult, and learning about nature without violating its secrets. Zilia is in society, yet she is different, in an ambiguous mode that is simultaneously inclusive—she does not renounce Déterville's or anyone's company—and separate—she not only wants to live on her own terms but she also wants to follow the dictates of both her own heart and her own mind. Graffigny leaves Zilia in a "library of one's own" where the heroine "in fiction controls precisely that which escapes control in a woman's life" (Miller, *Subject* 153, 157). In short, she remains in the position of the "stranger," a long-term outsider, and any discomfort about this conclusion may well betray a discomfort with the ambiguous figure of the stranger when no possibility of either assimilation or expulsion is envisaged. Zilia's way must be reckoned with, and her gift beckons to her readers who may decide that they prefer her womanly moves to any maneuver/man's oeuvre. We may well

Chapter Six

feel that her way more than compensates for love ("dédommager de l'amour"). Her last words are urgent and simple in renouncing passion (the emotions that one suffers) in favor of an intellectual and critical activity that will yield unending pleasures and may also change society—a duty mandated to the reader in the prefaces, and the reward achieved at the end of the novel, by reading it completely and very well.

Part 4
Nature Affirmed and Nature Denied

Chapter Seven

Voltaire's *L'Ingénu* and Claire de Duras's *Ourika*
The Aristocracy's Betrayals

> But the ability to contradict, the attainment of a good conscience when one feels hostile to what is accustomed, traditional, and hallowed—that is still more excellent and constitutes what is really great, new, and amazing in our culture; this is the step of steps of the liberated spirit: Who knows that?
>
> Nietzsche
> *The Gay Science*

This chapter will conclude the study by focusing on two works that have a stranger as chief protagonist, but have diametrically opposed philosophical positions regarding nature and society. On the surface, these authors and these texts seem very different. Voltaire and Claire de Duras are two figures who could be considered exemplary: one of the most central, prolific, and dominant male figures of the Enlightenment, and a woman from the highest ranks of her society who lived to see both the last years of that period and its brutal destruction, and who played a limited public role as the author of three novels. Voltaire's Huron man and Duras's Senegalese woman, both racially other visitors, come to very different ends during their sojourn in Europe. There is no direct connection between these works as there was between Montesquieu's novel and Graffigny's avowed response to it. One motivation for examining them in the same chapter is my interest in feminist criticism. I do not wish to reproduce the hegemony of male authorship nor to enclose women in a ghetto; I do wish to treat male and female authors on an equal footing; to highlight the depiction of a woman's struggle in a male-dominated society;

finally, to show that there is a variety of women's responses such that Graffigny and Duras, responding to the same social context, are diametrically different and yet echo each other. Like Julia Douthwaite, who finds advantages in the matching of male and female authors, I wish to stress the "interconnectedness of men's and women's roles in ancien régime society by comparing the male-female relationships found in novels by women with those of male-authored texts" (*Exotic Women* 6). One procedure is to perform the "reading 'in pairs'" suggested by Nancy Miller (*Subject* 129), which allows texts to interact with one another, just as they did in the culture at large.

Voltaire's and Duras's texts, moreover, have some unexpected meeting points. Both best-sellers in their times, both texts show a stranger interacting with a specific part of society, namely, its very highest levels, the Versailles court and the ruling aristocracy. Like the *Lettres persanes* and the *Lettres d'une Péruvienne*, both these texts use a stranger as a figure of ambiguity to critique society, but unlike Montesquieu and Graffigny, Voltaire and Duras erase the ambiguous stranger by opposite resolutions that are mirror images of each other: either integration (Voltaire) or complete rejection (Duras) of the stranger. Both texts self-consciously explore connections between various periods of history: they are deliberately set in an earlier period. Written in the later eighteenth century, *L'Ingénu* is set in the latter part of the seventeenth century, and *Ourika* is written in the nineteenth century and set in the latter part of the eighteenth century. Both stretch the boundaries of the time of the story by also including allusions to the period of their writing—though this stretching pales in comparison to the *Lettres d'une Péruvienne,* which merged the period of colonization and the eighteenth century. *L'Ingénu* and *Ourika* transcend the boundaries of their original space and time, thereby suggesting that having a retrospective viewpoint opens up the possibility of a broader reflection on history, both past and future.[1]

L'Ingénu, or Nature Confirmed

Critics have debated the message and the unity of Voltaire's story, and consensus does not seem achieved yet. Is its hero a devalued hero (Henein) or an example of the natural man of the highest order? Why does this story seem to have two distinct parts and tones, a philosophical tale and a sentimental novel, and how are these two connected (P. Clark, Levy)? Is the story unified (H. T. Mason, Wellington, Clouston), or does it contain two opposite and irreconcilable stories, one optimistic and one pessimistic, along with the two morals that conclude it?[2] I will not try to perform here a full analysis of *L'Ingénu*, but I will suggest that looking at this complex text as the story about a stranger helps make sense of its meaning. That the stranger theme is likely to be important is highlighted by the first two paragraphs about the tenth-century Irish saint Dunstan who comes to France on his "petite montagne," founds a priory there, and returns to Ireland by the same means of travel (285). Like the saint, the Ingénu comes from across an ocean, to bring not religion but the new philosophy of natural law. As Jacques van den Heuvel says, "le débarquement du Huron, c'est l'intrusion de la loi naturelle dans le domaine des superstitions" (302). Seven hundred years later, one stranger undoes the previous stranger's legacy on the very same shores.

It is obvious that the Ingénu is a man of nature not only by the way he speaks, but by the way he acts as he makes a graceful leap onto Breton shores. Right from the beginning of the story, he is presented as "très bien fait" (286) and acts with "un air si simple et si naturel" (287) that amazes all those who see him. Voltaire shows him as a person reconciling opposite characteristics effortlessly, such as having "l'air martial et doux" (286), being both a Huron and a white man with a "teint de lis et de rose" (287) (which will be explained by the fact that he is not a Huron at all), speaking with "assez de douceur, mais avec un peu de fermeté" (287). Not only is he a physical embodiment of complete nature, but he also thinks and speaks with the voice of nature, as he explains in his first self-definition: "je dis toujours naïvement ce que je pense, comme je fais tout ce que je veux" (288).[3] He listens to nature, and speaks and acts accordingly: for example, he has a natural passion for traveling, and here he is, having traveled from Canada to England to France (288).

In the figure of the Ingénu, furthermore, nature is not static, but is capable of being perfected through learning, as will happen when he is in prison. There the good Jansenist Gordon

Chapter Seven

educates him by giving him texts to read, but nature does the most work in forming the Huron. His learning gives true meaning to the word *e-ducation*, a drawing out of, as Clouston points out (162), because, as the Ingénu says himself at the conclusion of his study of theater, "J'ai parlé d'après la nature," which most human beings fail to do (320). In chapter 14, when the Ingénu concludes his course of study, Voltaire again repeats that he was "instruit par la nature," and that this nature gave him all his learning as well as a keen sense of his innate freedom: "je suis né libre comme l'air" (326)—a freedom that is lacking in prison and nevertheless operative, since it is this "nature outragée dans le premier de ses droits" (326) that gives him strength, insight, and even the capacity to convert a Jansenist, though to what is left unstated. In other words, even after having been baptized into the Catholic Church, thrown into prison by the king's confesseur, and educated by a Jansenist, he does not lose his innate nature. There is no opposition here between nature and civilization.

Although this stranger will become less of a stranger and will modify his characteristic of being only "ingénu" ("l'Ingénu, qui n'était plus l'*ingénu*" [337]), he keeps his basic gifts, but adds new capacities: "il avait appris à joindre la discrétion à tous les dons heureux que la nature lui avait prodigués" (341). The loss of stranger status is also what enables him to survive: more like Rica rather than like Usbek, he modifies his identity and melts into French society, but like Usbek and unlike Rica, he retains a sense of self without being an outcast. In the end, he acquires a place in society that exemplifies the highest possible accomplishment, for he becomes "à la fois un guerrier et un philosophe intrépide" (347)—note that in combining both the *via activa* and the *via contemplativa*, the life of a man of action and of the intellect, it is the life of the intellect that is called "intrépide" rather than the soldierly one, thus shifting the emphasis from the battleground of the army to that of ideas.

As he passes from his status as a sojourner to that of a citizen, he encounters obstacles that make this stranger's tale coherent and significant. It is the opposition to (his) nature that interests Voltaire and gives the story its basic unity. But in this ascent from an outcast on the shores of Brittany to the pinnacle of society, the line is not straight for our stranger. While his stranger status does not impede him from learning what the best of society has to offer—love, friendship, education, wisdom, bravery, and reknown—he is, however, a stranger to something else. There are certain aspects of society that remain impenetrable to the Huron: religious and social dogmas and practices, and the royal court, where these aspects are joined and carried to their ultimate and most dangerous development. His nature meets two principal enemies: first, Catholic religion and, second, a specific structure in society which is the monarch's court at Versailles—not society in general (à la Rousseau). This places *L'Ingénu* in the twin traditions of anticlerical and anticourt literature, and links the concerns of the seventeenth century to those of the eighteenth.

Catholic dogmas are the first and most persistent problem in the Ingénu's life: indeed, it is the interdiction of marriage between a godson (l'Ingénu) and his godmother (Mlle de Saint-Yves) that sets the entire plot into motion, i.e., his search for dispensation from the Pope or, more practically, from the king at Versailles, in order to marry Saint-Yves. The Ingénu can adapt to various ritual practices such as a particular form of baptism or confession, all the while making satirical remarks about the French people's lack of adherence to the letter and the spirit of the Bible (chapters 3 and 4). However, the refusal of Mlle de Saint-Yves to have sexual relations before marriage is harder to accept for him. It is ascribable both to religious law and to social practice, especially on the part of a person who is a proper lady and the sister of a priest, but for the Huron possessing "une vertu mâle et intrépide" (302), it is incomprehensible. In chapter 6, the disparity between human laws ("loi positive") and natural law is drawn in particularly sharp relief and pointed out with insistence by the helpless Ingénu: "[il] se défendit sur les privilèges de la loi naturelle, qu'il connaissait parfaitement" (303). When social propriety meets with religious law, together they form an insurmountable barrier to marriage between the Ingénu and Mlle de Saint-Yves.

The desire to marry begins the adventures of both the Ingénu and Mlle de Saint-Yves as they set off for Versailles to obtain the king's permission. In both their adventures the critique of the court and the critique of the Church are linked, though Mlle de Saint-Yves's story focuses mainly on the court. I will

Chapter Seven

examine each aspect, first the religious critique, then the anticourt critique, and their interrelation. In this analysis, the sentimental part of the story will be shown to be part of the philosophical critique, thus diminishing the gap that some critics (Levy, P. Clark) see between the first and second parts of the story.

By setting his story five years after the revocation of the Edict of Nantes, Voltaire targets not only Catholic hypocrisy and Jesuit intransigence, but also the persecution of the outlawed Huguenots, whose civil rights are being debated as Voltaire is writing his story. The fate of the Protestants is again a contested issue in the 1760s, and both periods are effortlessly merged in this story. Furthermore, the harsh treatment of the Jansenists by Louis XIV is also highlighted, the topic of Jansenism being by no means resolved at this time. While Voltaire admires neither the Jansenists nor the conservative Catholics, he does militate for civil rights and for tolerance and justice generally, more than for their freedom of conscience, as Samuel Taylor points out: "As a pragmatist, he looked forward to the limited objective of certain civil rights being extended to non-Catholics and little more" (128).

While the Protestant cause as major theme has attracted only a little attention from critics, as S. Taylor says (118), the anticourt thrust of the story has received even less attention. There is a long tradition of anticourt literature dating back to at least the sixteenth century, which authors such as Molière, Racine, Saint-Simon, and La Bruyère continued to mine in the seventeenth century.[4] Setting his story in the "grand siècle" allowed Voltaire to mine this material too, and to show its links with the current struggles against injustice, arbitrariness, abuse of "lettres de cachet," and the power of the king. Even before l'Ingénu reaches Versailles, the story focuses on the structure and the functioning of the court itself. The revocation of the Edict of Nantes is blamed not so much on the monarch as on the people around him, who give him bad and self-interested advice: "C'est qu'on l'a trompé, comme les autres grands rois [...] On lui a fait croire que, dès qu'il aurait dit un mot, tous les hommes penseraient comme lui, et qu'il nous ferait changer de religion, comme son musicien Lulli fait changer en un moment les décorations de ses opéras" (308). The weight of the courtiers' advice, among which are counted the Jesuits and the king's Jesuit confessor, is so great that Louis XIV is persuaded to take a decision that not only goes against the interest of his own people, but ironically makes him act in accordance with none other than the Pope, the king's bitter enemy. This view of Louis XIV, Voltaire's thesis, also reflects a more contemporary situation. While Louis XIV's motivations for revoking the Edict were complex, surely he was at the center of his own decision-making at least as much as he was pressured by his advisers: blaming only the advisers might reflect the later situation with Louis XV, a much weaker monarch than his predecessor.

The contrast between the Ingénu's mind set and the world of Versailles which he and Saint-Yves are about to enter is clearly highlighted at the beginning of chapter 13, when nature and Versailles are juxtaposed in the same paragraph: "Pendant que la nature, qui se perfectionnait en lui, le vengeait des outrages de la fortune, que devinrent monsieur le prieur et sa bonne sœur, et la belle recluse Saint-Yves? [. . .] M. et Mlle de Kerkabon apprirent [. . .] qu'un jeune homme semblable à l'Ingénu était arrivé un soir à Versailles" (321). There can be no place and no society more opposed to nature than Versailles, and the events that unfold at the palace for both the hero and the heroine make *L'Ingénu* a strong anticourt polemical piece.[5]

Each person undergoes trials at Versailles according to his and her status and character in life. The Ingénu, true to his status as a stranger and as a man of nature, does not even guess that there might be some formalities to observe, that he cannot simply ask the guard to see the king by saying, "'je viens parler au roi: je vous prie de me mener dans sa chambre'" (310). The Breton guard at the palace is surprised to find "un brave de sa province, qui ne paraissait pas au fait des usages de la cour" (310) and who never grasps the concept that a complicated etiquette must be observed at the court. He gets only as far as the "petite antichambre" of a low-ranking "premier commis" (310), and, in keeping with the anti-Jesuit theme, he is prevented from reaching the king by the Jesuit spy who had reported the sympathetic meeting between the fleeing Huguenots and l'Ingénu on his way to Versailles. For a man of nature, significantly and ironically, the only other place he gets to see

Chapter Seven

is the gardens, and no explanation is needed why those formal gardens bore him (311). He barely spends a day in the palace, being taken to prison that same night.

Contrast this with the longer, more elaborate story of Saint-Yves, who, unlike the Huron, knows all too well that there are rules and practices to follow. The women seem wiser in this respect than the men, for Mlle de Kerkabon had suspected correctly that the Huron "ne peut savoir comme on doit se comporter à la cour" (321). The main problem facing Saint-Yves is: "Mais comment se conduire à Versailles?" (324). Though a stranger at the court, she knows that she must seek intermediaries, even to speak to a guard of the king, starting with less powerful ones and working her way up the ladder of command, and cannot simply ask to go to the king's chamber. She knows that she must first "prendre des informations" and that she must speak not so much with the king as with his ministers: "Elle résolut [. . .] de se jeter aux pieds des ministres" (323), and she also knows that she must take gifts to these powerful people (in fact, she takes the gifts for her aborted wedding to another despised man). While her search for the right intermediaries is successful, it is also her undoing. After many travails, she reaches the right person, Saint-Pouange, who has the power to deliver the Huron from prison, but of course at a price which ultimately causes her so much guilt and pain that she dies, unable to confess to her beloved what she has done to liberate him. While still at Versailles, Saint-Yves exclaims: "'quel labyrinthe d'iniquités! quel pays! et que j'apprends à connaître les hommes!'" (332), which rings out with appropriate Voltairian indignation. In the end, both l'Ingénu and Saint-Yves are strangers to the world of the court, in different degrees, but degrees do not matter here. As Norbert Elias says of the court's exclusivity, "les chances de s'y intégrer, sans jamais tomber à zéro, se rétrécirent considérablement, autant pour les bourgeois que pour la noblesse de province" (205). The world of Versailles is the place where the critique of the Church and the critique of the court meet, where injustice, "lettres de cachet," and Jesuit spies converge on the court and the king, who has just outlawed the Protestants.

If the world of Versailles stayed there, that would be bad enough, but there is worse, for the world of Versailles comes to the world of lower Brittany and corrupts it too: both Saint-Pouange and the "amie" who shepherded Saint-Yves through the labyrinth of the court and enabled her to reach Saint-Pouange, come to visit. At the beginning of chapter 19, the Huron has barely returned home safe and sound, when "la bonne amie de Versailles" arrives in her splendid six-horse coach: "Elle entre avec l'air imposant d'une personne de cour qui a de grandes affaires" (337) in order to return the diamond earrings Saint-Yves had received from Saint-Pouange and left in the "friend"'s hands. That moment is a dramatic peripateia, as Saint-Yves utters the fatal words: "'Ah! madame, [. . .] vous m'avez perdue! vous me donnez la mort!'" (338). A statement that is prophetic, as it begins Saint-Yves's slow descent into a fatal illness. The world of Versailles is, literally, a death-giving world that the world of Brittany is powerless to resist. Voltaire emphasizes this by making everyone in that society unsuspecting and utterly amazed about the power of Saint-Yves to liberate the Huron: "L'admiration était mêlée de ce respect qu'on sent malgré soi pour une personne qu'on croit avoir du crédit à la cour" (337). The only person who does not take her actions as evidence of her sudden power at the court is her brother, who does wonder sometimes, "'Comment ma sœur a-t-elle pu faire pour obtenir sitôt ce crédit?'" (337), without ever guessing the terrible truth. Even the Huron, who overhears her complaint to the Versailles lady, cannot guess at the truth and is only vaguely disquieted. While it strains the reader's credulity that no one suspects what really happened to Saint-Yves, given earlier allusions to prelates meeting with ladies behind closed doors (chapter 9), this enables Voltaire to increase the distance between the world of Brittany and the corrupt world of Versailles, so corrupt that no one outside it can even come close to the truth—and with respect to the court, everyone who is not a courtier is an outsider.

There is a continuity (that critics tend to overlook) between the philosophical part of the story and the sentimental part: Voltaire makes a critical point by making his Breton society very naive. The sentimental novel is subsumed in the satire of the court, and is very much in the authorial control of the philosophical "conteur." The hand of the satirist shows itself clearly in the surprising change of heart of Saint-Pouange himself, who was "nourri dans les plaisirs" but not "né méchant" (346), and who is still capable of repenting and acting according to better principles, though no reference is made to his following nature—the word *nature*, never pronounced in his context, is reserved only for the Huron.

Finally, it must be noted that Voltaire makes no innovation in the ending of the story of the natural man, or the story of the woman. Saint-Yves is a devout woman, who falls in love, stays briefly in a convent, suffers at the hands of a corrupt and libertine aristocrat of the court, and subsequently dies of a broken conscience. Nothing could be more conventional than this woman's outcome. Ironically, but for a very different reason and with a very different critical significance, it is also Ourika's story: unmarried and, in her case, unmarriageable, she falls in love, and she has no choice but to join a convent and die there. Meanwhile, in a further stereotypical role, the Huron, like Charles in *Ourika*, goes on to succeed very well indeed in society: Charles is happily and appropriately married to an aristocratic woman, while the Huron, though not having the benefit of a wife, enjoys a close friendship with the former Jansenist. At the end of the story, Voltaire gives a double moral. The Huron's success is further emphasized by one moral, "*malheur est bon à quelque chose*" whereas, Voltaire says, the "honnêtes gens" of the world will disagree and exclaim, "*malheur n'est bon à rien!*" (347). Since the Ingénu showed many talents in learning and in his outstanding military man, then his misfortunes were good for something, and the first moral applies. From his perspective, the "honnêtes gens" would be wrong, but they are not entirely wrong: a woman pure of heart did die, without even the benefit of acquiring wisdom like the Persian wives, and so the second moral applies to the woman's sad fate. A slight tilt on the part of Voltaire to the women's side . . .

The opposition between the world of nature and the court suggests that Voltaire is using the figure of the outsider as a man of nature to make a critique of the court. As Elias says, the debate about nature in the eighteenth century has a historical context: the idealization of nature is used "comme antidote contre les contraintes de la cour et des conventions sociales qui marquent l'aristocratie curialisée" (254). Rousseau is of course the one associated with the so-called return to nature, which means that sometimes Voltaire meets with Rousseau against a common enemy, the courtly world, using nature which becomes "l'expression d'une opposition symbolique aux contraintes de l'autorité royale et de la cour considérées comme inéluctables" (Elias 255)—a dimension of Enlightenment reform and critique that is often understated or overlooked. In this sense, the stranger's final integration into society, but not into the court, shows that new possibilities are now opening up to a man of nature—the word *man* is used advisedly here. Once a stranger, he now finds himself at home in a new world of opportunities for advancement based on merit. Hence, Voltaire's story of the stranger solves the conundrum of how to live in a civilized society while following natural law by showing how this is possible if society changes from a world of inherited privilege, which thwarted nature, to a world of meritocracy that allows for fulfillment of one's (inner) nature—a decided tilt on the part of Voltaire toward men . . .

Ourika, or Nature Denied

Although Claire de Duras's short novel has attracted attention again since its re-editions by Claudine Herrmann and, more recently, by Joan DeJean and Margaret Waller, and has been the object of many critical studies, its story bears summarizing briefly, as this work has not yet overcome its disappearance from the literary canon after its initial success in the 1820s. Narrated in the first person by the heroine, Ourika, it is framed in the first person by the unnamed man to whom she tells it. This man is a young doctor who recently finished his medical studies at a prestigious school. The young heroine is a nun who is dying and wishes to seek some comfort by telling her unusual story before she dies. She recounts how she was brought as a baby from Senegal by its governor, and educated in the rich and intellectual aristocratic household of Mme de B., the governor's aunt and her benefactress, whom she adores and under whose tutelage she absorbs the aristocratic culture completely and happily. However, around the age of 12, she is made to realize suddenly that she is forever excluded from marrying into this society because of the color of her skin, a factor of exclusion that is complicated by her love for her benefactress's

Chapter Seven

grandson, Charles, a love that is culpable in several ways: because he is white and can never marry a black woman, and, because of the family proximity, this love has overtones of incest. She continues to love him even after he marries a highborn girl, Anaïs, which makes her feelings adulterous, and finally when she joins the convent, she vows eternal love to him, bringing suggestions of sacrilege to this already troubled passion. If marriage was impossible, the traditional avenues for women's stories and lives were the convent or death. The doctor's attempt to treat her with an early version of a talking cure does not succeed and in a short epilogue he states how she dies soon after telling her story during the symbolic season of autumn.

Written in the early 1820s, this work draws on the literary context of the Romantic period and on the political struggle against slavery that began gathering some momentum at that time. The novel's time line takes place in the years before the Revolution, the Terror, and the first few years of the Empire. This long context is woven continuously and seamlessly into the novel. The heroine has some affinities with other Romantic protagonists in that she is an outcast, melancholy, lonely, unfulfilled, but she is unlike them in that she does not feel herself superior, singled out for some spiritual or poetic privilege.[6] On the contrary, she desires nothing more than to integrate herself in the most conventional manner possible into the only society she knows, by marrying and having a family life. The strictures of society against her race are foregrounded in the novel, which militates for the author's abolitionist cause. Moreover, as most of its action takes place in the late eighteenth century, the novel also highlights the hypocrisy of that society, which was fully informed by the highest culture of the Enlightenment, but failed to live up to its own ideals of equality. She was brought to France as an outsider who from the beginning never knew her own culture, who is brutally wrenched from any natural family and land, and who never fully comprehends why she should be excluded so irremediably from her new society. She is the opposite of the natural man from the New World, having lived all her life in a society that is highly sophisticated, distanced from nature, and whose artificial aspect is highlighted by her dress "à l'orientale" (8), suggesting that she is a social descendant of the eighteenth-century Persians.

Ourika's story consists of a brief period of happiness, followed by two revelations: that because she is black she can never marry a white man equal to her social standing; that she is in love with Charles, a family member and later a married man and father. These revelations brutally change her status in the society in which she must live, but because she focuses on the restrictions against her race and internalizes them unquestioningly, her own critique stops there. Even at the time of her telling her story, which occurs at the end of her life, she does not acquire deeper insights. Hers is an example of a first-person narrative whose limitations recall what Genette describes (in *What Maisie Knew*) as a strictly restricted field of vision: "nous ne quittons presque jamais le point de vue de la petite fille, dont la 'restriction de champ' est particulièrement spectaculaire dans cette histoire d'adultes dont la signification lui échappe" (*Figures III* 207). The greater understanding is reserved for the readers, who can see that the causes of her exclusion and suffering are due not only to her race, but to her gender, and to the structure of society itself, which is organized and dominated exclusively by men, what can be called a patriarchal society.

I would like to show that there is a double perspective at work in *Ourika*, that of the heroine and that of the reader, and that while the abolitionist sentiment is evident to the heroine, the reader has access to a second, broader level of criticism leveled at society, and that the gap between the heroine's understanding and the reader's understanding carries the greatest critical charge of all. One way in which Duras emphasizes the social critique that lies only partially in the heroine's conscious thoughts is to structure the story as one of a trauma, or rather of multiple traumas that befall both the heroine and her society. In the reading that follows, rather than focus mainly on the heroine (as most studies of this novel have done), I will follow this double perspective, that of the heroine and that of the reader, since herein lies the greatest impact of the text's social critique by a stranger.

As has been noted by several critics, the doctor's short "Introduction" could not make it clearer that Ourika is a doomed, dying person: the setting for the storytelling is one of ruins, dismantled tombstones with half-erased names,[7] and she herself is completely covered by a large black veil, which

Chapter Seven

suggests an allegory of Death itself. The doctor's amazement at seeing a black nun is surpassed only by the fact that she is very polite or, in the earlier sense of "politesse," polished in manners and in speech, as if a black woman could not be expected to have the same degree of refinement as a white woman. This contrasts with the happiness evoked by Ourika at the beginning of her own storytelling: her being rescued from slavery and brought up by an exceptional woman, Mme la maréchale de B., in an atmosphere of gaiety, luxury, and good taste. Educated, protected, and loved, she knows that she is of a different color, but enjoys this difference, playing it up with her oriental dress and taking part willingly in an "African" dance, a "comba" in a kind of "coming of age" spectacle designed to show her accomplishments to the salon. The fact that this "African dance" is entirely re-created from books and learned treatises on African music and costumes does not prevent her from enjoying it.[8] She is even stimulated to dance it so well by "je ne sais quel instinct" (11) that would lie in her unremembered African origins. But the attentive reader will also have encountered other words right from the beginning of the text: "bâtiment négrier," "esclaves," "esclavage," and the violence of her being brought on board after her mother's death, "malgré mes cris" (7). The use of the passive voice in her narration contrasts with the violence and underscores the helplessness, the reduction to a piece of merchandise chosen without explanation other than a feeling of pity by the governor of Senegal, who orders her brought to France. She does not have any inkling of what lies ahead of her, but the reader already knows that her story originates in a violent wrenching away from her land, itself dominated by the institutions of colonization and slavery; and that the equilibrium between difference and acceptance that she finds in Mme de B.'s house is fragile and short-lived.

The first revelation that shatters her world happens in the scene, much commented on by critics, where the marquise de ... confronts Mme de B. with the fact that Ourika is unmarriageable, making her into a true outsider for the first time, whereas the reader already had had many reminders of this. This revelation, which Ourika overhears from behind a screen, "ouvrit mes yeux et finit ma jeunesse" (11). It not only ends the illusions of her happy childhood, but also prevents her from moving into adulthood and marriage, which is the standard option for women. This event can be illuminated by considering its analogies to a trauma, which can be defined "as the response to an unexpected or overwhelming violent event or events that are not fully grasped as they occur, but return later in repeated flashbacks, nightmares, and other repetitive phenomena" (Caruth 90). One of the main aspects of a traumatic event is that it "precipitates a violent fragmentation of the (perhaps fantasized) image of the integrated subject" (Henke xvi). Ourika's traumatic event (which will replay itself in the second revelation by the same marquise, that she is in love with Charles and that this passion is criminal) cannot be integrated into her previous experience by language and leads to dissociation, a splitting that accompanies trauma.[9] Not only does she split herself with the pronouns "je/me," as in "je me vis négresse,"[10] but she sees herself as two successively radically different people: "jusqu'ici un jouet, un amusement pour ma bienfaitrice, bientôt rejetée d'un monde où je n'étais pas faite pour être admise" (12). Trauma provokes a "psychic numbing" (*Diagnostic and Statistical Manual of Mental Disorders-IV*, qtd. in Henke xvii), which fixes Ourika on the very border between childhood and adulthood from which she is unable to move toward a broader and more adult perspective. This stasis in which she finds herself will limit, I suggest, her understanding of the larger reasons for her exclusion from society. However, her experience also is different from trauma: one difference is that she knows immediately, even before the marquise spells it out, what the factor of exclusion is, namely, her race. And in the second revelation by the marquise, Ourika likewise immediately understands that her passion is criminal, and again talks about herself in the third person, in an elevated style, reminiscent of classical tragedy: "Il faut qu'Ourika connaisse tous les genres d'amertume, qu'elle épuise toutes les douleurs!" (42). I will return to the significance of this aspect that seems to distinguish her experience from a true trauma after describing the larger issues at stake in the novel.

At the moment of this revelation, she is overwhelmed by it and sees immediately and clearly that society is so prejudiced against racial outsiders and interracial marriage that despite her

Chapter Seven

excellent upbringing she can never be accepted. This angry realization, repeated throughout the novel, carries the abolitionist message, and shows Ourika's understanding now catching up with what the reader had already understood: if there had been no slavery in Senegal and no slave trade, Ourika's unhappy story would never have taken place. The modern reader can go one step further and see an anticolonialist message, which would have been ahead of the book's time: no colonizing, hence no slavery.[11] A passage later in the book where Ourika wishes she were back in Senegal has her imagining herself as "la négresse esclave de quelque riche colon" cultivating "la terre d'un autre" (38); colonizing Africa is seen by her as a given, whereas prejudice against blacks in France where slavery is illegal is not. Readers knew that she was an outsider, and now she knows it too, and she can analyze the consequences of being brought up in a society whose capacity for accepting racial strangers is severely limited, no matter how well they conform to society's norms for education and refinement: "Depuis que je me sentais étrangère à tout, j'étais devenue plus difficile, et j'examinais, en le critiquant, presque tout ce qui m'avait plu jusqu'alors" (16).

However, by continually ascribing her lack of acceptance to the color of her skin, Ourika is blind to a much larger and more complex issue that the reader can see, but which Ourika never sees. It is her inability to move past the realization brought about by the traumatic revelation of her racial exclusion, that makes Duras's social critique exceptionally powerful through a kind of dramatic irony—the reader/spectator knows something the character does not. I will examine this divergence between the heroine's limited understanding and the far-reaching critique conveyed by the text by focusing first on Ourika's own statements about her longing for a state of nature, then on what the text says about French society in the last years of the ancien régime and the Revolutionary period.

Feeling completely estranged from society, Ourika speaks in a kind of litany, bemoaning her state of being a "négresse" (12),[12] "déplacée" (14), "étrangère à la race humaine tout entière!" (15), "étrangère à tout" (16), "étrangère à tous les intérêts de la société" (18), and does so obsessively in the same terms till the end of the novel. Seeking a solution, at first she can envisage only fleetingly that Mme de B. might send her back "dans mon pays; mais là encore j'aurais été isolée" (15). As she realizes more and more her exclusion from the proper role of a married woman, the return that she first thinks is impossible becomes halfway conceivable. This impossible return gradually takes hold of her imagination and becomes progressively more attractive, in this statement that mixes together unrealistic hope and cogent social critique: "j'aurais voulu être transportée dans ma patrie barbare, au milieu des sauvages qui l'habitent, moins à craindre pour moi que cette société cruelle qui me rendait responsable du mal qu'elle seule avait fait" (28). She even regrets not having died where she was born, "sur le sein de sa mère," and buried in the sand of her native Africa (32). As her hope for a life with Charles vanishes with his marriage and fatherhood, her dream of return becomes full blown: "je serais la négresse esclave de quelque riche colon; brûlée par le soleil, je cultiverais la terre d'un autre: mais j'aurais mon humble cabane pour me retirer le soir; j'aurais un compagnon de ma vie, et des enfants de ma couleur, qui m'appelleraient: Ma mère!" (38). The dream of identity is underscored by the repetition of the possessives, as she dreams of children resting on "mon front," "mon cou," "mes bras" (38), which focuses less on the actual children than on her own satisfaction. The final statement of this dream of return to her natural land, and her native condition even if it is that of being a slave, reaches its apogee in the wish to "tenir ma place dans la chaîne des êtres, ce besoin des affections de la nature," which occurs significantly after the second revelation by the marquise that her passion for Charles is "malheureuse" and "insensée" and that she is "folle d'amour" (41). The chain of being, as A. O. Lovejoy states, was "a conception of the complete and continuous Scale of Being" (288), and it was "in the eighteenth century that the conception of the universe as a Chain of Being" reached its "widest diffusion and acceptance" (183). It connoted "universality, obviousness to every rational mind as such, and uniformity of content" that was "oftenest carried by the protean term 'nature' in its ethical application" (289). The assumption of the age was that "man should conform as nearly as possible to a standard conceived as universal, uncomplicated, immutable, uniform for every rational being" (292).

Chapter Seven

What form does this dream take for Ourika? The form of natural existence that she desires is that of being loved, being a wife in a nuclear family, whereas she realizes that the opposite will be true for her: "moi qui jamais ne devais être la sœur, la femme, la mère de personne!" (17). Note the word "être": for her it is less the dream of *having* a family (and even that vision, as we just saw, was very self-centered), but of *being* a family member that would define her natural essence. Unlike Zilia, she cannot imagine living independently, supported by friendship and learning. Suddenly, even Mme de B.'s friendship becomes devalued: "ce que j'avais pour Mme de B. était plutôt un culte qu'une affection" (17). She closes off any middle avenue between death or death to the world in religious life, and life in the world and marriage, such as Graffigny's heroine had found—Zilia's kind of utopia is not even thinkable.

What Ourika does not realize is that the state of nature she envisages does not exist, that the state of being a wife and mother she so longs for is actually a societal role that passes itself off as natural. But the reader has known from the very beginning that the society in which Ourika finds herself is not only racist but sexist. From the male doctor who treats her in the framing story, to the governor of Senegal who takes her to his aunt, herself identified only by reference to her husband's social position as Mme la maréchale de B., to whom Ourika is given like an exotic pet (like the original person on whom the novel is based[13]), Ourika is passed along by male hands, down to the priest whom Mme de B. calls on in despair over Ourika's agony. This priest, likened to the archetypal figure of a wise and knowledgeable "vieux matelot" (43), will guide her to the only refuge possible, Christianity and the convent. She has a brief fleeting moment of insight into the patriarchal society where she was brought: at the beginning of her narration, Ourika recalls that she was a new "Galatée,"[14] saved from death and from slavery, but perhaps that story (which we suspect is male-authored) did not care to notice whether Galatée is happy in her new life (7).

The most significant woman in Ourika's life is depicted as helpless when faced with Ourika's social exclusion: Mme de B. can only say, "Hélas [. . .] lorsque je réfléchis à sa position, je la trouve sans remède. Pauvre Ourika! je la vois seule, pour toujours seule dans la vie!" (12). And despite her love for Ourika, she cannot devote herself completely to alleviating the young woman's pain, because, as Ourika says, "elle avait des intérêts qui passaient bien avant moi" and those much superior "intérêts" are the men mentioned in the next line, her grandsons and especially Charles (17), and specifically the property she wants to pass on to them during the Revolution. Mme de B. survives and keeps her property intact only thanks to the protection of powerful and influential men who owed her something and repaid the favor, but for whom she had first given many favors: she had been "liée avec M. de Choiseul" and "utile à bien des gens" (23).

As a representative of the patriarchal society that excludes and destroys Ourika, the marquise de . . . is fit for the role, described as "une personne d'une raison froide, d'un esprit tranchant, positive jusqu'à la sécheresse" (11), "inquisitive," a word that suggests the Inquisition. With good reason, Ourika dreads seeing her again: "je la vis avec effroi arriver près de moi" (38), at the moment of the second revelation, which stuns her like the first one and sends her into a state of illness stronger than the first, "un accablement qui ressemblait à la mort" (42). As a voice of "masculine" reason, she conveys a crucial message where all the threads of nature and society, trauma and death come together, in the following sentences: "la philosophie nous place au-dessus des maux de la fortune, mais elle ne peut rien contre les maux qui viennent d'avoir brisé l'ordre de la nature. Ourika n'a pas rempli sa destinée: elle s'est placée dans la société sans sa permission; la société se vengera." To which the helpless Mme de B. can only meekly reply, "Assurément [. . .] elle est bien innocente de ce crime; mais vous êtes sévère pour cette pauvre enfant" (13). The marquise's declaration is precise in showing the naturalization of society as an order of nature that she has ruptured ("brisé"). There is no recourse to this evil worse than the "maux de la fortune," which philosophy can overcome. The hypocrisy of this society is further underlined by its blaming the victim ("elle n'a point rempli sa destinée") for a transgression that was in fact carried out by a male governor on a two-year old child, a society for whose sins she must pay—for being brought into it "sans sa permission," she will then have vengeance wreaked upon her. The

Chapter Seven

marquise's final sentence on Ourika, "la société se vengera," falls from her mouth like a cutting knife equal to her "esprit tranchant," just like her judgment on the helpless Mme de B.: "je désire son bonheur, et vous la perdez" (13), which in a final show of hypocrisy reverses the positions: it is Mme de B. who desires Ourika's happiness and the marquise who condemns her.

This society is a profoundly patriarchal and racist one that can exist and justify its repression of women and blacks only by pretending to be natural—this is obvious to the reader of the text but not accessible to Ourika herself. As Michelle Chilcoat points out quoting the *Encyclopédie*, in the Enlightenment, the link between family and nature seems self-evident: "En effet, une famille est une société civile établie par la nature: cette société est la plus naturelle et la plus ancienne de toutes" (9). Aspiring to belong in this society, Ourika does not see the double-bind she is placed in, being made responsible for the transgression committed against her and having no way out except death. The only exception to her blindness comes when society changes around her and she begins to see that her own position might be different too. When in the Revolution the social order breaks down, Ourika has a glimpse of what might be if everyone were truly equal: under these new conditions, "tous les rangs confondus, tous les préjugés évanouis," maybe she would find her place: "je serais moins étrangère" (19). That equality might not be true equality, but only misery shared in the company of unhappy people: "je ne me sentais plus isolée depuis que tout le monde était malheureux" (22).

This brief insight is one Ourika never develops, but can be understood by the reader. The hopes that the Revolution could have given to disadvantaged groups were not fulfilled for women, and Claire de Duras, who lived through the end of the eighteenth century and experienced the reconstitution of society under the Empire and the Restoration, saw that neither the Enlightenment nor especially the Revolution brought about the sought-for emancipation for women. What Deborah Horvitz says of two *fin de siècle* periods, the end of the nineteenth century and the end of the twentieth, can apply to this novel, which is focused on a third *fin de siècle*: "promising to be emancipatory eras for women, the final decades of both centuries are periods in which investigations into psychic trauma, specifically violence against women, occur [...] only to precipitate an effective patriarchal backlash which silenced discussion and discredited its evidence" (3). Instead of fulfilling the Revolution's promise of a more just and equal society, society rebuilds itself in a conservative mode, with emphasis on separate gender roles, justifying this by the idea that this form of society is natural. That Ourika's story has parallels with Duras's own vision of women's position in society, even highborn women like herself, is suggested by the fact that Duras modified the dates of the life span of the real Ourika on which the story is based in order to coincide more closely with the dates of her own life: "née avant et morte après la vraie Ourika, l'héroïne du roman a une vie qui correspond davantage à l'enfance, à l'adolescence et à la jeunesse de l'auteur afin de permettre à ce dernier de retracer les bouleversements psychologiques et sociaux vécus par une jeune fille puis jeune femme du milieu aristocratique durant la période révolutionnaire et post-révolutionnaire" (Little, *Ourika* 49). In short, the story of a racial outsider is expanded into a story about other outsiders in that society, women.

Ourika's insight, however, is very limited, both in scope and in duration, as she describes the Revolution that would give birth to a new society accepting the equality of classes, genders, and races only as "ce grand désordre" (18–19). She is still bound in tight solidarity to her social context: "Je me disais quelquefois, que moi, pauvre négresse, je tenais pourtant à toutes les âmes élevées, par le besoin de la justice que j'éprouvais en commun avec elles" (22). Any hopes she might have had for a better society are dashed equally by the changes in both Saint-Domingue with the slave revolt and in France with the Terror that degenerate into "massacres" and "fureurs révolutionnaires" (20, 23). As soon as the Terror is over and society rebuilds itself, Ourika again uses the term *nature* to describe the process: "plus la société rentrait dans son ordre naturel, plus je m'en sentais dehors" (27), and the dream of returning to her country of origin, even if "barbare" (28), preoccupies her again. It is part of her emotional numbing and stasis mentioned earlier that she cannot learn from the experience of one of the most violent upheavals in European history and remains stuck in the dream of an impossible and desirable nature.

Chapter Seven

It is this incapacity to see beyond herself, and her full internalization of the double-bind in which society has placed her, which carries the greatest critical charge of the novel: educated in the society's highest ranks, but excluded by her race and disempowered by her gender, she cannot see much beyond the racial guilt that society inflicts upon her. Such is the power of society to pass itself off as natural that Ourika's wish to integrate herself into this society is equated as an integration into the "chain of being." She never perceives in the least "la mauvaise conscience d'un peuple à la fois civilisé et esclavagiste, c'est-à-dire vivant dans la contradiction" (10), in Hoffmann's words. It is here that another dimension of trauma in *Ourika* must be considered. For if trauma can be carried out against an individual person, as it was against the two-year-old child, this trauma is also a collective one, defined in the words of Deborah Horvitz as a "cultural or political trauma: an officially sanctioned, sadomasochistic system of oppression in which a targeted group, perceived by the dominant culture as an obstacle to the goals of the existing hegemony, are tortured, imprisoned, or killed" (11). And there can be a "convergence of individual and political traumas" as in the case of African-Americans (Horvitz quoting Michele Wallace 11). This is the case of *Ourika*, where the systems of colonization by the European powers, of slavery by the white masters, and of confinement of women to sex-specific roles by the dominant men, all converge on the heroine's head. Poor Ourika indeed. In short, the trauma of the revelation she overhears behind her lacquered screen (a luxury object evocative of exotic workmanship hides the exotic, oriental pet that she was) is itself a screen trauma, analogous to a screen memory that hides a more painful one, hiding the trauma evoked in the opening lines of Ourika's story: the death of her mother, her cries at being torn away (from whom?), her being carried on board a ship, all because the most powerful man in the colony took pity on her—all this hiding the immense trauma of slavery perpetuated on an entire race by another race.

However, in a final twist to this extraordinary tale, the habitual parameters of trauma, as currently understood, are modified in the novel. Ourika's experiences can be seen as both less than and more than traumas. As I noted earlier, her awareness of the marquise's revelations distinguishes them from a true trauma, which is not understood at the time it is experienced, because Ourika knows immediately what is meant; this makes them more like shocking experiences, bordering on the trauma with which they do share some characteristics. This experience dissociates her like a trauma, but being less than a trauma it only gives her a clear but limited perspective, like that of an adolescent. However, the greater initial trauma of separation from her mother and her country, unlike traumatic scenes that are repeated over and again in a compulsion to understand them belatedly,[15] is so completely repressed from memory that it is mentioned only once again in the novel, with the same terms of violence, when she is entering the convent: "Dieu, en me jetant sur cette terre étrangère, voulut peut-être me prédestiner à lui; il m'arracha à la barbarie [. . .] il me déroba aux vices de l'esclavage" (44). It is a trauma that she tells at the beginning of her narrative, but which she did not remember, and knows only because someone told her much later: "Je ne sus que longtemps après l'histoire des premiers jours de mon enfance" (7), thus illustrating what Caruth calls the "complex relation between knowing and not knowing" (3). The last level of strangerhood is conveyed by the language of others who tell her of her initial rupture. If the trauma is the "voice of the other" (Caruth 8), then Ourika is an example of someone who is not only other but so shot through with otherness that she is completely dispossessed: not even her own trauma belongs to her. There is perhaps only one place in which this sense of utter dispossession peeks through, in one prophetic sentence quoted in the doctor's initial framing story when Ourika says: "'J'éprouve [. . .] une oppression continuelle'" (4). Oppression indeed is the key word for Ourika: not only of her race and gender, but of her very psyche and language; in current psychoanalytic vocabulary, one might say that even her unconscious has been robbed from her. And the fact that this was robbed from her conveys the most scathing social critique of all, the complete blinding inflicted on her most intimate sense of self. The reader reads over her shoulder, so to speak, perceiving in a case of prolonged dramatic irony what Ourika is blind to. What was a personal and social death for the young black woman becomes a death "tout court," with

Chapter Seven

the evocation of the "dernières feuilles de l'automne" in the doctor's final words. "Elle mourut à la fin d'octobre," he notes, in a fitting time of year, just before All Saints' Day in the Catholic calendar (45).

Her strangerhood to society and to herself receives its final fulfillment in her turning to religion, to which, as one critic notes, more attention should be paid, as God saves her when all seems lost (DiMauro 205). Her entry into the convent makes her a permanent exile from the brilliant and empty life of the world, so that she is no longer a stranger in the true sense of the word like the other sojourners we have been looking at in this study. She does find true equality before God, because, as the wise priest says, "il n'y a pour lui ni nègres ni blancs: tous les cœurs sont égaux devant ses yeux" (43). One might think that she has finally found her place in the God-given chain of being that she so eagerly sought; however, that too is denied by the text. In an ultimate and bitter irony, she manages to remain estranged from the religious life even as she is preparing to enter it and telling her adoptive family of her decision. In her usual helplessness, Mme de B. can only be sad and recognize that she has done harm to Ourika even as she tried to do good (45). Charles, obviously more used to getting his way, resists her decision: "il me pria, il me conjura de rester" (45), in a moment of total incomprehension, equal to that of the marquise, and like his own complete lack of insight about Ourika's feelings for him earlier. Ourika replies to him, "Laissez-moi aller, Charles, dans le seul lieu où il me soit permis de penser sans cesse à vous . . ." (45), giving one final tableau of the divided young woman, for in consecrating herself to God, she is not renouncing Charles—on the contrary, she seems to be expressing an excessive and eternal devotion to him. Thus ends the nun's *récit*, with one final split between the religious and the amorous life that threatens language itself: "ici la jeune religieuse finit brusquement son récit," says the doctor (45). Although she has said several times that she has found peace and happiness in the convent (4, 43, 44), the text again diverges from her statements, and tells more than the heroine can say by suggesting a final confusion between erotic love and devotion to God in a sacrilege too awful to put into words.

L'Ingénu and *Ourika*

From the initial descent of the colonial master onto foreign lands and the institution of slavery there, to the final death of the heroine with the October leaves, the course of the story is fraught with ambiguities: a governor who takes pity (one of the most natural emotions in the state of nature according to Rousseau) on a black child giving her "deux fois la vie" (7) and who really brings her a twofold death, personal and social—the very kind of deaths he and his cohorts had brought to Africa; a benefactress who does harm while trying to do good and a severe woman who ironically does the same; a young man who wants to keep her in the world after having closed off permanently any possibility of a relationship with her by marrying someone else; finally, a heroine who criticizes over and again the racial prejudice while missing almost completely the larger picture of society's gender prejudice and its injustice toward her as a woman and toward all women. The ambiguities are unbearable, closing off possibilities for satire, for constructive criticism, for self-understanding, for language, for existence itself. In the end the heroine is completely annihilated, and the stranger passes into silence.

Conclusion
Ambiguous Strangers and
the Legacy of the Enlightenment

Ultimate Skepsis.—What are man's truths ultimately? Merely his *irrefutable* errors.
Nietzsche
The Gay Science

The purpose of this study was to survey in detail the best-known examples of the naive outsider novels that caught the imagination of the period, and along the way to consider how these novels, far from being only works of satire, raised profound questions about subjectivity, gender relations, social prejudice, and the knowability of nature. To conclude this study, I will focus first on the genre as a whole and its place in its historical context, then offer some broader reflections on the legacy of the Enlightenment for our own period.

The genre of the naive outsider novel was certainly innovative and imaginative, launched principally by the popularity of Montesquieu's novel. As some critics have noted, the genre represented a new way of writing, a reversal of perspective that seemed fresh and untried (Georges May, Jean-Paul Forster, Roger Caillois). Much like the Nouveau Roman in the twentieth century that also played with new perspectives and new narrative devices, the outsider novel looked at the world, and especially at the art of narration, differently—as if the Cannibals had been given an articulate voice. Roger Caillois calls it nothing less than a "révolution sociologique [. . .] qui consiste à se feindre étranger à la société où l'on vit, à la regarder du dehors et comme si on la voyait pour la première fois," an enterprise that calls for "une puissante imagination pour tenter une telle conversion et beaucoup de ténacité pour s'y maintenir" (xiii). I would like to suggest, however, that perhaps the

Conclusion

level of imagination and tenacity is not as great as Caillois supposes. In the eighteenth century, the effort to imagine and displace the narrative through interesting filters was in fact rather frequent. Consider the pastoral novel, the historical novel, the fairy tale, fictive memoirs, the use of Greek and Roman mythology and history—all these genres presuppose writing from an imaginary fictional standpoint and staying with it throughout the text. The effort required might seem great to us, accustomed as we are to various forms of realism since Balzac, Flaubert, and others in the nineteenth century redefined the novel in a way that is still alive in our own times, but would seem normal in earlier times for "high" literature.

To understand the particular originality of the naive outsider novel, we should situate the eighteenth century in its context of the preceding seventeenth century, whose esthetic system was built on "an aristocratic mold of analogy" as described by Erica Harth: "The various arts were unified by a set of correspondences between the visual and the verbal, the historical and the mythological, the ancient and the modern" (*Ideology* 17). There had to be a balance between the allegory and its content: "The allegory had to be decipherable to the restricted public [. . .]. If it was too obscure, it became pure diversion, enigma, depriving the representation of recognizable, imitative value. The absence of allegory, on the other hand, would have yielded a transparent, immediately recognizable truth" (*Ideology* 27). As heirs to this esthetic representational system, the eighteenth-century writers devised allegories of their own, no longer based in some mythical or historical past, but set in a spatially and culturally distant world. The heroes, gods, and princes of myth and history were replaced by contemporary travelers who were still foreign and mysterious, but less reliant on specific cultural knowledge and more understandable, except by the readers who, as Montesquieu said, want to be fooled. The truth was still veiled artfully, but the veil was more surprising, amusing, and seductive. These texts represent an intermediate stage between the seventeenth-century esthetics and its disintegration at the end of the eighteenth century along with the Old Regime's political and social structures.

The genre passed from the scene along with the Old Regime, and some critics have speculated on the brevity of its life and wondered why the genre lost its appeal and newness. I

Conclusion

would like to argue that its demise points to a deeper transformation of the relations between Europe and the remainder of the known world, a transformation that Edward Said's analyses of orientalism can illuminate. Said says that during approximately the last third of the century, there was a change in representations of the Orient, which greatly expanded and became more systematic, becoming "a corporate institution for dealing with the Orient [. . .] by teaching it, settling it, ruling over it [. . .] for dominating, restructuring, and having an authority over the Orient" (3). It is probably no coincidence that the last third of the century is when the genre of the outsider novel disappears, for at that time the dynamics between Europe and the known world were changing. A European culture that "gained in strength and identity by setting itself off against the Orient" (3) turns its efforts to colonizing, dominating, and transforming the Orient as well as the New World and Africa. It was the beginning of the colonial era, which would flourish until the struggles for decolonization. In the political and intellectual climate when other continents become the object of a more direct political rule, the outsider novel could not evolve with the new situation: a colonized world could no longer furnish to Western writers independent and keenly observant strangers from foreign shores. Born in a specific context, in a moment of balance between Europe and the rest of the world, after conquest and before colonization, the outsider novel disappeared when the relations between Europe and the rest of the world changed.

These ambiguous figures from elsewhere lent themselves to many occasions for satire, stemming from their amused and bewildered encounters with European society. What exactly did they focus on? All of them, the Persians, the Peruvian, the Huron (and his companion the lower Breton woman), and the Senegalese interact with one specific segment of society, the upper classes of France. If we set these texts in the context of Old Regime society, we can see that what these foreigners are looking at are the social and intellectual elites—this is the specific use to which the eighteenth-century writers put the descendants of the Cannibals, who were able to make only a very few pithy observations on the society at large. The elites offered commonly recognized cultural models to the rest of society, the "honnête homme" in the seventeenth century, and the "homme éclairé" in the eighteenth. The historian Robert Muchembled explains that the elites presented a cultural model of learning and behavior that was designed to repress the multiple and very diverse popular cultures that had existed in the culture throughout the medieval period and the Renaissance: "la société de cour, les lettrés, les nobles, les citadins aisés, les minorités privilégiées, en somme, élaborent un modèle culturel nouveau. [. . .] la centralisation et l'absolutisme engendrent obligatoirement un effort d'unification culturelle" (226–27). This cultural model, along with centralization of power, and the other models of knowledge that constituted the "cosmopolis," unified the cultural and the intellectual field and eliminated the ambiguities of the previous period. What the writers of the stranger fictions observed, I suggest, were the first obvious cracks in the "cosmopolis" system; they saw that the court, the aristocracy, the intellectuals, and the city elites, taken together, presented a model of culture that was not exemplary or admirable, in two different ways. One was that these various groups were often at odds with each other: the new aristocracy, the old nobility, the city elites, the intellectuals, and the monarchy were often competing for power and vying for recognition. Already in the seventeenth century the city elites and the court elites, "la cour" and "la ville," the king, the traditional nobility, and the high bourgeoisie felt that there were sometimes bitter rivalries between them. The second crack in the system was more insidious and more dangerous for these elites: simply put, the model of behavior they offered was often far from admirable. Hypocrisy, deception, unfaithfulness, corruption, and greed seemed to seethe under the cover of high social status.

All the novels studied show the foibles and the serious failings of the elites. Rica laughs at the antics of many a nobleman and noblewoman, priest, and intellectual, and so does Usbek; moreover, the latter continues to be a ruthless despot at home, and a cowardly one at that, preferring to leave the dirty job of repressing his wives to his eunuchs. Zilia is assailed by young savages who paw at her clothes and her breasts, and she meets a mother who is the image of coldness. She cannot understand why the men and especially the priests impose such a repressive education on women yet demand that these same women live up to that society's high standards. Her benefactor, Déterville, manipulates her in the manner of any libertine nobleman, barely mastering his own sexual impulses. Ourika finds a merciless double bind placed on the high-born women who rescue her from slavery but then reject her from their society, as she experiences racial and gender prejudice. The Ingénu meets with men who imprison him in the name of a charitable religion, and finds nothing but petty and vindictive officials at the Versailles court, while Mlle de Saint-Yves meets with aristocrats who use their power in order to obtain sexual favors. One function of the outside observer, then, was to point out the foibles, inconsequences, and gross contradictions in the upper class's actual behavior, as well as marveling at various customs that might seem simply funny, strange, or incomprehensible to anyone not familiar with them. The strangers can laugh at the ever-changing hairstyles of women and be appalled at the young nobleman who assaults a woman in an aristocratic salon, thus equalizing all features of the culture as strange, even inexplicable. They render unfamiliar, or denaturalize, both the details of daily life and the larger ethical failings evident in the culture.

The stranger novel was a new way of giving voice to the Enlightenment's double enterprise: critiquing the elites of society, and transforming a society based on customs and status into a more open, flexible society based on market exchanges, individual work and merit (analyzed by C. B. Macpherson and Alison Jaggar). The new liberal model that gradually evolved was obviously felt to be liberating, Alison Jaggar says: "When it was formulated, this conception of equality [entitlement to equal rights regardless of race, sex or economic class] was extremely progressive, and indeed it is progressive in many contexts even today" (46). Based on reason, respect for every individual, and citizenship, it offered equal chances for knowledge and advancement according to one's talents and work, without the restrictions of birth that could either impede or promote unfairly. If strangers, who took note of society's inequalities and contradictions, also enunciated foundational principles relating to nature, progress, and justice, then these strangers accomplished the double process of critique and reform. Strangers are both disquieting and consoling, able to pierce through the thickness of behavior and also arrive at underlying truths about human nature.

The eighteenth century continued the "flight from ambiguity" begun in the preceding period. Rejecting previous forms of authority based on aristocratic lineage, Church doctrine, and the divine rights of kings, the Enlightenment achieved much reform of society and sought to establish unambiguous, organized, and unified knowledge with, for example, the *Encyclopédie*, the search for unified systems of knowledge, the separation of public and private spheres, and the more abstract definition of the nation-state. The eighteenth century reformed, but did not dismantle the "cosmopolis" which it sought to readjust according to fairer, more progressive principles. Reform was counterbalanced by a search for certainty and foundations that was in keeping with the liberal model of society. Abstract laws of nature could be known apart from the facts, as Rousseau famously says; idealism sought to separate knowledge from its particular context and make it universal and objective; better, gentler forms of government that gave equal chances to individuals could be imagined; mastery of the self and of knowledge were possible. Only a very few writers did not subscribe to this totalizing, foundational philosophy, the chief example being Diderot, which makes him seem so congenial and anticipatory of the postmodern view (Brewer, Moscovici).

Our own postmodern period is on the far side of undoing the modern "cosmopolis." In the late nineteenth century, Nietzsche was one of the first thinkers to start tearing down the modern system with purpose and vigor, doing exactly what the eighteenth century did not want to do: emancipating itself completely from the "cosmopolis." In the book with the same title, Richard Rorty says our contemporary thought has taken a "linguistic turn" that irrevocably breaks with the previous model of knowledge by emphasizing that all knowledge takes place within language, and that philosophy must understand the language we use rather than explore traditional problems and search for universal truths outside language. To use Clifford Geertz's phrase, all knowledge has become "local" knowledge. Our epoch turns its back on the belief in foundations in nature—but has it accepted the artificialist point of view that

Conclusion

sees all foundational thought as deluded? Has the pendulum swung from naturalism to artificialism, as Clément Rosset claims is the case throughout history? Our postmodern epoch can certainly be considered to be closer to Montaigne's than to d'Alembert's, with its emphasis on deconstruction of presence, ambiguity, fragmentation of self, non-existence of absolute truth, and the refusal of groundedness in presence.

Yet the liberal model of society and the appeal of objective truth and universal principles still holds much persuasive power vis-à-vis how we view ourselves, our knowledge, and our institutions. In this way, we are both postmodern and the inheritors of the liberal model. Over two centuries later, we still value the principles of the liberal model of democracy, enshrined as they are in the constitutions of modern states. The difficult coexistence of the two models, liberal and postmodern, is reflected in two current debates: one is about the value of the Enlightenment's principles for the postmodern society, and the other questions the postmodern paradigm.

Opinions about the Enlightenment currently fall into several broad categories. One is positive, viewing it as liberating and progressive (Cassirer, Ehrard, Gay); another view is strongly negative, reproaching the Enlightenment for being repressive and hypocritical—Horkheimer and Adorno's *Dialectic of Enlightenment* is a scathing indictment of the Enlightenment as "totalitarian" (6), and Foucault's pithy sentence sums up the period as follows: "Les 'Lumières' qui ont découvert les libertés ont aussi inventé les disciplines" (*Surveiller* 224). Some other thinkers situate the Enlightenment in our current historical context, analyzing the unraveling of Enlightenment values in the postmodern era (Lyotard, Poster, Racevskis, Rorty, Saint-Amand, Tracy). With varying degrees of condemnation, they describe how the Enlightenment's beliefs in progress, liberalism, and the mastery over nature have lost their legitimacy and disappeared under the assault of various social and philosophical movements. Feminist critics, such as Jaggar, Keller, Kofman, and Pateman, point to the discrepancy between the Enlightenment re-evaluating the capacities of women and its placing women in a double-bind by confining them to a private sphere while demanding that they be educated and enlightened citizens. Jaggar makes a strong statement about the liberal model's inadequacy for bringing liberation to women: "I believe that the liberal conception of human nature and of political philosophy cannot constitute the philosophical foundation for an adequate theory of women's liberation" (47–48). Our postmodern era, with its emphasis on fragmentation, decentering, and simulacra, both condemns the Enlightenment for being too unified and centered, and remakes it into its own image, describing it as a complex, heterogeneous, and conflicted period with a decidedly dark side (Bates, Bender, Benrekassa, Saint-Amand). For some, the question remains open. Daniel Brewer asks a crucial question to which I will return: "If the eighteenth-century Enlighteners sought their freedom by refusing the paradigms and principles that unshakably grounded knowledge in religious and metaphysical terms, do they undo in the process the foundation of knowledge in general, including that of their own epistemological systems?" (5–6).

The struggle between the two models, liberal and postmodern, is considered from an opposite viewpoint by other contemporary thinkers, for example Charles Taylor. Taylor dismisses the artificialist position, as a "fallacy" (53), a position he calls, ironically, a "naturalist temper," contrary to Clément Rosset's artificialist position which seeks to "do without ontological claims altogether" (19). Taylor shows some conservative colors by wanting to counter naturalism (which corresponds to Rosset's artificialism) by a "recourse to the past" (104), which is necessary in an age dominated by "the neo-Nietzschean outlooks" (102). That these questions have no easy solution is demonstrated by the authors in the anthology *Pourquoi nous ne sommes pas nietzschéens*, whose preface ends with words that indicate the tenor of the book's ambivalent and soul-searching essays: "Certes, les écailles nous sont tombées des yeux: nul ne croit plus aujourd'hui au Savoir absolu, au sens de l'histoire ou à la transparence du sujet. Voilà précisément pourquoi c'est bien avec Nietzsche qu'il nous faut penser contre Nietzsche" (8). Despite Haraway's statement that we have moved into a period characterized by "The breakdown of clean distinctions between organism and machine and similar distinctions structuring the Western self" in a "simultaneity of breakdowns that cracks the matrices of domination and

Conclusion

opens geometric possibilities" (32), the tension is perhaps not finished between the flight from ambiguity and the flight into it. Even the more conservative thinkers do not think that absolute, universal knowledge is possible any more; the most progressive ones like Judith Butler and Donna Haraway are aware of the enormous difficulty of accepting artificialism in a comfortable manner. And one can wonder how much impact their thought has on the practices of the culture at large and one can worry about the return to forms of naturalist thought such as religious and other fundamentalisms.

Coming long after the total skepticism of Montaigne, and not as far removed from the Enlightenment, we postmoderns are tempted by the freedom of skepticism, and yet we harbor the nostalgic desire for fundamental values that was the hallmark of the Enlightenment. Perhaps we have to accept that our contemporary situation is characterized by a particular kind of ambiguity, the coexistence of the two models, as does Donald Levine. He sums up his study of ambiguity with the opinion that there are two kinds of rationality, a subjective one having to do with personal thought, and an objective one relating to goals and calculation observable by independent parties. Our situation contrasts with the Enlightenment, which exercised vigorous critiques in many areas, government, society, religion, but maintained fundamental values of nature and reason that legitimated their critiques. We criticize these fundamental, essentialist values as illusions and projections of our desires and social prejudices, but our social critique is harder to frame, lacks impact, and is generally "anemic" (Nicholson and Fraser 100), as we are not the heirs to the traditional elites who have long ago passed from power. So we are left with the question asked earlier by Brewer: can we now undo the epistemological systems which founded the Enlighteners' knowledge? This question is still ours to resolve. Freedom can appear to be without anchoring values, and foundational values can seem too restrictive. In the Enlightenment writers' struggle with these questions, we can recognize our own questions, but in their fear of ambiguity and in their endeavor to build rational and universal systems, we should not recognize our answers.

Notes

Part 1: Montaigne's Cannibals

Chapter One
Montaigne's Unknowable Cannibals

1. For a complete list and pictures of these creatures commonly known as "Plinian races," see Friedman.

2. The citations from the *Essays* are from the (a) stratum unless otherwise indicated. All emphasis is mine. (For similar statements by Montaigne on the amazement at the extent of the discovered lands, see also II, 12, 435 and 555; III, 6, 886). For a discussion of the shock of these encounters with the New World and the reliance on known concepts resulting in stereotypes, see Thorens; Duviols, especially chapter 2; Greenblatt; and Todorov.

3. On the Papal donation, see Bédouelle. In his *Marvelous Possessions*, Greenblatt discusses the relationship between the desire to possess and the mindset prevalent in the Renaissance that wanted to control and appropriate, and hence represented for itself the populations of the New World in such a way as to justify this appropriation. Marco Polo was not possessive, but interested in trade and commerce; even less materialistic was Mandeville's text (see Greenblatt's chapter 2). Thus Marco Polo stands halfway between the fantasy wanderings of Mandeville and the appropriation of Columbus. See also T. J. Reiss (especially chapters 1 and 5) for a detailed exposition of the rise of the willful self in the Renaissance and the differences from the medieval period.

4. Reiss and especially C. B. Macpherson have analyzed the possessive aspect of the individual and its nefarious impact on mercantile and democratic societies.

5. On the use of the words *discovery* and *conquest*, and on discovery as a process, see also the analysis of Seabra, in *1492: Le choc de deux mondes*, 138–47, and Todorov, especially the chapter "La découverte de l'Amérique." Seabra critiques Todorov (139) for emphasizing the uniqueness of the 1492 discovery as a reductionist vision of history, perhaps a bit unfairly, since Todorov makes the same point as Thorens does in *1492* on the surprising nature and the magnitude of the discovery for both sides: it is hard to imagine another discovery equally astonishing and heavy in consequences as that of Columbus.

6. Donald Frame's introduction to his translation of Montaigne's *Essays*, xii.

7. Reiss could have added Montaigne to Cusanus and Rabelais, who he says "represent [...] a critical moment of passage" between the medieval worldview and the "new certainty" (25) of the seventeenth century that occults the subject and strives for "absolute objective truth" (37). The possession of truth which Reiss sees as defining the seventeenth-century view was prepared by the already possessive strain in Renaissance culture relating to material goods, trade, commerce and to the definition of the self. Jacob Burckhardt has some eloquent descriptions of the attention paid to development of the self in Part 2 of *The Civilization of the Renaissance in Italy*, "The Development of the Individual."

8. I am disagreeing with Dalia Judovitz's otherwise excellent analyses, by suggesting that the difference between the Renaissance view of knowledge and the later, seventeenth-century, Cartesian view is not so clear cut; she says that the difference is based on "the lack of or dependence on a foundational principle which reifies the experiential relations of the self" whereas I suggest that the dependence on a foundational principle was already visible to the Renaissance culture—it was not dominant or exclusive yet. However, I do agree emphatically with her view that for Montaigne, "the endlessly proliferating circumstances" precluded any reliance on a foundational principle on his part. But then, as Judovitz says herself, "Montaigne's text, however, suggests a more complicated model" (13).

9. Cannibalism still has the power to evoke strong feelings in more modern centuries; witness the incidents of cannibalism used for survival in the US or in the Andes after a plane crash. A further indication of the deep and uneasy feelings stirred by cannibalism can be gleaned from reading the titles of books under the subject heading "Cannibalism" on the library's data base at Northwestern University. Under the general heading "Cannibalism," the titles are mostly sober, such as *Unspeakable Crimes*, *Cannibalism in the Neolithic*, *Eating People Is Wrong*, with only Desmond Morris daring to be a little flip with his *A Taste for Their Own Kind*. But turning to the subheading "Cannibalism (Animals)," one finds an array of surprisingly amusing or odd titles: *Cannibals Eat Their Way to an Early Death; Consuming Passion for Distant Relatives; The Days of Swine and Roses; Honey, I Ate the Kids; Relative Hunger;* and even *You Eat What You Are: In Costa Rica It's a Frog-Eat-Frog World*. It is as if the uneasiness with human cannibalism is transferred to the animal kingdom, in a kind of "joking relationship" that anthropologists say we maintain with difficult relatives whom we do not like but have to live with.

10. On the use of negatives to describe the Golden Age, see Levin (10–11); the reference to Rousseau is to his description of primitive man in the *Discours sur l'origine de l'inégalité*: "errant dans les forêts sans industrie, sans parole, sans domicile, sans guerre, et sans liaisons, sans nul besoin de ses semblables [. . .] l'homme sauvage sujet à peu de passions, et se suffisant à lui-même" (218), with the significant and original difference that Rousseau has introduced time in precivilized life, a kind of history before history.

11. Reiss 25–27; the subsequent, seventeenth-century "analytico-referential" discourse of Reiss corresponds to Clément Rosset's view that Descartes's fundamental project was to restore Aristotelian naturalism on new epistemological bases, thus bringing about the demise of the short "artificialist" interlude of the sixteenth and early seventeenth centuries, and preparing the resurgence of "naturalist" philosophies in the Enlightenment (39). Toulmin's "cosmopolis" covers the same vision of the seventeenth century as Reiss.

12. The question about Montaigne's use of cosmographers whom he has just reprimanded is the object of some disagreement among critics. Michel de Certeau says that the text hides its sources beneath the discourse of the simple man (*Heterologies* 74), and Gérard Defaux says that Montaigne is lying but tells us that he is lying about the uselessness of the cosmographers whom he does use in his long description of the "cannibals" (938) in order to imitate the impossibility of objective, historical narrative: "Montaigne ne l'assume [le récit historique] que pour mieux en démontrer l'impossibilité" (956). My interpretation owes much to Defaux's reading.

13. Fragment 91 in the Lafuma edition.

14. Diderot, *Supplément* 146. In the same text, concerning the speech "Les adieux du vieillard," given originally in Tahitian, A. says: "à travers je ne sais quoi d'abrupt et de sauvage, il me semble retrouver des idées et des tournures européennes" (151), with good reason, for here also there is the problem of too many languages and translations: the original Tahitian is translated into Spanish and then translated again into French.

15. Edward Rothstein, "When Worlds Collide, on the Operatic Stage."

16. I am taking this word from Roman Jakobson's discussion of "embrayeurs," defined by him as having the following property: "la signification générale d'un embrayeur ne peut être définie en dehors d'une référence au message" (178). What he uses in linguistic analysis I am applying to cultural texts.

Part 2: Montesquieu's Persians

Chapter Two
The Men's Quest for Knowledge:
The Impossibility of Transcendence

1. I am following Donald Levine's distinction of stranger relationships: the guest who remains an outsider to the community, the sojourner who resides in it, and the newcomer who aspires to membership in the community, as outlined in the introduction.

2. On tourism in the ancien régime and on the grand tour of the eighteenth century, see Adams, Graburn, Hibbert, Valene Smith, and Van den Abbeele (*Travel* and "Utopian").

3. Valene Smith, in her introduction to *Hosts and Guests*, classifies travelers on a scale of 1 to 7, ranging from the rare category 1 Explorer, to the innumerable Charter travelers of category 7: the explorers, few in number, have to understand, and integrate themselves into, the local culture, while the masses demand every familiar amenity. Usbek and Rica fall probably in category 2, the Elite few, not discoverers of unknown lands, but perhaps not in category 3, the "Off-beat," who are more numerous.

4. Percy Adams suggests that these novels of travels, transitional between adventure and touring are the "nouveau roman" of the post-1700 years which evoked discovered societies with geographical accuracy and local color for satirical ends (109–16). Into this category he puts Montesquieu's text, as well as some of the texts Montesquieu drew on, such as *L'Espion turc* of Marana, Chardin, and Tavernier (115–16). I will later draw a difference between texts about actual travels and the imagined travelers of Montesquieu.

5. On the critiques of court life, see Pauline Smith, and on the evolution of the courts generally in Western Europe, see Elias and Scaglione.

6. On the separation from the maternal body, and the stages of growth, I am thinking of Kristeva's analyses. I note that an allusion is made to Rica's mother (Letter 5), as well as to the virgin mother and to the wives in the same group of Letters, 1–6), a feminine world the men leave behind in their bold adventure. The Orient has sometimes been coded as immature, feminine, and maternal by the West, according to Said.

7. Suzanne Gearhart analyzes the critique of nature in *L'Esprit des lois* in terms that could easily apply to this earlier novel: "The task *De l'Esprit des lois* sets for itself is that of situating all ideals of nature and theories of history according to specific contexts [. . .] Montesquieu constructs his own theory of history and explores the possibility of a history without a simple origin or a simple end, without a concept of nature" ("Reading *De l'Esprit des lois*" 177); see also her discussion in chapters 3 and 4 of *The Open Boundary of History*, especially 141–42 and 126–27.

8. Georges Van den Abbeele discusses the "transvestism" of the English travelers, who upon arriving on the Continent "went native," and its risks to one's identity, because "it also carries the risk of being nowhere at home" (51).

9. Many critics have discussed the contrast between Usbek and Rica, and I will not rehearse it here again; I will point to Gearhart's discussion of the contrast specifically in terms of alienation or integration into society in her "The Place and Sense of the 'Outsider'" and to Saint-Amand, who wants us to "take Rica seriously" (*Laws of Hostility* 34). As a counter-balancing view, see Stewart's article, "Toujours Usbek," though I disagree with his conclusion that Usbek finds "un peu d'équilibre" (150).

10. Many critics have traced this evolution, using various labels, from one episteme (to use Foucault's word) to another, and the crisis of the modern; e.g., Jardine (22–24) and Hunt, Appleby, and Jacob (198–207), the former's "modernity" being equivalent to the latter's "post-modernism." I also refer the reader to the discussions of Reiss's "analytico-referential discourse" (41), of Toulmin (who labels what I call modern as the "cosmopolis"), and Racevskis (the "Cartesian-Kantian paradigm"). Levine traces in detail the development from "ambiguous discourse" to "univocal discourse" in culture and society (chapter 2). In the course of this study, I will often use Toulmin's term "cosmopolis."

11. Hence his subverting chronology in order to put at the end of the novel Roxane's final statement of her finding new knowledge. The importance of this letter and its place as a conclusion to the search for a foundation of knowledge will be discussed in Chapter 3.

12. On the general evolution within the ancien régime from the traditional societies of the seventeenth century to the reshaped social order of the eighteenth, see, for example, Harth, *Ideology*, chapter 6, and Chaussinand-Nogaret; on the impact of the increasing dominance of new bourgeois society, see Macpherson and, for the impact of the destabilization of the old social categories and the rise of new ones on the novel, see McKeon, especially chapter 4.

Chapter Three
Women's Knowledge: The Temptation of Equality

1. Curiously enough, in his "What Is Enlightenment?" Foucault does not comment on this sentence about women when he discusses how widely applicable Kant's definition of humanity might be.

2. On plot lines that are defined by men and their point of view, see Brooks, de Lauretis.

3. On the eunuchs, see Delon, who views them as more ambivalent than the women who are able to undo the dominant system. I would disagree with this position, since the eunuchs are unambiguously, if differently, male, and they remain in power at the end. No one undoes the dominant system in this text. See also Kempf, Pucci (especially her remarkable "Letters from the Harem"), and Vartanian. Vartanian was one of the first to take both the women and the eunuchs seriously, and in his succinct, powerful article he makes the case for taking the erotic intrigue as a serious moral and political commentary.

4. Schneider and Ehrard ("Signification") have examined the chronology in detail and the latter especially has drawn important conclusions on the political meaning that results.

5. In my article "La quête," I developed the analysis of various forms of knowledge in the novel, but drew a different conclusion with respect to the women.

6. For discussions of this topic, see especially Althusser, who identifies a split between Montesquieu's tendency to view society as devoid of first principles, and his search for some general explanatory foundation; Benrekassa also views Montesquieu as heterogeneous, dispersed among several tendencies.

7. On the tension between these two aspects in Montesquieu's major work, see especially Gearhart's clear discussion in "Reading."

8. Carol Blum emphasizes that neither the middle class nor the aristocratic women had any special advantages, and indeed that they envied each others' privileges.

9. A good recent description of women's education and lives is contained in Rapley's work. Huppert, in his study of the education of women in the Renaissance, makes some allusions to the fact that education was reserved for male elites until 1918, but then continues to write his history of schools with few further references to women's education. Julia also makes the point that women were excluded from "collèges," and discusses the various attitudes toward women's education in the Old Regime.

10. Ian Maclean emphasizes perhaps a bit too much the triumph of women in the first half of the seventeenth century. Contemptuous works also abound in the same period.

11. I am basing this discussion of women's learning on Erica Harth, *Cartesian Women*.

12. Brissenden links Locke's emphasis on the senses as the source of ideas to the rise of emphasis on the senses generally and the rise of the sentimental novel in particular. Grimsley and Oake make similar arguments.

13. Keller analyzes the shifting polarization of gender, the domination of man over woman, and the implications for science's attempt to dominate nature in a mutually reinforcing development of practice and thought in her chapter "Spirit and Reason at the Birth of Modern Science." She also analyzes the simultaneous "appropriation and denial of the feminine" (41) by Francis Bacon, who stands at the threshold of modern science. For a non-feminist treatment of the relation between reason and gender, see Walker's essay on images of women in Locke.

14. Asymmetry of women with respect to men is discussed by Harth, Moi, and Butler, among others. It means that, to borrow a term from linguistics, women are "marked" as opposed to men, who are unmarked. An example of this from recent scholarship is the contrast between two titles, *Public Schools in Renaissance France* (by G. Huppert) and *The Dévotes: Women and Church in Seventeenth-Century France* (by E. Rapley). The first title does not specify the gender for its readers and talks only about men, dismissing the subject of women's schooling in about six pages.

15. Susan Moller Okin explains why some equality, such as the franchise, has not succeeded in bringing about equality for women, because the entire structure of the family and the individual has not been rethought: integrating women into an existing system that presupposed their inequality in order to function is no integration at all. Other arguments concerning the political reforms needed for equality of men and women have been made by Lorenne Clark, Lorraine Code, and Lynda Lange.

16. The identification of woman and body in narrative has been studied by E. Spelman and Helena Michie, the latter with special attention to the fact that the point of entry of women in novels is often focused on their bodies.

17. Sandra Bartky has defined this double-bind as that of a society that affirms human values and bars some people from excercising those functions that give value, resulting in alienation (31).

18. On the role of women as objects of exchange in the patriarchal system, see Gayle Rubin.

19. According to Richard Terdiman, Roxane's loss of her battle for autonomy and freedom prefigures nineteenth-century plots that, after 1830, show the death of the protagonist, thus indicating the pessimism and closing of opportunities for action in the world (9). Suicide or alienation are the only outcomes possible, e.g., the cases of Roxane and Usbek, or else complete integration and loss of self, as Rica shows.

20. Though I disagree with Pucci's ultimate conclusion that Montesquieu is "throughout the *Lettres persanes*, writing like a woman" ("Letters" 131). On the contrary, Montesquieu is fighting mightily against any such possibility.

21. Marie-Claire Vallois makes the point that Montesquieu was already adumbrating the later, nonhierarchial model of sexuality.

Chapter Four
Who Are the Eunuchs?

1. See the works of Delon, Grosrichard, Harari, Kempf, Singerman, and Vartanian.

2. Montesquieu read Chardin and Ancillon; Taisuke Mitamura writes on Chinese eunuchs, Charles Humana sketches a broad history of eunuchs in the world, and Zia Jaffrey describes eunuchs in contemporary India. The phenomenon of the castrato is discussed in connection with the history of opera, and is the object of a film, *Farinelli*.

3. For historical accounts, see Humana and especially Mitamura. On the psychoanalytic interpretations as they relate to the *Lettres persanes*, see Delon and Kempf.

4. Barthes himself suggests that it is pure chance or mere convenience, though the parenthetical interrogation suggests something else: "Quant au texte qui a été choisi (pour quelles raisons? Je sais seulement que je désirais depuis assez longtemps faire l'analyse d'un court récit dans son entier et que mon attention fut attirée sur la nouvelle de Balzac par une étude de Jean Reboul [qui] disait tenir son propre choix d'une citation de Georges Bataille" (*S/Z* 23). Thus under Barthes's Balzac lurks Reboul's Bataille. Perhaps Bataille had been the reason all along for Barthes's choice, and not chance; the hidden presence of the thinker of eroticism suggests that Barthes studied a figure emblematic of deprivation

of erotic power in its literal sense and over-endowment with imaginary and symbolic power in other senses.

5. These are Letters 2, 4, 7, 9, 15, 20, 21, 22, 41, 42, 43, 47, 53, 64, 79, 96, in the first grouping; in the second grouping are Letters 147–154 and 156–160.

6. In his chapter "The Eunuch's Tale" Harari suggests analogies between Montesquieu's view of the body as a place of such mechanical interactions and of the political body of an empire or monarchy (94–97). Here I suggest that this same principle works between individuals in bilateral directions: as Usbek becomes powerless, his eunuchs acquire power. In a similar fashion, in Chapters 2 and 3 I showed how the men either lost or gave up their identities, while the women acquired a self and self-knowledge. And as the women acquired these, they lost their lives. The use of the word *organ* in Harari's quotation in the context of the subject matter of this chapter is pure, delightful serendipity.

7. I am indebted to Marjorie Schreiber Kinsey for drawing my attention to the existence and the meaning of this painting, located in the Cleveland Museum of Art.

8. Here is the one place where I part with Aram Vartanian's remarkable and path-breaking analysis: he locates the desire for liberty and the struggle of sexuality against "the 'unnaturalness' and 'inhumanity' of despotic rule" (26) as an essential part of human nature; perhaps those quotation marks show the author's slight hesitation about making them essentially unnatural and inhuman. Despotism can also be considered as part of human nature. Vartanian was one of the first critics to see the importance of despotism and of the eunuchs as a general symbol of the malaise in the "interregnum following the establishment of autocratic power under Louis XIV, with the resultant abasement of the aristocracy to a position of servile obedience to the royal will. [. . .] The satire on despotism was thus intended, if not as an exact depiction of the political condition of France around 1721, at least as an imaginative interpretation—with its implied warning—of what the future under the Bourbons might well hold in store" (32–33).

9. As it is in our time, in the thought of Georges Bataille, for example. Our view of sexuality as a powerful force that is hard to suppress is obviously not present in Montesquieu's thinking at the time he writes his novel. In *L'Esprit des lois*, he will show himself to be somewhat more preoccupied by free sexuality, especially among women, a traditional locus of such anxieties (book 7, chapter 8, for example).

Chapter Five
Montesquieu's "Introduction" and "Réflexions," and the Question of the "Secret Chain"

1. I refer the reader to the notes in Vernière's edition of the novel, which contains the "Réflexions" (3–5). All quotations of the "Réflexions" are from this edition.

2. For references to other articles on the "secret chain," see note 4 in Braun's article.

3. I have analyzed the use of showing rather than telling in *L'illusion chez Descartes*, especially chapter 4.

4. I am indebted to Sarah Kofman for pointing out that the image of the chain of eloquence occurs in Plato's *Ion*.

Part 3: Graffigny's Elusive Peruvian

Chapter Six
Graffigny's *Lettres d'une Péruvienne:*
Giving (and) Reading

1. Janet Altman bemoans the lack of close readings of Graffigny's novel ("Graffigny's Epistemology" 199n8). This chapter is an attempt to remedy that lack, though other critics have also given fuller treatment since her 1989 article.

2. For the seventeenth century, Ehrmann and Reiss, for example, have studied tensions between various modes of exchange. See also my article on Racine's *Bajazet*.

3. Altman's two articles were the first to examine the novel as focused on the experience of colonization; she also mentions the "work of the prefaces" as a challenge to the dominant European culture of the readers. See Julia Douthwaite's articles and book in which she analyzes the works of Graffigny and Montesquieu along lines that are different from, but not contradictory to, my own views.

4. For an insightful analysis of the role of footnotes by Graffigny, I refer the reader to the article by Aurora Wolfgang. Her thesis is that Graffigny was deliberately mixing the genres of the philosophical and the sentimental novel by introducing footnotes that normally do not belong in a love story, thereby creating a disturbance in the novel of sensibility. Many readers have commented on the dual heritage of Graffigny's text; but these various strands do not simply coexist, they echo and reinforce each other throughout the text.

5. There have been some doubts regarding the exact authorship of this second prefatory text added to the 1752 edition. Joan DeJean and Nancy K. Miller mention this question in a note. In any case, Graffigny obviously endorsed its contents or she would not have put it in between her "Avertissement" and her novel.

6. The barbarous and wild states of the prehistorical Troglodytes and of the Peruvians are reminiscent of a Hobbesian state of war, yet unlike Hobbes's, this state of war precedes the civilized, more peaceful state in being prehistorical—the Peruvians have barely four centuries of written history, Graffigny states in her opening paragraph, but a much longer, nonwritten prehistory of "barbarie." Unlike Hobbes's state of war which can recur at any time, Graffigny's and Rousseau's states of nature occurred in a time that is irrevocably past.

7. Thus for once I disagree with Ross Chambers, who has inspired my reading of Graffigny's text, when he states in a footnote that "The only textual site in which 'textual function' seems to be clearly separate from 'narrative function' is the area of paratext" (272). I do not see any such clear-cut distinction between the paratexts and texts, both capable of having textual and narrative functions. The "on" of the French regrettably disappears in the passive English construction.

8. Stressing the critique of European society, and the Incan society's utopian aspect, Douthwaite notes that Graffigny omits the fratricidal battles and bellicose spirit that Graffigny had read in her main source, Garcilaso's history of the Incas (*Exotic Women* 110).

9. Douthwaite quotes Graffigny's witty reply about the accusation of anachronism: everyone thought it all took place "l'année passée" (*Exotic Women* 136n70).

10. See John Berger, E. Ann Kaplan, Laura Mulvey, and Teresa de Lauretis on woman as gazer and as spectacle. In Graffigny's novel, the relations are reversed: Zilia is the observer of spectacles, and the observer of her observers, except for the brief moment of extreme despair when she is kidnapped by the French and contemplates death (3: 31).

11. That the love story is a hook, and less important than other functions of the text, accounts for the reduction of that aspect of the story (which ties it to the sentimental genre) to some repetitive, almost ritualistic, phrases of Zilia's longing for Aza at the beginning and end of each letter. It is as if Graffigny is putting in just enough sentiment to satisfy the reader's expectation, but not enough to make it a full-blown sentimental novel. The reader may feel that she is winking at us, indicating that the substance of the novel is to be found elsewhere.

12. Altman in "Graffigny's Epistemology" makes a reference to the existential drama of the heroine (184), and Jack Undank's interpretation starts from the premise that this novel goes beyond "ethnological differences" to "a devastating critique of being itself" (297–98). But see below, note 16.

13. This explains the question asked by Zilia, who wonders where she really fits in the hierarchy around her, "O ciel! dans quelle classe dois-je me ranger?" (20: 85). Critics such as Douthwaite are right in not erasing the importance of class, but in my opinion, Graffigny does not have in mind modern economic classes, but a more elementary necessity of knowing which rung of the social hierarchy is hers. As noted below in note 15, Graffigny's own experience led her to feel the disjunction between a noble birth and a difficulty of living according to the expectations of the noble lifestyle.

14. Already in Letter 14, she was amazed by the contradiction between the kindness and the contempt coexisting simultaneously in the women around her, and by the excessive familiarity of the French "sauvages," one of whom tries to touch her breast. She cries out, showing that she knows the laws of civility better than he (68).

15. Another sense in which it might be utopian might be found in Graffigny's life: a gift of money in order to live in the noble lifestyle, to fulfill the obligation to "vivre noblement," very hard to do for the petty and impoverished nobility from which Graffigny came. As English Showalter bluntly states, Madame de Graffigny "dit, et répète, qu'elle n'écrit que pour gagner de l'argent" ("Les Lettres" 15). During the seventeenth and eighteenth centuries, the gap between revenues and noble lifestyle became wider: see J. Meyer, "Relativité de la pauvreté de la noblesse" and "Les difficultés économiques de la noblesse de Cour," and G. Chaussinand-Nogaret, "Noblesse et capitalisme" and other studies and excerpts from ancien régime writers quoted in the volume *Une histoire des élites 1700–1848*. A highly generous gift would have put an end to the author's money woes, which are noted by all her biographers. For an interesting discussion of exceptional and fortunate events which would provide freedom from want, see Kavanagh, "Reading."

16. Many critics have discussed the ending of Graffigny's novel: Douthwaite, Fourny, Miller, Robb, Roulston, and Undank. I particularly agree with Jack Undank, who stresses the novel's paradoxes and the ending's transgressivity, which exists only in the eyes of readers expecting something other than "tendre amitié" at the end of a sentimental love story. But we know that this is not primarily a love story. It seems to be a love story that, according to Undank, in turn gives "an ostensible message about the ethnological differences between Peru and France" that, in turn, "slowly becomes subsumed to a devastating critique of being itself" (297–98); however, I do not concur with the third level of critique as stated here by Undank.

On imitation and exemplarity in *La Princesse de Clèves*, see John Lyons's article. See also the entire volume dedicated to this topic, *An Inimitable Example: The Case for the Princesse de Clèves*.

17. The word *superficial* (173) chosen by the novel's English translator, David Kornacker, to translate *légère* (167) perhaps betrays the difficulty we still have in appreciating positively Zilia's final attitude. I might have said "slight" or even "gentle." Thus unlike the anthropologists' "thick" descriptions, Zilia's would be a "thin" one.

18. My only point of disagreement with Altman's interpretation of Zilia lies in that I do not believe that Zilia ever experienced sexual love with Aza, but remained a virgin ("Graffigny's Epistemology" 190). This makes her even more exceptional, as Douthwaite says, "that unusual creature—a woman happily alone" (*Exotic Women* 125).

19. In fact, Graffigny emphasizes the difference between Céline and her lover, whom Zilia describes as "un jeune sauvage d'une figure aimable" (17: 76). Similarly, Aza's fiancée, a Spanish Catholic woman, is known only in the most generic terms.

20. Most critics who discuss Graffigny's novel also discuss the ending; see also Brooks's and especially MacArthur's discussion of endings.

21. When I teach the *Lettres persanes*, I am always struck by the students' approval of the ending, which they find ennobling and positive. On the other hand, having read Graffigny's text for the first time only a few years ago, I can still remember distinctly my own surprise at the ending.

22. I would like to note here that Chambers's universe in *Room for Maneuver* is quite masculine, both in the authors he analyzes and in the content of the works analyzed. Yet women, at least as much as men, have also their reasons for being oppositional; even more than men they have reasons for finding "moyen de moyenner" (253); they do it, also, personally and differently.

Part 4: Nature Affirmed and Nature Denied

Chapter Seven
Voltaire's *L'Ingénu* and Claire de Duras's *Ourika:* The Aristocracy's Betrayals

1. Most critics analyze *L'Ingénu* in its historical context, but a few critics (Levy, Clouston) have noted the actuality of Voltaire's advocacy for an open meritocracy, religious tolerance, freedom, and justice, still actual themes for today. O'Connell has written on the resonance for today between Ourika's predicament and the analyses of Frantz Fanon pertaining to the dual identity of black people living in white societies.

2. Other critics also treat these problems, for example, Carroll, S. Taylor. The most complete study on *L'Ingénu* is that of Clouston.

3. *Naïvement* in classical language meant "avec naturel." To call l'Ingénu "naïf" (P. Clark) is to introduce a term not necessarily implied by the adverb and needlessly complicates the discussion of the hero.

4. On anticourt writing, see Pauline Smith and Aldo Scaglione. On the structure and functioning of the court itself, see especially Elias.

5. Voltaire emphasizes the importance of the court with some of his chapter titles: the eighth chapter is (partially), "L'Ingénu va en cour"; the ninth chapter is "Arrivée de l'Ingénu à Versailles. Sa réception à la cour"; chapter 13 is titled "La belle Saint-Yves va à Versailles."

6. See Chantal Bertrand-Jennings ("Problématique"), and Roger Little (*Ourika*), who differentiate between the typical romantic heroes and Ourika.

7. On the signification of the tombstones, see especially Woshinsky.

8. Little, who investigated the name of Ourika ("Le nom"), can find no source for the "comba" danced by Ourika: perhaps in addition to being taken from books, as Duras says, it is also completely imaginary.

9. According to the *Diagnostic and Statistical Manual of Mental Disorders-IV-TR,* dissociation, "a disruption in the usually integrated func-

tions of consciousness, memory, identity, or perception," is included among the symptoms of trauma (qtd. in Henke 519).

10. See Bertrand-Jennings's remarkable analysis in "Problématique" of the splitting of Ourika's enunciation and her ultimate disintegration.

11. On the depiction of the effects of slavery and of colonization on the colonized's psyches, and the parallels between Duras's descriptions of Ourika's mental state and the analyses of Frantz Fanon in his *Peau noire, masques blancs*, see O'Connell. The twentieth- and twenty-first-century readers are free to imitate the feminist readers and see an anticolonialist message that neither Ourika nor Duras could see, but which the insightful text conveys.

12. Her use of the word *négresse* to identify herself is significant of her self-devaluation: as Serge Daget notes, the abolitionists prefered the word *noir*, while the word *nègre* underwent an eclipse in the years 1819–33, exactly at the time of the writing of the novel.

13. See Little's quotes from Boufflers, the governor of Sénégal, who brings back to France such gifts as beautiful fabrics, exotic birds, a horse, along with a young black boy and girl (Little, *Ourika* 38–39). On the patriarchal nature of that society, see especially Bertrand-Jennings's "Problématique."

14. On Ourika as a "Galatée" but as a "Galatée" in reverse, who is given life but also reverts back to stone, see Damon DiMauro's very interesting article.

15. On recurrence as a defining part of trauma, see Caruth: "trauma is not locatable in the simple violent or original event in an individual's past, but rather in the way that its very unassimilated nature—the way it was precisely *not known* in the first instance—returns to haunt the survivor later on" (4; Caruth's emphasis). Ourika's traumatic experiences dissociate her like traumas, but unlike traumas they do give her immediate understanding and have a revelatory nature. Her traumas, like the rest of text, are fraught with ambiguity.

Bibliography

1492: Le choc de deux mondes: Ethnocentrisme, impérialisme juridique et culturel, choc des cultures, droits de l'homme et droits des peuples. Actes du Colloque international organisé par la Commission Nationale Suisse pour l'UNESCO. Genève. 17 and 18 Sept. 1992. [Genève]: La Différence, 1993.

Adams, Percy G. *Travel Literature and the Evolution of the Novel*. Lexington: UP of Kentucky, 1983.

Affergan, Francis. *Exotisme et altérité: Essais sur les fondements d'une critique de l'anthropologie*. Paris: Presses Universitaires de France, 1987.

Alberti, Leon Battista. *The Family in Renaissance Florence*. A translation by Renée Neu Watkins of *I Libri della Famiglia*. Columbia, SC: U of South Carolina P, 1969.

Albistur, Maïté, and Daniel Armogathe. *Histoire du féminisme français du moyen âge à nos jours*. Paris: Editions des Femmes, 1977.

Althusser, Louis. *Montesquieu: La politique et l'histoire*. Paris: Presses Universitaires de France, 1959.

Altman, Janet Gurkin. *Epistolarity: Approaches to a Form*. Columbus: Ohio State UP, 1982.

———. "Graffigny's Epistemology and the Emergence of Third World Ideology." *Writing the Female Voice*. Ed. Elizabeth C. Goldsmith. Boston: Northeastern UP, 1989. 172–202.

———. "Making Room for 'Peru': Graffigny's Novel Reconsidered." *Dilemmes du Roman: Essays in Honor of Georges May*. Ed. Catherine Lafarge. Stanford: Anma Libri, 1989. 33–46.

Anderson, Benedict. *Imagined Communities: Reflections on the Origin and Spread of Nationalism*. Rev. ed. London: Verso, 1991.

Annas, Julia, and Jonathan Barnes. *The Modes of Scepticism: Ancient Texts and Modern Interpretations*. Cambridge: Cambridge UP, 1985.

Axelos, Kostas. *Problèmes de l'enjeu*. Paris: Minuit, 1979.

Bacon, Francis. *Selected Writings*. Ed. Hugh G. Dick. New York: Modern Library, 1955.

Barthes, Roland. *Mythologies*. Paris: Editions du Seuil, 1957.

———. *S/Z*. Paris: Editions du Seuil, 1970.

Bartky, Sandra Lee. *Femininity and Domination: Studies in the Phenomenology of Oppression*. New York: Routledge, 1990.

Bibliography

Bates, David. "The Epistemology of Error in Late Enlightenment France." *Eighteenth-Century Studies* 29 (1996): 307–27.

Bédouelle, Guy. "La donation Alexandrine et le traité de Tordesillas (1493–1494)." *1492* 193–209.

Bender, John. "Eighteenth-Century Studies." *Redrawing the Boundaries: The Transformation of English and American Literary Studies*. Ed. Stephen Greenblatt and Giles Gunn. New York: Modern Language Association of America, 1992. 79–99.

Benjamin, Walter. *Illuminations*. Ed. Hannah Arendt. Trans. Harry Zohn. New York: Schocken, 1969.

Benrekassa, Georges. *Le concentrique et l'excentrique: Marges des lumières*. Paris: Payot, 1980.

Bernheimer, Richard. *Wild Men in the Middle Ages: A Study in Art, Sentiment, and Demonology*. New York: Octagon, 1979.

Berger, John. *Ways of Seeing*. London: BBC and Penguin, 1972.

Bertrand-Jennings, Chantal. "Condition féminine et impuissance sociale: Les romans de la duchesse de Duras." *Romantisme* 63 (1989): 39–50.

———. "Problématique d'un sujet féminin en régime patriarcal: *Ourika* de Mme de Duras." *Nineteenth-Century French Studies* 23 (1994–95): 42–58.

Blanchard, Marc Eli. "Writing the Museum: Diderot's Bodies in the *Salons*." *Diderot: Digression and Dispersion: A Bicentennial Tribute*. Ed. Jack Undank and Herbert Josephs. Lexington, KY: French Forum Publishers, 1984. 21–36.

Blum, Carol. *Rousseau and the Republic of Virtue: The Language of Politics in the French Revolution*. Ithaca: Cornell UP, 1986.

Blumenberg, Hans. *The Legitimacy of the Modern Age*. Trans. Robert M. Wallace. Cambridge, MA: MIT P, 1983.

Brady, Patrick. "Are Digression and Dispersion Necessarily 'Rococo'? The Diderot of Spitzer, Laufer, Minguet." *Diderot: Digression and Dispersion: A Bicentennial Tribute*. Ed. Jack Undank and Herbert Josephs. Lexington, KY: French Forum Publishers, 1984. 37–43.

———. "The Present State of Studies on Period Style." *L'Esprit Créateur* 33 (1993): 3–8.

———. *Rococo Style versus Enlightenment Novel: With Essays on "Lettres persanes," "La vie de Mariane," "Candide," "La Nouvelle Héloïse," "Le Neveu de Rameau."* Genève: Editions Slatkine, 1984.

Braun, Theodore. "'La chaîne secrète': A Decade of Interpretations." *French Studies* 42 (1988): 278–91.

Brewer, Daniel. *The Discourse of Enlightenment in Eighteenth-Century France: Diderot and the Art of Philosophizing.* Cambridge: Cambridge UP, 1993.

Brissenden, R. F. *Virtue in Distress: Studies in the Novel of Sentiment from Richardson to Sade.* London: Macmillan, 1974.

Brodzki, Belle, and Celeste Schenk. Introduction. *Life/Lines: Theorizing Women's Autobiography.* Ithaca: Cornell UP, 1988. 1–15.

Brooks, Peter. "Freud's Masterplot." *Yale French Studies* 55/56 (1977): 280–300.

Burckhardt, Jacob. *The Civilization of the Renaissance in Italy.* Vol 1. Introd. Benjamin Nelson and Charles Trinkaus. New York: Harper, 1958.

Butler, Judith. *Gender Trouble: Feminism and the Subversion of Identity.* London: Routledge, 1994.

Caillois, Roger. Preface. Montesquieu, *Œuvres complètes.* Paris: Gallimard–Bibliothèque de la Pléiade, 1949.

Carroll, M. G. "Some Implications of 'Vraisemblance' in Voltaire's *L'Ingénu.*" *Studies on Voltaire and the Eighteenth Century* 183 (1980): 35–44.

Caruth, Cathy. *Unclaimed Experience: Trauma, Narrative, and History.* Baltimore: Johns Hopkins UP, 1996.

Cassirer, Ernst. *The Philosophy of the Enlightenment.* 1932. Trans. Fritz C. A. Koelln and James P. Pettegrove. Princeton: Princeton UP, 1986.

Célestin, Roger. *From Cannibals to Radicals: Figures and Limits of Exoticism.* Minneapolis: U of Minnesota P, 1996.

Certeau, Michel de. *Heterologies: Discourse on the Other.* Trans. Brian Massumi. Foreword by Wlad Godzich. Minneapolis: U of Minnesota P, 1986.

———. *L'invention du quotidien.* Vol. 1. *Arts de faire.* 1980. Paris: Folio, 1990.

Chambers, Ross. *Room for Maneuver: Reading (the) Oppositional (in) Narrative.* Chicago: U of Chicago P, 1991.

Charpentrat, Pierre. *Living Architecture: Baroque: Italy and Central Europe.* New York: Grosset and Dunlap, 1967.

Chartier, Roger. "Formation sociale et économie psychique: La société de cour dans le procès de civilisation." Préface. *La société de cour.* By Norbert Elias. Paris: Flammarion, 1981. i–xxviii.

Bibliography

Chaussinand-Nogaret, Guy. *La noblesse au XVIIIe siècle: De la Féodalité aux Lumières*. Paris: Hachette, 1976.

Chilcoat, Michelle. "Confinement, the Family Institution, and the Case of Claire de Duras's *Ourika*." *L'Esprit Créateur* 38 (1998): 6–16.

Clark, Lorenne M. G., and Lynda Lange, eds. *The Sexism of Social and Political Theory: Women and Reproduction from Plato to Nietzsche*. Toronto: U of Toronto P, 1979.

Clark, Priscilla P. "'L'Ingénu': The Uses and Limitations of Naïveté." *French Studies* 27 (1973): 278–86.

Clouston, John S. *Voltaire's Binary Masterpiece "L'Ingénu" Reconsidered*. Bern: Peter Lang, 1986.

Code, Lorraine. *What Can She Know? Feminist Theory and the Construction of Knowledge*. Ithaca: Cornell UP, 1991.

Condillac, Etienne Bonnot de *Essai sur l'origine des connaissances humaines*. Ed. Aliénor Bertrand. Paris: Vrin, 2002.

Corneille, Pierre. *Le Cid. Œuvres complètes*. Vol. 1. Ed. Georges Couton. Paris: Gallimard–Bibliothèque de la Pléiade, 1980.

Crichfield, Grant. *Three Novels of Madame de Duras: "Ourika," "Edouard," "Olivier."* The Hague and Paris: Mouton, 1975.

Crocker, Lester G. *An Age of Crisis: Man and World in Eighteenth-Century French Thought*. Baltimore: Johns Hopkins UP, 1959.

Crumpacker, Mary M. "The Secret Chain of the *Lettres persanes*, and the Mystery of the B Edition." *Studies on Voltaire and the Eighteenth Century* 102 (1973): 121–41.

Daget, Serge. "Les mots esclave, nègre, Noir, et les jugements de valeur sur la traite négrière dans la littérature abolitionniste française de 1770 à 1845." *Revue Française d'Histoire d'Outre-mer* 60 (1973): 511–48.

Darnton, Robert. *The Literary Underground of the Old Regime*. Cambridge, MA: Harvard UP, 1982.

Dauphiné, Claude. "Pourquoi un roman de sérail?" *Europe* 574 (1977): 89–96.

Davis, Natalie Zemon. *Society and Culture in Early Modern France: Eight Essays*. Stanford: Stanford UP, 1965.

Découvertes européennes et nouvelle vision du monde (1492–1992). Paris: Publications de la Sorbonne, 1994.

Defaux, Gérard. "Un cannibale en haut de chausses: Montaigne, la différence et la logique de l'identité." *Modern Language Notes* 97 (1982): 919–57.

Bibliography

De Lauretis, Teresa. *Alice Doesn't: Feminism, Semiotics and Cinema.* Bloomington: Indiana UP, 1982.

Delon, Michel. "Un monde d'eunuques." *Europe* 574 (1977): 79–88.

De Man, Paul. *Blindness and Insight: Essays in the Rhetoric of Contemporary Criticism.* New York: Oxford UP, 1971.

Derrida, Jacques. *De la grammatologie.* Paris: Minuit, 1967.

———. *Positions.* Paris: Minuit, 1972.

Desan, Philippe. *Les commerces de Montaigne: Le discours économique des "Essais."* Paris: Nizet, 1992.

Descartes, René. *Œuvres et Lettres.* Ed. André Bridoux. Paris: Gallimard–Bibliothèque de la Pléiade, 1953.

Diderot, Denis. *Supplément au Voyage de Bougainville.* Paris: Garnier–Flammarion, 1972.

Didier, Béatrice. "Anthropologie," "Exotisme," "Libertinage." *Le siècle des Lumières.* Paris: MA Editions, 1987.

Dieckmann, Herbert. "The Concept of Knowledge in the *Encyclopédie.*" *Essays in Comparative Literature*, 1961. 73–107.

———. "Themes and Structure of the Enlightenment." *Essays in Comparative Literature.* St. Louis: Washington University Studies, 1961. 41–72.

DiMauro, Damon. "Ourika, or Galatea Reverts to Stone." *Nineteenth-Century French Studies* 28 (2000): 187–211.

Douthwaite, Julia. *Exotic Women: Literary Heroines and Cultural Strategies in Ancien Régime France.* Philadelphia: U of Pennsylvania P, 1992.

———. "Female Voices and Critical Strategies: Montesquieu, Madame de Graffigny and Madame de Charrière." *French Literature Series, Feminism* 16 (1989): 64–77.

———. "Relocating the Exotic Other in Graffigny's *Lettres d'une Péruvienne.*" *Romanic Review* 82 (1991): 456–74.

Duchet, Michèle. *Anthropologie et histoire au siècle des lumières: Buffon, Voltaire, Rousseau, Helvétius, Diderot.* Paris: Maspéro, 1971.

Duclos, Charles Pinot. *Les confessions du comte de ***.* In *Romanciers du XVIIIe siècle.* Ed. Etiemble. Vol. 2. Paris: Gallimard–Bibliothèque de la Pléiade, 1965. 197–301.

Duras, Claire de. *Ourika.* Ed. Joan DeJean. Introd. Joan DeJean and Margaret Waller. New York: Modern Language Association of America, 1994.

Bibliography

Duviols, Jean-Paul. *L'Amérique espagnole vue et rêvée: Les livres de voyages de Christophe Colomb à Bougainville*. Paris: Promodis, 1985.

Eco, Umberto. *A Theory of Semiotics*. Bloomington: Indiana UP, 1976.

Ehrard, Jean. *L'idée de nature en France dans la première moitié du XVIIIe siècle*. 1963. Paris: Albin Michel, 1994.

———. "La signification politique des *Lettres persanes*." *Archives des Lettres Modernes* 116 (1970): 32–49.

Ehrmann, Jacques. "Structures of Exchange in *Cinna*." *Yale French Studies* 36–37 (1966): 169–99.

Elias, Norbert. *La société de cour*. 1969. Paris: Calmann-Lévy, 1974.

Eriksen, Svend. *Early Neo-classicism in France: The Creation of the Louis Seize Style in Architectural Decoration, Furniture, and Ormolu, Gold and Silver, and Sèvres Porcelain in the Mid-Eighteenth Century*. Trans. Peter Thornton. London: Faber and Faber, 1974.

Exoticism in the Enlightenment. Ed. G. S. Rousseau and Roy Porter. Manchester: Manchester UP, 1990.

Fauchery, Pierre. *La destinée féminine dans le roman européen du dix-huitième siècle, 1713–1807: Essai de gynécomythie romanesque*. Paris: Armand Colin, 1972.

Forster, Jean-Paul. "Avec les yeux d'un étranger: *Les Lettres d'un Persan* de George Lyttelton." *Philosophiques: Revue de la Société de Philosophie du Québec* 23 (1996): 139–49.

———. "From 'Persian Letters' to 'Chinese Letters': Inquiry into the Premature Disappearance of this Eighteenth-Century Genre." International Congress on the Enlightenment. Dublin, 31 July 1999.

Foucault, Michel. *Histoire de la folie à l'âge classique*. Paris: Gallimard, 1972.

———. *Les mots et les choses: Une archéologie des sciences humaines*. Paris: Gallimard, 1966.

———. *Power/Knowledge: Selected Interviews and Other Writings 1972–1977*. Ed. Colin Gordon. New York: Pantheon, 1980.

———. *Surveiller et punir: Naissance de la prison*. Paris: Gallimard, 1975.

———. *La volonté de savoir. Histoire de la sexualité*. Vol. 1. Paris: Gallimard, 1976.

———. "What Is Enlightenment?" *The Foucault Reader*. Ed. Paul Rabinow. New York: Pantheon, 1984. 32–50.

Fourny, Diane. "Language and Reality in Françoise de Grafigny's *Lettres d'une Péruvienne*." *Eighteenth-Century Fiction* 4 (1992): 221–38.

Frautschi, R. L. "The Would-be Invisible Chain in *Les Lettres persanes*." *French Review* 40 (1967): 604–12.

Freccero, Carla. "Economy, Woman, and Renaissance Discourse." Migiel and Schiesari 192–208.

Freud, Sigmund. *The Interpretation of Dreams*. 1900. Trans. James Trachey. New York: Avon, 1965.

Fried, Michael. *Absorption and Theatricality: Painting and Beholder in the Age of Diderot*. Berkeley: U of California P, 1980.

Friedman, John Block. *The Monstrous Races in Medieval Art and Thought*. Cambridge, MA: Harvard UP, 1981.

Furetière, Antoine. *Dictionnaire Universel*. 1690. Genève: Slatkine Reprints, 1970.

Gay, Peter. *The Enlightenment: An Interpretation*. New York: Knopf, 1966.

Gearhart, Suzanne. *The Open Boundary of History and Fiction: A Critical Approach to the French Enlightenment*. Princeton: Princeton UP, 1984.

———. "The Place and Sense of the 'Outsider': Structuralism and the *Lettres persanes*." *Modern Language Notes* 92 (1977): 724–48.

———. "Reading *De l'Esprit des lois*: Montesquieu and the Principles of History." *Yale French Studies* 59 (1980): 175–200.

Gebert, Clara. Introduction. *An Anthology of Elizabethan Dedications and Prefaces*. Ed. Gebert. New York: Russell and Russell, 1966. 3–26.

Geertz, Clifford. *Local Knowledge: Further Essays in Interpretive Anthropology*. New York: Basic Books, 1983.

Genette, Gérard. *Figures III*. Paris: Editions du Seuil, 1972.

———. *Seuils*. Paris: Editions du Seuil, 1987.

Godinho, Vitorino Magalhaes. "Rôle du Portugal aux XVe–XVIe siècles: Qu'est-ce que découvrir veut dire? Les Nouveaux Mondes et un monde nouveau." *1492* 55–92.

Goodman, Dena. *The Republic of Letters: A Cultural History of the French Enlightenment*. Ithaca: Cornell UP, 1994.

Graburn, Nelson H. H. "Tourism: The Sacred Journey." V. Smith 21–36.

Bibliography

Graffigny, Madame de. *Lettres d'une Péruvienne*. Introd. Joan DeJean and Nancy K. Miller. New York: Modern Language Association of America, 1993.

———. *Letters from a Peruvian Woman*. Trans. David Kornacker. Introd. Joan DeJean and Nancy K. Miller. New York: Modern Language Association of America, 1993.

Greenblatt, Stephen. *Marvelous Possessions: The Wonder of the New World*. Chicago: U of Chicago P, 1991.

Grimsley, Ronald. *From Montesquieu to Laclos: Studies on the French Enlightenment*. Genève: Droz, 1974.

Grosrichard, Alain. *Structure du sérail: La fiction du despotisme asiatique dans l'Occident classique*. Paris: Editions du Seuil, 1979.

Grosz, Elizabeth. "Conclusion: A Note on Essentialism and Difference." Gunew 332–44.

Gunew, Sneja, ed. *Feminist Knowledge: Critique and Construct*. London: Routledge, 1990.

———. "Feminist Knowledge: Critique and Construct." Gunew 13–35.

Harari, Josué. *Scenarios of the Imaginary: Theorizing the French Enlightenment*. Ithaca: Cornell UP, 1987.

Haraway, Donna. "A Manifesto for Cyborgs: Science, Technology, and Socialist Feminism in the 1980s." 1985. *The Haraway Reader*. New York: Routledge, 2004.

Harth, Erica. *Cartesian Women: Versions and Subversions of Rational Discourse in the Old Regime*. Ithaca: Cornell UP, 1992.

———. *Ideology and Culture in Seventeenth-Century France*. Ithaca: Cornell UP, 1983.

Havens, George R. "Voltaire's *L'Ingénu*: Composition and Publication." *Romanic Review* 63 (1972): 261–71.

Hayes, Julie Candler. *Reading the French Enlightenment: System and Subversion*. Cambridge: Cambridge UP, 1999.

Heidegger, Martin. "Dépassement de la métaphysique." *Essais et conférences*. Trans. André Préau. Paris: Gallimard, 1958. 80–115.

Henein, Eglal. "Hercule ou le pessimisme: Analyse de *L'Ingénu*." *Romanic Review* 72 (1981): 149–65.

Henke, Suzette A. *Shattered Subjects: Trauma and Testimony in Women's Life-Writing*. New York: St. Martin's, 1998.

Heuvel, Jacques van den. *Voltaire dans ses contes: De "Micromégas" à "L'Ingénu."* Paris: Armand Colin, 1967.

Bibliography

Hibbert, Christopher. *The Grand Tour*. London: Weidenfeld and Nicolson, 1969.

Histoire de la famille. Vol. 3: *Le choc des modernités*. Ed. André Burguière, Christiane Klapisch-Zuber, Martine Segalen, Françoise Zonabend. Paris: Armand Colin, 1986.

Une Histoire des élites, 1700–1848. Ed. Guy Chaussinand-Nogaret. Paris: Mouton, 1975.

A History of Private Life. Vol. 3: *Passions of the Renaissance*. Ed. Roger Chartier. Trans. Arthur Goldhammer. Cambridge, MA: Belknap, 1989.

Hobbes, Thomas. *Leviathan*. Ed. Michael Oakeshott. New York: Collier, 1962.

Hoffmann, Léon-François. *Le nègre romantique: Personnage littéraire et obsession collective*. Paris: Payot, 1973.

Horkheimer, Max, and Theodor W. Adorno. *Dialectic of Enlightenment*. 1944. Trans. John Cumming. New York: Continuum, 1996.

Horvitz, Deborah M. *Literary Trauma: Sadism, Memory, and Sexual Violence in American Women's Fiction*. Albany: SUNY P, 2000.

Hulliung, Mark. *Montesquieu and the Old Regime*. Berkeley: U of California P, 1976.

Humana, Charles. *The Keeper of the Bed: The Story of the Eunuch*. London: Arlington, 1973.

Hunt, Lynn. *Politics, Culture and Class in the French Revolution*. Berkeley: U of California P, 1984.

Hunt, Lynn, Joyce Appleby, and Margaret Jacob. "Postmodernism and the Crisis of Modernity." *Telling the Truth about History*. New York: Norton, 1994. 198–237.

Huppert, George. *Public Schools in Renaissance France*. Urbana: U of Illinois P, 1984.

An Inimitable Example: The Case for the "Princesse de Clèves." Ed. Patrick Henry. Washington, DC: Catholic U of America P, 1992.

Jaffrey, Zia. *The Invisibles: A Tale of the Eunuchs of India*. New York: Pantheon, 1996.

Jaggar, Alison M. *Feminist Politics and Human Nature*. Totowa, NJ: Rowman and Allanheld, 1983.

Jakobson, Roman. *Essais de linguistique générale*. Trans. Nicolas Ruwet. Paris: Minuit, 1963.

Jardine, Alice A. *Gynesis: Configurations of Woman and Modernity*. Ithaca: Cornell UP, 1985.

Bibliography

Judovitz, Dalia. *Subjectivity and Representation in Descartes.* Cambridge: Cambridge UP, 1988.

Julia, Dominique. *Les trois couleurs du tableau noir: La Révolution.* Paris: Belin, 1981.

Kant, Immanuel. *Perpetual Peace and Other Essays.* Trans. Ted Humphrey. Indianapolis: Hacket, 1983.

Kaplan, E. Ann. "Is the Gaze Male?" *Powers of Desire: The Politics of Sexuality.* Ed. Ann Snitow, Christine Stansell, and Sharon Thompson. London: Virago, 1983. 309–27.

Karl, Frederick R. *Modern and Modernism: The Sovereignty of the Artist.* New York: Atheneum, 1985.

Kavanagh, Thomas M. "*Jacques le fataliste*: An Encyclopedia of the Novel." *Diderot: Digression and Dispersion: A Bicentennial Tribute.* Ed. Jack Undank and Herbert Josephs. Lexington, KY: French Forum Publishers, 1984. 150–65.

———. "Reading the Moment and the Moment of Reading in Graffigny's *Lettres d'une Péruvienne.*" *Modern Language Quarterly* 55 (1994): 125–47.

Keller, Evelyn Fox. *Reflections on Gender and Science.* New Haven: Yale UP, 1985.

Kempf, Roger. "Les *Lettres persanes* ou le corps absent." *Tel Quel*, no. 22 (1965): 81–86.

———. *Sur le corps romanesque.* Paris: Editions du Seuil, 1968.

Kofman, Sarah. *Le respect des femmes (Kant et Rousseau).* Paris: Editions Galilée, 1982.

Kra, Pauline. "The Invisible Chain of the *Lettres persanes.*" *Studies on Voltaire and the Eighteenth Century* 23 (1963): 7–60.

Kristeva, Julia. *La révolution du langage poétique: L'avant-garde à la fin du XIXe siècle, Lautréamont et Mallarmé.* Paris: Editions du Seuil, 1974.

Kritzman, Lawrence D. *Destruction/Découverte: Le fonctionnement de la Rhétorique dans les "Essais" de Montaigne.* Lexington, KY: French Forum Publishers, 1980.

La Bruyère. *Les caractères ou les Mœurs de ce siècle.* Ed. Robert Garapon. Paris: Garnier, 1962.

Lacan, Jacques. "Le stade du miroir comme formateur de la fonction du Je telle qu'elle nous est révélée dans l'expérience psychanalytique." *Ecrits.* Paris: Editions du Seuil, 1966. 93–100.

Lafayette, Madame de. *Romans et Nouvelles.* Ed. A. Niderst. Paris: Garnier, 1997.

Bibliography

Landes, Joan. *Women and the Public Sphere in the Age of the French Revolution*. Ithaca: Cornell UP, 1988.

Lange, Lynda. "Rousseau: Women and the General Will." *The Sexism of Social and Political Theory: Women and Reproduction from Plato to Nietzsche*. Toronto: U of Toronto P, 1979. 41–52.

Laporte, Roger. "Une double stratégie." *Ecarts: Quatre essais à propos de Jacques Derrida*. Paris: Fayard, 1973. 219–64.

Laqueur, Thomas. "Orgasm, Generation and the Politics of Reproductive Biology." *The Making of the Modern Body: Sexuality and Society in the 19th Century*. Ed. Catherine Gallagher and Thomas Laqueur. Berkeley: U of California P, 1987.

Laufer, Roger. "La réussite romanesque et la signification des *Lettres persanes* de Montesquieu." *Revue d'Histoire Littéraire de la France* 61 (1961): 188–203.

Lazzaro, Claudia. "The Visual Language of Gender in Sixteenth-Century Garden Sculpture." Migiel and Schiesari 71–113.

Lecomte du Nouÿ, Jules-Jean-Antoine. *A Eunuch's Dream*. The Cleveland Museum of Art, Cleveland.

Lee, Bongjie. *Le roman à éditeur: La fiction de l'éditeur dans "La Religieuse," "La Nouvelle Héloïse," et "Les Liaisons Dangereuses."* Bern: Peter Lang, 1989.

Leiner, Wolfgang. *Der Widmungsbrief in der französischen Literatur (1580–1715)*. Heidelberg: Carl Winter Universitätsverlag, 1965.

León-Portilla, Miguel. "Le Nouveau Monde, 1492–1992: Un débat interminable." *Diogènes* 157 (1992): 3–26.

Lestringant, Frank. *Le Cannibale: Grandeur et décadence*. Paris: Perrin, 1994.

Levin, Harry. *The Myth of the Golden Age in the Renaissance*. Bloomington: Indiana UP, 1969.

Levine, Donald N. *The Flight from Ambiguity: Essays in Social and Cultural Theory*. Chicago: U of Chicago P, 1985.

Lévi-Strauss, Claude. *Anthropologie structurale*. Paris: Plon, 1958.

Levy, Zvi. "L'Ingénu ou l'Anti-Candide." *Studies on Voltaire and the Eighteenth Century* 183 (1980): 45–67.

Little, Roger. *Claire de Duras, "Ourika." Présentation et étude*. Exeter: Exeter UP, 1993.

———. "Le nom et les origines d'Ourika." *Revue d'Histoire Littéraire de la France* 98 (1998): 633–37.

Lloyd, Genevieve. *The Man of Reason: "Male" and "Female" in Western Philosophy*. Minneapolis: U of Minnesota P, 1984.

Bibliography

Lovejoy, Arthur O. *The Great Chain of Being: A Study of the History of an Idea*. 1936. Cambridge, MA: Harvard UP, 1953.

Lowe, Lisa. *Critical Terrains: French and British Orientalisms*. Ithaca: Cornell UP, 1991.

Lyons, John D. "Narrative, Interpretation and Paradox: *La Princesse de Clèves*." *Romanic Review* 72 (1981): 384–400.

Lyotard, Jean-François. *La condition postmoderne: Rapport sur le savoir*. Paris: Minuit, 1979.

MacArthur, Elizabeth J. "Devious Narratives: Refusal of Closure in Two Eighteenth-Century Epistolary Novels." *Eighteenth-Century Studies* 21 (1987): 1–20.

Maclean, Ian. *Woman Triumphant: Feminism in French Literature, 1610–1652*. Oxford: Clarendon, 1977.

Macpherson, C. B. *The Political Theory of Possessive Individualism: Hobbes to Locke*. London: Oxford UP, 1962.

Mannsåker, Frances. "Elegancy and Wildness: Reflections of the East in the Eighteenth-Century Imagination." *Exoticism* 175–95.

Marana, G. P. *L'Espion turc*. Cologne, 1710.

Martin, Henri-Jean. *Livre, pouvoirs et société à Paris au XVIIe siècle (1598–1701)*. 2 vols. Genève: Droz, 1969.

Mason, Haydn T. "The Unity of Voltaire's *L'Ingénu*." *The Age of Enlightenment: Studies Presented to Theodore Besterman*. Ed. W. H. Barber, J. H. Brumfitt, R. A. Leigh, R. Shackleton, and S. S. B. Taylor. Edinburgh and London: Oliver and Boyd, 1967. 93–106.

Mason, Sheila. "The Riddle of Roxane." *Women and Society in Eighteenth-Century France: Essays in Honor of John Stephenson Spink*. Ed. Eva Jacobs, W. H. Barber, J. H. Block, F. W. Leakey, and E. Le Breton. London: Athlone, 1979. 28–41.

Mass, Edgar. "Le développement textuel et les lectures contemporaines des *Lettres persanes*." *CAIEF* 35 (1983): 185–200.

———. *Literatur und Zensur in der frühen Aufklärung: Produktion, Distribution und Rezeption der "Lettres persanes"*. Frankfurt: Klostermann, 1981.

Mauzi, Robert. *L'idée de bonheur dans la littérature et la pensée française au XVIIIe siècle*. Paris: A. Colin, 1965.

May, Georges. *Le dilemme du roman au XVIIIe siècle: Étude sur les rapports du roman et de la critique (1715–1761)*. Paris: Presses Universitaires de France, 1963.

Bibliography

———. "One Way and in Both Directions: Considerations on Imaginary Voyages." *Diogenes* 152 (1990): 1–18.

May, Gita. "Neoclassical, Rococo or Preromantic?" *Diderot: Digression and Dispersion: A Bicentennial Tribute.* Ed. Jack Undank and Herbert Josephs. Lexington, KY: French Forum Publishers, 1984. 180–92.

McKeon, Michael. *The Origins of the English Novel, 1600–1740.* Baltimore: Johns Hopkins UP, 1987.

Merleau-Ponty, Maurice. *Sens et non-sens.* Paris: Nagel, 1966.

Michie, Helena. *The Flesh Made Word: Female Figures and Women's Bodies.* New York: Oxford UP, 1987.

Miel, Jan. "Ideas or Epistemes: Hazard Versus Foucault." *Yale French Studies* 49 (1973): 231–45.

Miething, Christoph. "Die Erkenntnisstruktur in Montesquieus *Lettres persanes.*" *Archiv für das Studium der neueren Sprachen* 223 (1986): 64–81.

Migiel, Marilyn, and Juliana Schiesari. *Refiguring Woman: Perspectives on Gender and the Italian Renaissance.* Ithaca: Cornell UP, 1991.

Miller, Nancy K. *The Heroine's Text: Readings in the French and English Novel, 1722–1782.* New York: Columbia UP, 1980.

———. "Men's Reading, Women's Writing: Gender and the Rise of the Novel." *Yale French Studies* 75 (1988): 40–55.

———. *Subject to Change: Reading Feminist Writing.* New York: Columbia UP, 1988.

Mitamura, Taisuke. *Chinese Eunuchs: The Structure of Intimate Politics.* 1963. Trans. Charles A. Pomeroy. Rutland, VT: Charles E. Tuttle, 1970.

Moi, Toril. *Sexual/Textual Politics: Feminist Literary Theory.* London: Routledge, 1985.

Montaigne, Michel de. *The Complete Essays of Montaigne.* Trans. Donald M. Frame. Stanford: Stanford UP, 1948.

———. *Œuvres complètes.* Ed. Maurice Rat. Paris: Gallimard–Bibliothèque de la Pléiade, 1962.

Montesquieu. *Lettres persanes.* Ed. P. Vernière. Paris: Garnier, 1960.

Montiel, Edgar. "L'Amérique ancienne dans le miroir de l'Europe." *1492* 109–20.

Moscovici, Claudia. *From Sex Objects to Sexual Subjects.* New York: Routledge, 1996.

Bibliography

Muchembled, Robert. *Culture populaire et culture des élites dans la France moderne (XVe–XVIIIe siècles)*. Paris: Flammarion, 1978.

Mulvey, Laura. "Feminism, Film and the 'Avant-garde.'" *Women Writing and Writing about Women*. Ed. Mary Jacobus. New York: Barnes and Noble, 1979. 177–95.

———. "Visual Pleasure and Narrative Cinema." *Screen* 16 (1975): 6–18.

Nancy, Jean-Luc. *Ego sum*. Paris: Flammarion, 1979.

Newmark, Kevin. "Leaving Home without It." *Stanford French Review* 11 (1987): 17–32.

Nicholson, Linda J. *The Play of Reason: From the Modern to the Postmodern*. Ithaca: Cornell UP, 1999.

Nicholson, Linda J., with Nancy Fraser. "Social Criticism without Philosophy: An Encounter between Feminism and Postmodernism." Nicholson 99–115.

Nietzsche, Friedrich. *The Gay Science*. Trans. Walter Kaufmann. New York: Vintage, 1974.

———. *On the Genealogy of Morals*. Trans. Walter Kaufmann and R. J. Hollingdale. New York: Vintage, 1969.

Oake, Roger B. "Montesquieu's Religious Ideas." *Journal of the History of Ideas* 14 (1953): 548–60.

O'Connell, David. "*Ourika*: Black Face, White Mask." *French Review* 47, spec. issue no. 6 (1974): 47–56.

Okin, Susan Moller. *Women in Western Political Thought*. Princeton: Princeton UP, 1979.

O'Reilly, Robert F. "The Structure and Meaning of the *Lettres persanes*." *Studies on Voltaire and the Eighteenth Century* 67 (1969): 91–131.

Pascal, Blaise. *Pensées*. Ed. Louis Lafuma. Paris: Editions du Seuil, 1962.

Pateman, Carole. "The Fraternal Social Contract." *Civil Society and the State: New European Perspectives*. Ed. John Keane. London: Verso, 1988. 101–27.

Piroux, Lorraine. *Le livre en trompe l'œil ou le jeu de la dédicace: Montaigne, Scarron, Diderot*. Paris: Editions Kimé, 1998.

Plato. *Ion. Plato in Twelve Volumes*. Vol. 8. Trans. W. R. M. Lamb. Cambridge, MA: Harvard UP, 1925.

Poe, George. "The Eighteenth-Century French Rococo: Some Terminological, Methodological and Theoretical Considerations." *L'Esprit Créateur* 33 (1993): 57–68.

Poggioli, Renato. *The Theory of the Avant-Garde*. Trans. G. Fitzgerald. New York: Harper and Row, 1971.

Popkin, Richard H. *The History of Scepticism from Erasmus to Descartes*. New York: The Humanities Press, 1964.

Poster, Mark. *Critical Theory and Poststructuralism: In Search of a Context*. Ithaca: Cornell UP, 1989.

Pourquoi nous ne sommes pas nietzschéens. Paris: Bernard Grasset, 1991.

Pucci, Suzanne L. "The Discrete Charms of the Exotic: Fictions of the Harem in Eighteenth-Century France." *Exoticism* 145–74.

———. "Letters from the Harem: Veiled Figures of Writing in Montesquieu's *Lettres persanes*." *Writing the Female Voice: Essays on Epistolary Literature*. Ed. Elizabeth C. Goldsmith. Boston: Northeastern UP, 1989. 114–34.

———. "Patriarcat et domesticité dans les *Lettres persanes* de Montesquieu." *Sciences, musiques, Lumières. Mélanges offerts à Anne-Marie Chouillet*. Ferney-Voltaire: Centre international d'étude du XVIIIe siècle, 2002. 289–99.

Rabelais, François. *Œuvres complètes*. Ed. Jacques Boulenger. Paris: Gallimard–Bibliothèque de la Pléiade, 1955.

Rabine, Leslie. "History, Ideology, and Femininity in Manon Lescaut." *Stanford French Review* 5 (1981): 65–83.

Racevskis, Karlis. *Postmodernism and the Search for Enlightenment*. Charlottesville: U of Virginia P, 1993.

Ranum, Orest. "Personality and Politics in the *Persian Letters*." *Political Science Quarterly* 84 (1969): 606–27.

Rapley, Elizabeth. *The Dévotes: Women and Church in Seventeenth-Century France*. Montréal: McGill–Queens UP, 1990.

Raymond, Agnès G. "Encore quelques réflexions sur la 'chaîne secrète' des *Lettres persanes*." *Studies on Voltaire and the Eighteenth Century* 89 (1972): 1337–47.

Reiss, Timothy J. *The Discourse of Modernism*. Ithaca: Cornell UP, 1982.

Robb, Bonnie Arden. "The Easy Virtue of a Peruvian Princess." *French Studies* 46 (1992): 144–59.

Romanowski, Sylvie. "The Circuits of Power and Discourse in Racine's *Bajazet*." *Papers on French Seventeenth Century Literature* 10 (1983): 849–67.

———. *L'illusion chez Descartes: La structure du discours cartésien*. Paris: Klincksieck, 1974.

Romanowski, Sylvie. "La quête du savoir dans les *Lettres persanes.*" *Eighteenth-Century Fiction* 3 (1991): 93–111.

Rorty, Richard, ed. and introduction. *The Linguistic Turn: Recent Essays in Philosophical Method.* Chicago: U of Chicago P, 1967.

Ross, Susan A. *Extravagant Affections: A Feminist Sacramental Theology.* New York: Continuum, 1998.

Rosset, Clément. *L'anti-nature: Eléments pour une philosophie tragique.* Paris: Presses Universitaires de France, 1973.

Rosset, François. "Les nœuds du langage dans les *Lettres d'une Péruvienne.*" *Revue d'Histoire Littéraire de la France* 96 (1996): 1106–27.

Rothstein, Edward. "When Worlds Collide, on the Operatic Stage." *The New York Times,* 8 Oct. 1994, Arts and Leisure section, 31.

Roulston, Christine. "Seeing the Other in Madame de Graffigny's *Lettres d'une Péruvienne.*" *Eighteenth-Century Fiction* 9 (1997): 309–26.

Rousseau, G. S., and Roy Porter. "Introduction: Approaching Enlightenment Exoticism." *Exoticism* 1–22.

Rousseau, Jean-Jacques. *Discours sur l'origine et les fondements de l'inégalité parmi les hommes.* Paris: Garnier–Flammarion, 1971.

Rubin, Gayle. "The Traffic in Women: Notes on the 'Political Economy' of Sex." *Towards an Anthropology of Women.* Ed. Rayna R. Reiter. New York: Monthly Review P, 1975. 157–210.

Sahlins, Marshall. *Stone Age Economics.* New York: Aldine-Atherton, 1972.

Said, Edward. *Orientalism.* New York: Vintage, 1978.

Saint-Amand, Pierre. *The Laws of Hostility: Politics, Violence and the Enlightenment.* 1992. Trans. Jennifer Curtiss Gage. Minneapolis: U of Minnesota P, 1996.

———. "Original Vengeance: Politics, Anthropology, and the French Enlightenment." Trans. Jennifer C. Gage. *Eighteenth-Century Studies* 26 (1993): 399–417.

Saisselin, Rémy G. *The Enlightenment against the Baroque: Economics and Aesthetics in the Eighteenth Century.* Berkeley: U of California P, 1992.

Scaglione, Aldo D. *Knights at Court: Courtliness, Chivalry, and Courtesy from Ottonian Germany to the Italian Renaissance.* Berkeley: U of California P, 1991.

Schalk, Ellery. *From Valor to Pedigree: Ideas of the Nobility in France in the Sixteenth and Seventeenth Centuries.* Princeton: Princeton UP, 1986.

Schneider, Jean-Paul. "Les jeux du sens dans les *Lettres persanes*: Temps du roman et temps de l'histoire." *Etudes sur le XVIIIe siècle.* Strasbourg: Faculté des Lettres Modernes, 1980.

Seabra, José Augusto. "La découverte de l'autre dans la 'lettre' de Pero Vaz de Caminha." *1492* 138–47.

Shackleton, Robert. *Montesquieu: A Critical Biography.* London: Oxford UP, 1961.

Showalter, English, Jr. *The Evolution of the French Novel, 1641–1782.* Princeton: Princeton UP, 1972.

———. "Les *Lettres d'une Péruvienne*: Composition, Publication, Suites." *Actes du 6e Congrès International des Lumières. Archives et Bibliothèques de Belgique* 54 (1983): 14–28.

Simmel, Georg. *The Sociology of Georg Simmel.* Trans. and ed. Kurt H. Wolff. Glencoe, IL: Free Press, 1950.

Singerman, Alan J. "Réflexions sur une métaphore: Le sérail dans les *Lettres persanes*." *Studies on Voltaire and the Eighteenth Century* 185 (1980): 181–98.

Smith, Pauline M. *The Anti-Courtier Trend in Sixteenth-Century French Literature.* Genève: Droz, 1966.

Smith, Valene L., ed. *Hosts and Guests: The Anthropology of Tourism.* 2nd ed. Philadelphia: U of Pennsylvania P, 1989.

Spelman, Elizabeth V. "Woman as Body: Ancient and Contemporary Views." *Feminist Studies* 8 (1982): 109–31.

Stafford, Barbara Maria. *Artful Science: Enlightenment Entertainment and the Eclipse of Visual Education.* Cambridge, MA: MIT P, 1994.

Starobinski, Jean. "Les *Lettres persanes*: Apparence et essence." *Neohelicon* 1–2 (1974): 83–112.

———. *Montesquieu.* Paris: Editions du Seuil, 1953.

Steadman, John M. *The Hill and the Labyrinth: Discourse and Certitude in Milton and His Near-Contemporaries.* Berkeley: U of California P, 1984.

Stewart, Philip. *Le masque et la parole: Le langage de l'amour au XVIIIe siècle.* Paris: José Corti, 1973.

———. "Toujours Usbek." *Eighteenth-Century Fiction* 11 (1999): 141–50.

Strong, Susan C. "Why a Secret Chain?: Oriental Topoi and the Essential Mystery of the *Lettres persanes*." *Studies on Voltaire and the Eighteenth Century* 230 (1985): 167–79.

Bibliography

Taylor, Charles. *Sources of the Self: The Making of the Modern Identity.* Cambridge, MA: Harvard UP, 1989.

Taylor, Samuel S. B. "Voltaire's L'Ingénu, the Huguenots and Choiseul." *The Age of Enlightenment: Studies Presented to Theodore Besterman.* Ed. W. H. Barber, J. H. Brumfitt, R. A. Leigh, R. Shackleton, and S.S. B. Taylor. Edinburgh and London: Oliver and Boyd, 1967. 106–36.

Terdiman, Richard. *The Dialectics of Isolation: Self and Society in the French Novel from the Realists to Proust.* New Haven: Yale UP, 1976.

Thomas, Ruth P. "The Death of an Ideal: Female Suicide in the Eighteenth-Century French Novel." *French Women and the Age of Enlightenment.* Ed. Samia I. Spencer. Bloomington: Indiana UP, 1984. 321–31.

Thorens, Justin. "Le 12 octobre 1492, date charnière dans l'histoire de l'humanité." *1492* 23–49.

Todorov, Tzvetan. *La conquête de l'Amérique: La question de l'autre.* Paris: Editions du Seuil, 1982.

Toldo, Pietro. "Dell' 'Espion' di Giovanni Paolo Marana e delle sue attinenze con les *Lettres persanes* del Montesquieu." *Giornale Storico della Letteratura Italiana* 29 (1897): 46–79.

Toulmin, Stephen. *Cosmopolis: The Hidden Agenda of Modernity.* Chicago: U of Chicago P, 1992.

Tracy, David. *Blessed Rage for Order: The New Pluralism in Theology.* New York: Harper, 1988.

———. "The Hidden God: The Divine Other of Liberation." *Cross Currents* 46 (1996): 5–16.

Undank, Jack. "Grafigny's Room of Her Own." *French Forum* 13 (1988): 297–318.

Valéry, Paul. "Préface aux *Lettres persanes.*" *Variété II.* Paris: Gallimard, 1930. 53–73.

Vallois, Marie-Claire. "'Rêverie orientale' et géopolitique du corps féminin chez Montesquieu." *Romance Quarterly* 38 (1991): 363–92.

Van den Abbeele, Georges. *Travel as Metaphor: From Montaigne to Rousseau.* Minneapolis: U of Minnesota P, 1992.

———. "Utopian Sexuality and Its Discontents: Exoticism and Colonialism in the *Supplément au Voyage de Bougainville.*" *L'Esprit Créateur* 24 (1984): 43–52.

Vartanian, Aram. "Eroticism and Politics in the *Lettres persanes*." *Romanic Review* 60 (1969): 23–33.

Vattimo, Gianni. *La fin de la modernité: Nihilisme et herméneutique dans la culture post-moderne*. Trans. Charles Alunni. Paris: Editions du Seuil, 1987.

Vernière, Paul. "Une ligne directrice dans l'œuvre de Montesquieu: Le problème de l'acculturation." *Parcours et rencontres: Mélanges de langue, d'histoire et de littérature françaises offerts à Enea Balmas*. Vol 2. Paris: Klincksieck, 1993. 1113–17.

Versini, Laurent. "La phrase miroitante de Montesquieu dans les *Lettres persanes*." *Langue, Littérature du XVIIe et du XVIIIe siècle. Mélanges offerts à M. le Professeur Frédéric Deloffre*. Ed. Roger Lathuillère. Paris: SEDES, 1990. 357–65.

Voltaire. *L'Ingénu*. In *Romans et contes*. Ed. Frédéric Deloffre and Jacques van den Heuvel. Paris: Gallimard–Bibliothèque de la Pléiade, 1979.

Walker, William. "Locke Minding Women: Literary History, Gender and the *Essay*." *Eighteenth-Century Studies* 23 (1990): 245–68.

Weisgerber, Jean. *Les masques fragiles: Esthétique et formes de la littérature rococo*. Lausanne: Editions L'Age d'Homme, 1991.

Wellington, Marie. "Hercule, Mlle de Saint-Yves, and the Unity of *L'Ingénu*." *Australian Journal of French Studies* 28 (1991): 5–16.

Wolfgang, Aurora. "Intertextual Conversations: The Love-Letter and the Footnote in Madame de Graffigny's *Lettres d'une Péruvienne*." *Eighteenth-Century Fiction* 10 (1997): 15–28.

Wollstonecraft, Mary. *A Vindication of the Rights of Woman*. In *The Works of Mary Wollstonecraft*. Ed. Janet Todd and Marilyn Butler. Vol. 5. New York: New York UP, 1989. 61–266.

Woolf, Virginia. *Three Guineas*. 1938. New York: Harcourt, 1966.

Woshinsky, Barbara R. "Tombeau de *Phèdre*: Repression, Confession and *Métissage* in Racine and Claire de Duras." *Dalhousie French Studies* 49 (1999): 167–81.

Index

Adams, Percy G., 221n2, 222n4
Adorno, Theodor W., Max Horkheimer and, 216
Affergan, Francis, 7
Alberti, Leon Battista, 90–93, 103
Alembert, Jean Le Rond d', 9
Althusser, Louis, 223n6
Altman, Janet Gurkin, 154, 227nn1 and 3 (chap. 6), 228n12, 229n18
ambiguity, 3–4, 8, 11, 43–44, 46, 93, 107, 122, 181, 209, 215, 231n15. *See also* Levine, Donald N.
Annas, Julia, and Jonathan Barnes, 18
Appleby, Joyce, Lynn Hunt, and Margaret Jacob, 222n10
artificialism, 6–7, 83, 94, 116. *See also* Rosset, Clément
Axelos, Kostas, 62

Bacon, Francis, 18, 41, 224n13
Barnes, Jonathan, Julia Annas and, 18
Barthes, Roland, 86, 169, 225n4
Bartky, Sandra Lee, 225n17
Bataille, Georges, 226n9
Bates, David, 217
Bédouelle, Guy, 219n3
Bender, John, 217
Benjamin, Walter, 1–3, 11
Benrekassa, Georges, 217, 223n6
Berger, John, 71, 228n10
Bernheimer, Richard, 19
Bertrand-Jennings, Chantal, 230n6, 231nn10 and 13
Blanchard, Marc Eli, 129
Blum, Carol, 224n8
Blumenberg, Hans, 35
Brady, Patrick, 129
Braun, Theodore, 124–25, 227n2 (chap. 5)

Brewer, Daniel, 215, 217–18
Brissenden, R. F., 224n12
Brodzki, Belle, and Celeste Schenk, 82
Brooks, Peter, 80, 223n2, 230n20
Burckhardt, Jacob, 220n7
Butler, Judith, 218, 224n14

Caillois, Roger, 210–11
Carroll, M. G., 230n2
Caruth, Cathy, 199, 207, 231n15
Cassirer, Ernst, 9–10, 216
Certeau, Michel de, 138, 221n12
Chambers, Ross, 138–39, 153, 181, 228n7, 230n22
Charpentrat, Pierre, 42
Chartier, Roger, 162–63
Chaussinand-Nogaret, Guy, 223n12, 229n15
Chilcoat, Michelle, 204
Clark, Lorenne M. G., and Lynda Lange, 224n15
Clark, Priscilla P., 187, 190, 230n3
Clouston, John S., 187–88, 230nn1–2
Code, Lorraine, 69, 224n15
Condillac, Etienne Bonnot de, 156, 158
Corneille, Pierre, 124
court, 8, 42, 45, 47–48, 54, 186, 189–94, 213–14, 222n5, 230nn4–5. *See also* Elias, Norbert
Crumpacker, Mary M., 124

Daget, Serge, 231n12
Dauphiné, Claude, 124
Davis, Natalie Zemon, 92
Defaux, Gérard, 221n12
DeJean, Joan, 195, 227n5
De Lauretis, Teresa, 71, 82, 223n2, 228n10

253

Index

Delon, Michel, 223n3, 225nn1 and 3
De Man, Paul, 61
Derrida, Jacques, 47, 60–61, 97–98, 165–66, 175
Desan, Philippe, 142
Descartes, René, 4, 10, 68, 122, 127, 160, 220n11
Diderot, Denis, 20, 35–36, 61, 104, 156, 215, 221n14
Dieckmann, Herbert, 8
DiMauro, Damon, 208, 231n14
double-bind, 72, 171, 204, 206, 214, 216, 225n17
Douthwaite, Julia, 152, 161, 186, 227n3 (chap. 6), 228nn8–9 and 13, 229nn16 and 18
Duclos, Charles Pinot, 8
Duviols, Jean-Paul, 219n2

Eco, Umberto, 164
Ehrard, Jean, 6, 8, 53, 216, 223n4
Ehrmann, Jacques, 227n2 (chap. 6)
Elias, Norbert, 162, 192, 194–95, 222n5, 230n4

Fanon, Frantz, 230n1, 231n11
Fontenelle, Bernard Le Bovier de, 76
Forster, Jean-Paul, 210
Foucault, Michel, 5, 28, 60–61, 104, 107–08, 112, 216, 222n10, 223n1
Fourny, Diane, 229n16
Frame, Donald, 219n6
Fraser, Nancy, Linda J. Nicholson with, 218
Freccero, Carla, 92
Freud, Sigmund, 60, 86, 102
Friedman, John Block, 219n1
Furetière, Antoine, 126

Gay, Peter, 216
Gearhart, Suzanne, 101, 222nn7 and 9, 223n7
Gebert, Clara, 119

Geertz, Clifford, 215
Genette, Gérard, 118, 140, 197
Godinho, Vitorino Magalhaes, 22
Goodman, Dena, 172
Graburn, Nelson H. H., 221n2
Greenblatt, Stephen, 21, 23, 33, 162, 219nn2–3
Grimsley, Ronald, 224n12
Grosrichard, Alain, 100–01, 225n1
Grosz, Elizabeth, 82
Guyon, Jeanne, 68

Harari, Josué, 88, 105, 225n1, 226n6
Haraway, Donna, 6–7, 217–18
Harth, Erica, 28, 42, 68, 211, 224nn11 and 14
Hayes, Julie Candler, 93
Heidegger, Martin, 61–62
Henein, Eglal, 186
Henke, Suzette A., 199
Herrmann, Claudine, 195
Heuvel, Jacques van den, 187
Hibbert, Christopher, 221n2
Histoire de la famille, 102
Histoire des élites, 1700–1848, Une, 229n15
History of Private Life, A, 90
Hobbes, Thomas, 53, 56, 67, 101–02, 113, 227n6
Hoffmann, Léon-François, 206
Horkheimer, Max, and Theodor W. Adorno, 216
Horvitz, Deborah M., 204, 206
Hulliung, Mark, 108, 114–16
Humana, Charles, 225nn2–3
Hunt, Lynn, Joyce Appleby, and Margaret Jacob, 222n10
Huppert, George, 224n14

Jacob, Margaret, Lynn Hunt, Joyce Appleby, and, 222n10
Jaffrey, Zia, 225n2
Jaggar, Alison M., 9, 214, 216
Jakobson, Roman, 221n16

254

Index

Jardine, Alice A., 222n10
Judovitz, Dalia, 160–61, 220n8
Julia, Dominique, 224n9

Kant, Immanuel, 50, 65, 223n1
Kaplan, E. Ann, 71, 228n10
Karl, Frederick R., 61
Kavanagh, Thomas M., 229n15
Keller, Evelyn Fox, 69, 216, 224n13
Kempf, Roger, 106, 223n3, 225nn1 and 3
Kofman, Sarah, 171, 216
Kra, Pauline, 124
Kristeva, Julia, 222n6
Kundera, Milan, 157

La Bruyère, Jean de, 51, 169
Lacan, Jacques, 161–62
Lafayette, Madame de, 176–77
Landes, Joan, 68
Lang, Lynda, Lorenne Clark M. G. and, 224n15
Laporte, Roger, 61
Laqueur, Thomas, 162
Laufer, Roger, 124
Lecomte du Nouÿ, Jules-Jean-Antoine, 95
Lee, Bongjie, 121
Leiner, Wolfgang, 119–20
Levin, Harry, 33, 220n10
Levine, Donald N., 3–4, 218, 221n1, 223n10
Lévi-Strauss, Claude, 6, 178
Levy, Zvi, 187, 190, 230n1
Little, Roger, 205, 230nn6 and 8, 231n13
Lloyd, Genevieve, 69
Locke, John, 10, 68, 224nn12–13
Lovejoy, Arthur O., 201
Loy, J. Robert, 127
Lyons, John D., 229n16
Lyotard, Jean-François, 61, 216

MacArthur, Elizabeth J., 230n20
Machiavelli, Niccolò, 107

Maclean, Ian, 224n10
Macpherson, C. B., 42, 214, 219n4, 223n12
Marana, G. P., 125
Mason, Haydn T., 187
Mass, Edgar, 87
May, Georges, 132, 210
May, Gita, 129
McKeon, Michael, 42, 223n12
Merleau-Ponty, Maurice, 155
Mersenne, le p. Marin, 4
Meyer, J., 229n15
Michie, Helena, 225n16
Middle Ages, 18–19, 85
Miething, Christoph, 125
Miller, Nancy K., 81, 178, 181, 186, 227n5, 229n16
Mitamura, Taisuke, 225nn2–3
Moi, Toril, 82, 224n14
Montiel, Edgar, 34
Moscovici, Claudia, 82, 215
Muchembled, Robert, 5, 213
Mulvey, Laura, 71, 228n10

Nancy, Jean-Luc, 53
Newmark, Kevin, 80
Nicholson, Linda J., 9
Nicholson, Linda J, with Nancy Fraser, 218
Nietzsche, Friedrich, 17, 37, 60–61, 135, 185, 210, 215, 217

Oake, Roger B., 224n12
O'Connell, David, 230n1, 231n11
Okin, Susan Moller, 224n15

Pascal, Blaise, 7, 34, 55, 85, 99, 110, 115, 167
Pateman, Carole, 216
Piroux, Lorraine, 118
Plato, 131
plot, 66, 80–81, 86, 128, 223n2, 225n19
Poggioli, Renato, 61
Popkin, Richard H., 4
Poster, Mark, 216

255

Index

postmodern, 4, 10, 45, 59–60, 62–63, 116–17, 215–16
Poullain de la Barre, François, 68
Pourquoi nous ne sommes pas nietzschéens, 217
Pucci, Suzanne L., 84, 115, 223n3, 225n20

Rabelais, François, 18, 124
Racevskis, Karlis, 216, 223n10
Rapley, Elizabeth, 224nn9 and 14
Raymond, Agnès G., 124
Regency (*Régence*), 8, 41–43, 63, 68, 107
Reiss, Timothy J., 23, 29, 59–60, 219nn3–4 and 7, 221n11, 227n2 (chap. 6)
Renaissance, 4, 7, 17, 21, 24, 29, 47, 90, 131, 142, 219n3, 219–20nn7–8, 224n9
Robb, Bonnie Arden, 229n16
rococo, 128–30
Romanowski, Sylvie, 66, 223n5, 227n3 (chap. 5), 227n2 (chap. 6)
Rorty, Richard, 215–16
Rosset, Clément, 6–7, 61, 82–83, 114, 216–17, 220n11
Rothstein, Edward, 221n15
Roulston, Christine, 229n16
Rousseau, Jean-Jacques, 20, 28, 32, 47, 98, 102, 166, 169, 189, 194, 209, 220n10, 227n6
Rubin, Gayle, 225n18

Sade, Donatien, marquis de, 61
Sahlins, Marshall, 142–43, 145, 173–75
Said, Edward, 49–50, 212, 222n6
Saint-Amand, Pierre, 216–17, 222n9
Saisselin, Rémy G., 42
Scaglione, Aldo D., 222n5, 230n4
Schalk, Ellery, 142

Schenk, Celeste, Belle Brodzki and, 82
Schneider, Jean-Paul, 223n4
Seabra, José Augusto, 219n5
seventeenth century, 4–5, 7, 23, 29, 41–43, 59, 63, 67–68, 83, 108, 126, 189, 211, 213, 219–20nn7–8, 220n11, 223n12, 224n10, 227n2 (chap. 6), 229n15. *See also* Toulmin, Stephen
Showalter, English, Jr., 229n15
Simmel, Georg, 1–2, 11, 122
Singerman, Alan J., 225n1
skepticism, 4, 6, 17–18, 42, 86, 218
Smith, Pauline M., 222n5, 230n4
Smith, Valene L., 221nn2–3
Spelman, Elizabeth V., 225n16
Stafford, Barbara Maria, 42
Steadman, John M., 131
Stewart, Philip, 83–84, 222n9
Strong, Susan C., 125

Taylor, Charles, 217
Taylor, Samuel S. B., 190, 230n2
Terdiman, Richard, 225n19
Thorens, Justin, 22, 219nn2 and 5
Todorov, Tzvetan, 219nn2 and 5
Toulmin, Stephen, 4, 9, 83, 116, 221n11, 222–23n10
Tracy, David, 216
trauma, 199, 206–07, 231n15

Undank, Jack, 228n12, 229n16

Valéry, Paul, 85–86, 89, 98, 105
Vallois, Marie-Claire, 225n21
Van den Abbeele, Georges, 221n2, 222n8
Vartanian, Aram, 80, 99–101, 223n3, 225n1, 226n8
Vattimo, Gianni, 62–63
Vernière, Paul, 50, 76, 121, 226n1
Versini, Laurent, 123

Walker, William, 224n13
Waller, Margaret, 195
Weisgerber, Jean, 129
Wellington, Marie, 187
Wolfgang, Aurora, 227n4 (chap. 6)
Wollstonecraft, Mary, 76, 81–82

women, education of, 65, 67–69, 76, 171, 213, 224nn9 and 14
Woolf, Virginia, 65
Woshinsky, Barbara R., 230n7

Zola, Emile, 86